THE LIST
SERVES
POPULATION CONTROL
AND POWER
KENNETH C. WERBIN

Theory on Demand #22
The List Serves: Population Control and Power

Kenneth C. Werbin
With a foreword by Geert Lovink

Edited by: Miriam Rasch
Cover design: Katja van Stiphout
Design: Leonieke van Dipten
EPUB development: Leonieke van Dipten
Publisher: Institute of Network Cultures, Amsterdam, 2017
ISBN: 978-94-92302-15-1

The research was supported by Le Fonds Québecois de la recherche sur la société et la culture and The Social Sciences and Humanities Research Council of Canada.

Contact
Institute of Network Cultures
Phone: +3120 5951865
Email: info@networkcultures.org
Web: http://www.networkcultures.org

This publication is available through various print on demand services and freely downloadable from http://networkcultures.org/publications

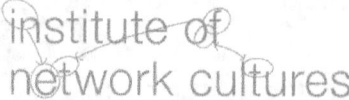

CONTENTS

This book is dedicated to my late mother, Eleanor Moss-Werbin, and late grandfather, Irwin Moss, both of whom epitomized the value of life-long learning and instilled a profound sense of social justice in me.

ACKNOWLEDGMENTS

A first draft of this manuscript was completed in fulfillment of the requirements for my Ph.D. at Concordia University in Montréal, Canada in 2008. Although that draft was completed some years ago, the analysis and theorizing of lists as instruments of population control and power continues to resonate and remains pertinent. If anything, since that draft was finished, there has been an intense proliferation of lists wielded as apparatuses of security in conjunctions of power. No-fly lists continue to expand and continue to erroneously and unjustly contain the names of innocent people whose sole crime is to have a name identical or similar to 'known' threats. Getting one's name off such a list continues to be a Kafkaesque affair. Moreover, the conjunction of data, lists, and algorithmic logics has been taken up in an even wider array of efforts to control the movement of populations, including but not limited to lists of illegal immigrants, lists of risks to the hotel and hospitality industry, and lists of risks to the banking industry. There is no doubt that lists will continue to problematically serve the classification, delineation and policing of populations of 'them' as they have since the advent of the written record. It is my hope that the publication of this work will help others to problematize and theorize the use of lists as instruments of population control and power and further resistance to this form of governmentality.

This work would not have been possible without the help, support, and encouragement of a wide group of people who I would like to take a moment to acknowledge. First and foremost, I would like to thank my Ph.D. supervisor, Dr. Kim Sawchuk (Concordia University) who thoughtfully and diligently saw the dissertation through to completion with me. Her sophis-ticated theoretical insights contributed invaluably to the work. I would also like to thank my committee members, beginning with Dr. Leslie Regan Shade (University of Toronto) who continues to be a close research collaborator and friend. I was also honoured to have the late Dr. Martin Allor (Concordia University) as a member of my dissertation committee, as well as Dr. Steven Shaw (Concordia University), and Dr. Greg Elmer (Ryerson University). I would also like to extend special thanks to Dr. Geert Lovink (University of Applied Sciences Amsterdam) of the Institute of Network Cultures for all of his support, encouragement and belief in these ideas throughout the development and publication of this work.

Thanks also to the following people for their contributions to my thinking and providing me with a rich intellectual community in which to grow: Monika Kin-Gagnon, Gaëtan Tremblay, Charles Perraton, Rae Staseson, Charles Acland, Chantal Nadeau, Owen Chapman, Inderbir Riar, Eric Abitbol, Fenwick McKelvey, Zach Devereaux and Ganaele Langlois. I would also like to thank my current research collaborators who make being an academic a whole pile of fun: Mark Lipton, Leslie Regan Shade, Judith Nicholson and Ian Reilly. Special thanks to my current colleagues at Wilfrid Laurier University who inspire me on a daily basis: James Cairns, Sue Ferguson, Robert Feagan, Ken Paradis, Kate Rossiter, Charles Wells, Heidi Northwood, Rob Kristofferson, Tarah Brookfield, Kofi Campbell, Abby Goodrum, Nathan Rambukkana, Greg Bird and Penelope Ironstone. I would also like to thank my research assistant, Alison Leonard, who helped with the formatting of this book.

Very special thanks are extended to my family who have stood beside me through thick and thin: my brother, Robert Werbin, his wife Heidi, and my three nephews, Ryan, Evan and Brendan Werbin. I also want to thank ma belle-mère Claire van Belle, my aunt and uncle Beverly and Ernie Shapiro, cousins David Moss, Louise Bloom, and Murray, Lorne and Debra Shapiro. Thanks also to my closest friends for all of their support through the years: Andrew Gelber, Matt Nuss, Ben Duffield, Sandy Fleischer, Robert Robert Landau, Brandee Diner, Sandy Mamane, Pamela Teitelbaum, Lienne Sawatsky, Dan Williams, Samantha Cogan and Doron Sommer.

Finally, I want to thank the three people who make me the luckiest person in the world: the love of my life, my confidante and shelter from the storm, Alix-Jeanne Loewenguth, and my intensely loving and ever-inspiring daughters, Celeste-Eléonore and Annabelle Werbin – without you three, nothing else matters!

This work was funded by the Fonds Québecois de la recherche sur la société et la culture and the Social Sciences and Humanities Research Council of Canada.

Kenneth C. Werbin
Brantford, Canada
November 2016

PREFACE BY GEERT LOVINK

'Hacktivism is not always about breaking into a system, sometimes it's about breaking out of it.' Anon

'The vile pogroms of 1940's were by-products of the industrial revolution. Today's pogroms are by-products of the digital revolution.' Max Keiser

The Institute of Network Cultures is proud to present Kenneth Werbin's study on lists in its Theory on Demand series. It was our wish to publish this important work that was finished as a PhD in 2008, and we are very happy that we remained patient and reminded Kenneth time and again of the utmost strategic-political importance of his research.

It was around 1984 that I discovered lists as a separate sociological category. The fact that lists do not merely exist but are a distinguished concept, a mode of power along the lines of Michel Foucault's philosophy, a specific way to organize subjects and matters, was a real insight for me. This happened during an era when lines of people, waiting in the street for a bakery or office, had all but disappeared and was associated with disfunctioning 'real existing socialism' and collapsing Third World economies elsewhere. Lists empower, lists repress, lists order. What could be better than publishing a comprehensive study about lists?

When I grew up in the early 1970s the list was the Radio Veronica Top 40, a folded sheet of paper we picked up in the record shop for free. Later on, lists became a piece of software, a small and simple, yet powerful internet tool. The electronic mailinglist – also called list serv, running on 'majordomo', which I got to know in 1993 – was a list of subscribers. Internet lists turned out to play an important part in my life. The most famous of them is 'nettime', which I founded in 1995 together with Pit Schultz. This practice of organizing networks for debate culminated in the 'mailman' domain called 'listcultures.org' that our Institute of Network Cultures has been running for the past decade.

One of my early political memories concerns the Dutch protest campaign against the 1970 census. My mother, who as a teenager during World War II had been a courier, transporting newspapers and false food stamps on her bike in the Dutch southern town of Breda, signed up. It was the first time I heard of the Nazi logic of registration, counting, and selecting, leading up to transportation and extermination. The German 'Wehrt den Anfängen' ('stop the beginnings') had to be applied to the counting of populations itself, even if this meant civil disobedience, like sabotage the making of lists. Lists are not innocent. This fight was not just about opinions, convictions, prejudices, ideologies. It was about taking the toys from the authorities.

By asking the question what lists are all about, we're entering dark territory. Lists are not innocent, and not by definition 'useful'. There is more to the topic than the shopping or to-do list. In his 1960 magnum opus *Crowds and Power*, Elias Canetti describes the various cultural techniques that rulers have used over time to prevent a crowd turning into a dangerous, unpredictable mass. An example is separating people and putting one after the other, in a line. Following Canetti we could say that lists are abstract lines, cues that wait to be processed. In contrast to the open crowd that grows and then suddenly disintegrates, the list is stable and fixed. Surprisingly few items can, and will be, taken on or off the list. The list is a symbol of hierarchy, power, and stability.

As a symbol for rational order, the list prevents the atomized subjects from forming unwanted articulations of collective energies. Chaos has been overcome, now we just wait and see how number crunching is progressing. The institution will eventually deal with each and every single item. A list is not dead information, it is not a residue but a potent, dense form of rule that shows us the power of organization, and the organization of power. The list is living evidence, a reminder of the technological violence that inhabits our cybernetic machines.

*

It is in this context that I want to discuss Detlef Hartmann's *The Alternative: Life as Sabotage, on the Crisis of Technological Violence* from 1981, a bitter post-utopian document of my own in-between generation, born around 1960, squashed between hippies and yuppies, disco and punk. No one is using the phrase 'technological violence' anymore; in the same way as we no longer talk about 'West-Germany'. There is a good reason for this. The topos is associated with the greyness of the post-war concrete deserts, symbolized in the Raststätten and Autobahnen that I frequented as hitch-hiker. Think of Kraftwerk, the Rote Armee Fraktion, Tatort and Wiedergutmachung.

Hartmann is one of the many harsh critics of his own generation of '68 (other heroes were Wolfgang Pohrt, Eike Geisel, and Hendrik Broder, all writing in the tradition of Adorno and Arendt). For Hartmann, life is not sacrifice; its essence is sabotage. What remains of our human qualities will rebel. His central argument is that humans are not machines. This a priori does not grow out of some superior, sentimental, let alone nostalgic humanism. Neither does it stem from the holistic wisdom of the selected few, the super humans that hover above our petty concerns. According to Hartmann, life remains an unnoticed factor on the side, yet it often disturbs processes and thus needs to be controlled, tamed, if not erased. 'Life has become sabotage, precisely because it is life.' Humans are defined by Hartmann and other members of his German autonomist generation as a remainder, a non-productive rest, a left-over of a useless entity that is refusing to be utilized, quantified, and optimized. A core he calls 'subjective strangeness': the non-value that refuses to be measured, incorporated, and exploited. From a bureaucratic perspective it is this worthless remainder that is a threat to the entire system and cannot be ignored, and thus needs to be removed aka exterminated.

In line with late 1970s brutalist reality we are all subjected to the violence of institutions, from shopping malls to schools, hospitals, traffic systems, and jails (today we might add social media to the list). These pedagogical institutions all follow the logic of the machine (so well described by the 'early' Michel Foucault). No matter how different their purposes, their architectures are identical and follow the primitive logic of the Machine. For Hartmann, our richness, language, games, and feeling cannot be captured by the poverty of these machines.

This is a different perspective from the dominant one in progressive circles forty years later, which sees life, everyday life with all its oddities and anomalies, as the mean source of capitalist exploitation. Data are extracted out of tiny differences in taste, consumer behavior, and opinions, are then run through various computational procedures, visualized and sold to the highest bidder.

According to Hartmann, the Machine is neither progress nor a necessary evil or a monstrosity born out of the mind. The machine is defined as violence against life. The machine is not some accidental side effect. Reading Hartmann I interpret it as a vector, a vitalist force. The machine is a 'strategy of violence, destruction, power and expropriation'. This is deeply written into the cybernetic logic that we deal with in the context of the internet. Life is not defined by victimhood. Life is a revolt (for example against the list), an uprising, a strategy of freedom and autonomy and subjective richness. The rise against the Machine, in defense of the human remainder, is what Hartmann calls the 'technological class struggle'. For Hartmann the technological struggle has always been at the core of the class struggle. This may be true, but it has not always been perceived as such. In retrospect we can easily read this as an avant-garde statement. It feels like we're still at the very beginning of this process.

To see the destruction of the outside environment (in the case of Hartmann this was capitalist city planning) against the backdrop of the inner destruction of life: here we need to take into account a parallel understanding of 'subculture' as an element that capitalism can no longer absorb, and fend our culture against the cynical reading that every outcry, no matter how disturbing and unusual, can and will be sublimated and integrated into the capitalist machine. Resistance is not futile, it is fertile as long as it explicitly takes apart power.

Detlef Hartmann was member of the West-German collective that published the early 1980s radical theory zine *Autonomie*. Its subtitle is 'Materials Against the Factory Society' (and its lists, we could add). The first issue reported about the 1979 revolution in Iran in support of the Shia opposition and Bani Sadr, while nr. 2 focused on 'new prisons' and the trails against German armed struggle. The issue is an infamous one on the 'second destruction of Germany': the desolate concrete suburbs, the social housing pedagogy meant to tame the working class, and the strategies of squatters movement. In all these struggles 'autonomy' is a central motive, with the aim to create independent lives that hold off and undermine the Machine (including the Party), in particular the rational ones that are filled with good intentions.

The Hamburg doctor Karl-Heinz Roth was, and still is, a key figure in the German autonomist Left. While living in a West-Berlin squat on Potsdammer Strasse in 1983-84, I read, sitting in Sharoun's then brand new Staatsbibliothek, *Die restlose Erfassung* (translated as *The Nazi Census)* which Roth wrote together with the historian Götz Aly in 1984, a book that is also featured in Kenneth's research. It is a historical study on census and the role of statistics during the Nazi period. It is here that I read for the first time about the widespread use of IBM's punch card technology by the Nazis in their 1933 census, its use within the military-industrial complex under Todt and Speer to coordinate forced labor and ultimately the counting and selection of Jews in the Holocaust. The authors point out that while writing the book the same punch cards were still in use; indeed, I followed an SPSS course how to use punch cards that were fed into an IBM mainframe computer back in 1978 at the University of Amsterdam.

Aly and Roth present first sketches of what could be a history of the role of statistics during the Nazi period and showcase individual careers of statistics experts that span well into the West-German post-war period. The political aim of this short study is to show that collecting population statistics to single out social groups has a frightening continuity. The book was in fact written to support the census boycott movement, which had just celebrated a rare victory in German court. Statistics were not just created to process information about large groups; the Nazi tactics were aimed at individualizing single cases out of large databases. The methods used were both scientific and rational, with the aim to take the subject out of the social struggle.

Although mentioned occasionally, we can't say that IBM's punch card technology and its role in the Holocaust is part of current internet discourse. When Edwin Black's monumental study on the 'strategic alliance between Nazi Germany and America's most powerful corporation' came out in 2001 (in the midst of the dotcom crash and 9/11), it received some airplay but it couldn't be well positioned in the light of the internet revolution that unfolded at the time. The symbolic fifty years after the war-commemorations were over and IBM itself seemed to have lost out against baby boom giants such as Microsoft. As Werbin's study makes clear, in the chapter on the no-fly lists, this all changed in that very same year 2001, after 9/11 took place.

*

Authorities require we're on the list – and that we obey their rules. Once we're captured by the spatial order of the list, we cannot jump the line or simply leave. This is by far the most dangerous aspect of list governance. Once we're on, how do we get off? From a database perspective, the list as an 'organized collection of data' (Wikipedia) is a given. For officials and managers lists condense knowledge, putting it in a specific order (often alphabetic or numeric). As an abstract experience, the itemized and organized data are ready to be pro-cessed. Once entered into the database management systems, the list as such disappears and transforms into tabs, numbers, entries, forms, numbers, or simply 'data' as it's called these days. It is only in the database that data become relational. As part of a list, data can be related to other data, but this is tedious labor, a task which has been taken over by the com-puter and earlier calculation machines that have become operational since the early 1900s.

Kenneth Werbin's study is confronting. It not only makes a powerful, and potentially deadly, form of power visible. It takes us deep inside the cybernetic logic itself, in which the 'order of information' is a prerequisite to virtually any move we take in our computerized, networked society.

Geert Lovink
Amsterdam, The Netherlands
January, 2017

INTRODUCTION. IN LISTS WE ARE...

In short, the point of view adopted in all these studies involved the attempt to free relations of power from the institution, in order to analyze them from the point of view of technologies; to distinguish them also from the function, so as to take them up within a strategic analysis; and to detach them from the privilege of the object, so as to resituate them within the perspective of the constitution of fields, domains, and objects of knowledge.[1]

The list serves. Indeed, the list serves the all-encompassing work of classifying and developing all fields, domains, and objects of knowledge as related to all living beings, things, and events. Equally, since ancient times, the list has served an instrumental role in managing security, territory, and population, albeit in a series of radically different political power/knowledge formations, and in a variety of roles. The list is a technology that serves the administration, organization, management, policing, and circulation of things and populations, as well as the development of knowledge, and in this way, the list is a political technology that has served, and continues to serve different formations of power, or *governmentality*.

From ancient administrative lists that logged the kings' reigns and served as the basis for early history, to contemporary apparatuses of security that list predicted terrorist threats boarding planes; from early lists of prohibitions, rules, and laws like the Ten Commandments, to censuses and their attendant analyses of populations; from the Nazis' lists of Jews and threats to the *Volk*[2] to McCarthy's blacklists of communist threats; from ancient lexicons scrawled on scrolls, to the emergence of cybernetics and computers; from lists underpinning classification and naming systems in 'natural history', to lists pivoting global classification infrastructures and flows of populations across the world; from no-fly lists, to no-fill-in-the-blank list culture – the list is a simple, yet highly powerful critical support technology of modern and contemporary forms of government that somehow has received very little attention from scholars. Moreover, the combination of its historical, cultural, and contemporary dimensions also makes the list a political technology that serves juridical-legal mechanisms, disciplinary mechanisms, and apparatuses of security, playing a key instrumental role in what Michel Foucault termed 'governmentality'.[3]

---

1   Michel Foucault, '8 February 1978 *Governmentality*', in M. Senellart and A.I. Davidson (eds), *Security, Territory, Population: Lectures at the College de France, 1977-1978*, Houndmills, Basingstoke, Hampshire, New York: Palgrave Macmillan, 2007, pp. 115-134.
2   German for 'people', see 'Volk', from *The Concise Oxford-Duden German Dictionary*, ed. Michael Clark and Olaf Thyen, Oxford University Press, 2004; *Oxford Reference Online*, Oxford University Press, Concordia University Library, Montreal, 31 January 2008.
3   Foucault, '1 February 1978 *Governmentality*', in Senellart and Davidson (eds), *Security, Territory, Population*, pp. 87-114.

So, since there has to be an imperative, I would like the one underpinning the theoretical analysis we are attempting to be quite simply a conditional one: If you want to struggle, here are some key points, here are some lines of force, here are some constrictions and blockages. In other words, I would like these imperatives to be no more than practical pointers. Of course, it is up to me, and those working in the same direction, to know on what fields of real forces we need to get our bearings in order to make a tactical effective analysis. But this is after all the circle of struggle and truth, that is to say, precisely of philosophical practice.[4]

Drawing on the lines of force, constrictions and blockages Foucault[5] articulates for struggle around contemporary apparatuses ('*dispositifs*') of security and governmentality in his seminal lecture series at the Collège de France in 1977-1978 on *Security, Territory, Population*, and through the examination of two events in modern governmentality and two events in contemporary governmentality, this work explores how lists are political technologies – fields of real forces – that have served and continue to serve formations of power.

The deployment of lists as instruments of security is inextricably intertwined with the emergence of modern computing and the abundance of data that began to be amassed with the advent of the earliest forms of computers developed in the late 1800s. Although the concept of 'big data'[6] is one that has increasingly been written about, there is no work that traces the history of big data back to the earliest forms of punch cards, sorters and tabulators emerging in the late 19th century when these technologies of population control were first developed by Herman Hollerith (founder of IBM) while working at the US Census Bureau as does this work. Developments in computing and data accumulation and their inextricable links to lists are examined here through the theoretical lens of population control and power: from the earliest conjunctions of lists, computing technologies and the accumulation of data emerging with Hollerith's punch cards, sorters and tabulators, through to the Nazis' use of these same technologies to not only control, but also eradicate populations, and onto the ways that contemporary conjunctions of lists, data, and computation are engaged in contemporary apparatuses of security and arrangements of power, like no-fly lists, no-work lists, no-buy lists, and no-stay lists deployed to control populations.

The first event explored in this work is the emergence of what this work calls 'Nazi Governmentality' in chapter 1: a modern event wherein juridical-legal and disciplinary mechanisms underpinned by list technologies were redeployed in a milieu of circulation ('*circulation*') that privileged pseudo-scientific articulations of biology and taxonomy in the establishment

4   Michel Foucault, '11 January 1978', in Senellart and Davidson (eds), *Security, Territory, Population*, pp. 1-28

5   Michel Foucault, Graham Burchell, Colin Gordon, and Peter Miller, *The Foucault Effect: Studies in Governmentality: With Two Lectures by and an Interview with Michel Foucault*, Chicago: University of Chicago Press, 1991; Michel Foucault and James D. Faubion, 'Power', in P. Rabinow (ed.), *Essential Works of Foucault 1954-1984, vol. 3*, New York: The New Press, 2000, pp. xliii, 484; Senellart and Davidson (eds), *Security, Territory, Population*.

6   Viktor Mayer-Schonberger and Kenneth Cukier, *Big Data*, New York, NY: Houghton Mifflin Harcourt Publishing Company, 2013; Lisa Gitelman, *'Raw Data' is an Oxymoron*, Cambridge, MA: The MIT Press, 2013.

of caesuric fractures between 'normal' and 'abnormal' populations. Herein we will see how this modern society installed an apparatus of security that interwove calculation, probability, population, and risk assessment – the techniques of statistics – with a natural history 'truthfully' articulated through eugenics and Nazi race theory, which sought to classify and normalize all people, things, and knowledge to the biological body of the German people, or the *Volk*. This chapter argues that crucial to the installation of this apparatus of security – this art of governmentality – was the critical support technology of lists; not only a way of *seeing* and *doing* law, discipline, circulation, and security under the Third Reich, but also a way of operationalizing the fracture of threatening populations from general populations in the constitution of regimes of truth about the battles between 'us' and 'them'. Moreover, this chapter reveals how the Nazi's use of these technologies was in fact the first instance of lists derived through the mining of data and deployed as apparatuses of security to control the movement and circulation of populations. In this way, chapter 1 explores how 'The List Served: Nazi Governmentality'.

Overlapping in time with the first event is the second, explored in chapter 2, 'The List Serves: Entropy and Governmentality', which traces the birth of modern computer technologies and their attendant cybernetic, game, and system theories in the 1940s and 1950s, and how this event came to install global milieus of circulation characterized by the physical law of entropy and the accumulation of data. This chapter argues that in these entropic milieus we begin to see ourselves and our societies as technoscientific cultural constructions of cyborg elements and populations, circulating in disordered and ever-expanding environments, where the boundaries between people, objects, and knowledge are completely eviscerated. While the emergence of modern computers ushered in awe-inspiring developments, it also served to increasingly isolate cyborgs in global classification infrastructures, subjecting them to evermore pervasive and ubiquitous monitoring, data accumulation, delimitation, policing, and listing.

In the era of the Cold War, when myths relating to us vs. them were heightened, and ultimately transformed into epic global battles between *communists* and the *free world*, black and white classifications of opposing forces, and wars over meaning – like the current one on terror – began to appear as ongoing and never-ending, further necessitating the self-elaborating operations of assemblages of policing involving delimiting, predicting, and policing the movements of unknown threats through listing practices. As computers and statistics were increasingly deployed to comb ever-expanding and ever-disordered – entropic – sets of social (big) data for regularities and patterns of 'threatening' living beings and things since World War II, these self-elaborating processes have produced the teleological effect of establishing natural and global good versus evil relationships, and the further need to redeploy lists to delimit and police the movement and control of populations.

Moving onto a contemporary examination of the interweaving of juridical-legal mechanisms, disciplinary mechanisms, and apparatuses of security hinged by the conjunction of list technologies and data is the third event of this research project, as recounted in chapter 3, 'Fear and No-fly Listing in Canada', an interrogation of the emergence of contemporary no-fly lists, wherein Foucault's lines of force, blockages and constrictions are brought to bear on a examination of lists as technologies of security installed under contemporary governmentality. This event is followed up with an event called 'No-blank List Culture, or How Technoscience Constructs the Terrorist', in chapter 4: an analysis of how list apparatuses of security continue to grow, evolve, and expand outside any perceived territorial boundaries, installing and normalizing the juridical-legal and disciplinary mechanisms of list technologies of security and the broad accumulation of data in more and more milieus of everyday circulation.

The List Served: Ancient Times

While there is little specific research into lists, let alone how they relate to people, things, and knowledge, an invaluable chapter called 'What's in a list?' by Jack Goody[7] reveals that the majority of ancient writings were in fact constituted in lists, and further, that much of early social order and organization revolved around listing practices and early forms of data accumulation. In the only direct and substantive examination of lists as technologies on record, Goody explores lists as they relate to transformations from oral to literate societies, suggesting through a material analysis of ancient documents, that while lists pre-date literacy, they were radically transformed by writing and reading, ultimately contributing to their emergence as powerful 'technologies of the intellect'.[8] For Goody, the 'power' associated with lists as 'technologies of the intellect' and specifically to the development of knowledge in ancient societies, was a factor of the dual-role they played; wherein lists at once brought order through the clear delimitation of boundaries between things and/or people – visualizing classes – and at the same time, they brought contradiction, through the questions they raised regarding the veracity of the 'classes' they constituted and called into existence.

> In saying the list transforms (or at least embodies) the class, I mean that it establishes the necessity of a boundary, the necessity of a beginning and an end. In oral usage, there are few if any occasions when one is required to list vegetables or trees or fruit … But the question: is a tomato a fruit or a vegetable? is the kind that would seem pointless in an oral context, but which may be essential to the advance of systematic knowledge about the classification and evolution of natural species. And it is this kind of question generated by written lists.[9]

Using as his corpus ancient Sumerian, Mesopotamian and Assyrian writings, Goody argues through a taxonomic material analysis of the characteristics of these early writings that there were three kinds of lists in these ancient societies; each of which at once carved out clear categories of knowledge, and at the same time opened up questions about the truth and nature of the classes they constituted and represented. In this way, Goody's taxonomic dual-role understanding of lists as 'intellectual technologies' positions them as

---

7   Jack Goody, *The Domestication of the Savage Mind*, Cambridge, New York: Cambridge University Press, 1977.
8   Goody, *The Domestication of the Savage Mind*, p. 106.
9   Goody, *The Domestication of the Savage Mind*, p. 105.

a source of ongoing friction between truth and falsity; on the one-hand cementing clearly delimited boundaries through the invocation of written classes, and on the other, calling into question the very lines in the sand they draw through the scanning and consideration of their contents.

This research argues that Goody's lists, understood as dual-role 'intellectual technologies', critical to both the administration and organization of people and things, and further 'to the classification and evolution of the natural species',[10] are assertions that bear out well beyond ancient Sumerian, Mesopotamian, and Assyrian times. In fact, his analysis can be extended into the era Foucault takes up his seminal 1977-1978 lectures series on *Security, Territory and Population*, which is the end of the Classical age with its series of sovereign and disciplinary mechanisms, and further into the era of 'governmentality', which takes shape in the seventeenth and eighteenth centuries. Indeed, the 'intellectual technology' role that lists play continues to bear out through to modern and contemporary political formations and their apparatuses of security. As we shall see, the list's dual-role that Goody describes is in fact characteristic of all technologies of security – what Foucault calls their 'double integration' effects.[11]

But for now, what Goody gives this investigation into lists and the governance of people, is an understanding of lists as critical technological supports of formations of power involving the accumulation of data dating back to ancient times. And more instrumentally, he provides us with a taxonomy for the operations of lists as 'intellectual technologies' on three levels: (a) as retrospective tools of administration, (b) as administrative tools for managing the future, and finally, (c) as lexical repertoires enabling the development of knowledge through the contradictory operations of at once delimiting, and at the same time, posing questions as to the veracity of the classes they constitute.

'Retrospective lists' were 'record[s] of outside events, roles, situations, persons, a typical early use of which would be the king-list. It is a kind of inventory of persons, objects or events'.[12] For Goody these administrative lists were used to store and sort data in the short and long term, and indeed, two-thirds of Goody's ancient corpus consisted of such written lists, which began to crystallize economic and legal problems in ancient society, interweaving people, things, and events in a manageable and viewable form. 'Shopping lists', for Goody, were those intended to administer the future, where items got checked off, mentally or physically, providing new levels of organization and complexity for ancient societies.[13] A news article from the BBC with the headline and byline '300-year-old shopping list found: A Chinese shopping list thought to have been written 300 years ago has been found stuffed inside an 18th century vase in a York stately home', is evidence of how the list continued to serve this administrative, organizational and knowledge development role through the Classical age and

---

10 Goody, *The Domestication of the Savage Mind*, p. 105.
11 Michel Foucault, '25 January 1978', in Senellart and Davidson (eds), *Security, Territory, Population*, pp. 55-86.
12 Goody, *The Domestication of the Savage Mind*, p. 80.
13 Goody, *The Domestication of the Savage Mind*, p. 81.

in a range of literate societies.[14] Finally, 'lexical lists', like those that would seek to classify the tomato as fruit or vegetable, provided an 'inventory of concepts'; acting in ancient times as 'proto-dictionaries' and 'embryonic encyclopedias'.[15]

Lexical lists were the least represented lists in Goody's ancient corpus, as characteristically they appeared only in educational situations. But at the same time, these least represented lists are crucial to the history of the development of knowledge in how they acted as 'abstractions', 'de-contextualizations', and 'conceptual prisons', which 'crystallized problems of classification' and 'led to increments of knowledge, to the organization of experience'.[16] Goody argues that, 'it was the keeping of such chronicles and the re-ordering of materials by means of visual inspection of the written word that permitted wider developments in the growth of human knowledge'.[17] For Goody, ancient administrative lists, like lists of the kings' reigns, were the incunabula for the development of 'event lists',[18] which ultimately played a significant role in the development of history:

> Lists were arranged in varying order, including chronological and were soon used for recording daily events or facts behind a given situation. Thus "king-lists", year formulae and other data necessary to law became the basis of historical writing ... Such records were of fundamental importance in enabling writers to draw out histories of particular sequences of events from the more general records, some of which accounts seem to have been used for composing the books of the Old Testament. Archives are a pre-requisite of history.[19]

The dual delimiting and knowledge development roles of Goody's overall conception of lists as 'intellectual technologies' – their double integration – that on the one hand establishes boundaries and encourages hierarchies, and on the other, leads to '...questions about the nature of the classes through the very fact of placing items together'[20] is not only key to understanding lists as critical support technologies of formations of power/knowledge, but also to understanding literacy as a communication technology and cultural phenomenon. Goody's work can be situated in a whole stream of research related to understanding the technologies of writing and reading as spaces of tension; epitomized in the work of Harold Innis[21], James Carey[22], and Walter Ong.[23] But where Goody's emphasis on the techniques of lists and how they operate as 'intellectual technologies' is productive in terms of generating a rough taxon-

14 British Broadcasting Corporation, BBC News, 31 January 2008, http://news.bbc.co.uk/go/pr/fr/-/2/hi/uk_news/england/north_yorkshire/7220717.stm.
15 Goody, *The Domestication of the Savage Mind*, p. 80.
16 Goody, *The Domestication of the Savage Mind*, p. 94.
17 Goody, *The Domestication of the Savage Mind*, p. 90.
18 Goody, *The Domestication of the Savage Mind*, p. 90.
19 Goody, *The Domestication of the Savage Mind*, p. 90.
20 Goody, *The Domestication of the Savage Mind*, p. 102.
21 Harold Adams Innis, *The Bias of Communication*, Toronto: University of Toronto Press, 1991.
22 James W. Carey, *Communication as Culture: Essays on Media and Society*, Boston: Unwin Hyman, 1989.
23 Walter J. Ong, *Orality and Literacy: The Technologizing of the Word*, London, New York: Routledge, 1991.

omy for the operations of listing, it only offers a glimpse into how lists in conjunction with the accumulation of data operate as political technologies of security in modern and contemporary formations of power, or more specifically governmentality. And it is precisely here that my research bifurcates from such communications research traditions, not discounting them, but suggesting an alternate and perhaps complementary trajectory.

Where such traditions examine what writing and reading are, or examine literacy as commu-nication technology, and where Goody in particular taxonomically investigates what lists are and describes the list as a technology of the intellect, I am less concerned with the objective characteristics of lists – the whats of taxonomic structures – and more with the hows of listing practices; the techniques that are deeply subsumed in the constitution of meanings, fields, domains, and objects of knowledge. In other words, this research concerns itself with how listing techniques in conjunction with the accumulation of data have been redeployed in jurid-ical-legal and disciplinary mechanisms, and instrumentalized in modern and contemporary apparatuses of security that serve governmentality.

This work argues that it is insufficient to characterize and classify lists as 'intellectual technologies', but rather one must consider them as political technologies, that oper-ate in conjunction with a wide range of myths, stories, ideologies, practices, and other technologies – *ways of doing* and *ways of seeing* – that together operate in, and as, an economy of discourses; all overlapping, competing, and collaborating with one another. In this way, lists are ultimately explored here as critical support technologies of modern and contemporary articulations of security, territory, and population – understood broadly as governmentality. Indeed, Foucault's conception of governmentality[24] is central to a key question this work asks: How do lists at once provide a technological way of doing, and at the same time enable us to see truth?

The List Served: The Classification of the Human Species

> What is this field in which nature appeared sufficiently close to itself for the individual beings it contained to be classified, and yet so far removed from itself that they had to be so by the medium of analysis and reflection?[25]

In his chapter in *The Order of Things* related to 'Classifying', Foucault traces the evolution of the field of 'natural history', wherein roughly between the seventeenth and mid eigh-teenth centuries, the difficulties surrounding linking together diverse attempts at establish-ing taxonomies à la Aristotle, Descartes, and Newton, began to butt theoretical heads with attempts at microscopic observation that were emerging in the new sciences surrounding 'evolution, the specificity of life, and the notion of organism',[26] which ultimately culminat-

---

24 Michel Foucault, 'Governmentality', in J.D. Faubion (ed.), *Power: Essential Works of Foucault 1954-1984, vol. 3,* New York: The New Press, 2000, pp. 201-222.
25 Michel Foucault, *The Order of Things: An Archaeology of the Human Sciences,* London and New York: Routledge, 2001 (1970), p. 139.
26 Foucault, *The Order of Things,* p. 140.

ed in the work of Charles Darwin (1809-1882) in the nineteenth century. For Foucault, the tensions inherent in 'dividing knowledge into these two interwoven fabrics',[27] which for him, were 'alien to one another', are ultimately reconciled by Darwin's new focus on an analysis of populations, epitomized above all by the classification of living beings. In this way, according to Foucault, the event of natural history marks the emergence of a new 'classifying' regime that concerns itself with the all-encompassing task of 'truthfully' categorizing everything and everyone.

Before the seventeenth century, writes Foucault, 'the history of a living being was that being itself', understood as existing 'within the whole semantic network that connected it to the world',[28] an existence wherein divisions and classifications that we now take for granted, including those of the human species, did not exist. In such times, argues Foucault, signs were a part of things themselves, for it was only in the seventeenth century that signs began to take on modes of representation, articulated according to their structure, numbers and magnitude, forms and arrangements. With this event, Foucault sees the biological begin to be suffused with the natural, in the constitution of an emergent regime of truth, which would come to pivot the classification of all living beings. In short, the emergence of 'man as the human species', homo sapiens, further subdivided and listed as elements in populations circulating amongst many in a field, domain, and object of knowledge that would come to be called natural history.

With the emergence of 'natural history' – this 'double integration' of taxonomy and biology – the boundaries between living beings, things and events are rendered irrelevant; all categorized, classified and listed as elements in populations. At the same time, with the event of natural history, the historian was transformed from one who retold what they read, heard, and experienced, to one who undertook to meticulously examine things themselves, in microscopic detail, seeing people, living beings, and objects as they truthfully were; transcribing, classifying and finally, listing their findings in the 'smooth, neutralized and faithful words'[29] that came to constitute the elements of natural history; the 'interweaving and classification' of all living beings, things, and events.

> Natural history in the Classical age is not merely the discovery of a new object of curiosity; it covers a series of complex operations that introduce the possibility of a constant order into a totality of representations. It constitutes a whole domain of empiricity as at the same time describable and orderable.[30]

With the emergence of natural history, a gap was left between words and things, and in this space, representation emerged as an interweaving force. 'Natural history' found its locus in the articulation of the elements of representation, 'those same elements that can now without let

---

27 Foucault, *The Order of Things*, p. 141.
28 Foucault, *The Order of Things*, p. 141.
29 Foucault, *The Order of Things*, p. 172.
30 Foucault, *The Order of Things*, p. 172.

or hindrance be named'[31]; those same elements that self-elaborate themselves as a regime of 'natural' truth. Foucault argues that natural history as a field and domain is characterized by a classifying space of representation; by an analysis that anticipates the possibility of naming; the possibility of seeing, at a distance, the truth of order between living beings, things and events, rendered indistinct in representation. In this way, for Foucault, representation is the 'language of language',[32] in how it intermediates between words and things, particularly as this concerns the theory of natural history, which takes as its chief concern the 'fundamental arrangement of knowledge, which orders the knowledge of beings so as to make it possible to represent them in a system of names'.[33] And all such systems of classifying, naming, representing, and ordering take as their basis the ancient technology of lists.

As such, it is argued here that the practices of classification in 'natural history', and equally in all fields and domains where classification is practiced, all rely on the critical support technology of lists, which continue to serve administration, organization, and the lexical development of knowledge with the event of natural history, but also now become critical support technologies of classification in and of themselves, deployed to bring order to populations and thus control them. So, it is not just the act of classifying in natural history that renders the boundaries between living beings, things, knowledge, and events increasingly irrelevant as Foucault argues, but this is also a factor of the effects of lists as critical support technologies operationalized in these biologically driven modes of representation.

Through the Classical age, the list continued to serve its delimiting power/knowledge role, but at the same time, it also began to be taken up in new tasks, in other disciplines, in new ways, including to order and control the circulation of populations. As such, the history of how lists serve modern and contemporary apparatuses of security and governmentality is 'a history restored to the irruptive violence of time'[34], one in which the political events and data of the day are understood as providing the 'natural history' around which populations are calculated, predicted, controlled, and secured through the technology of lists.

The List Serves: Disciplinary and Juridical-legal Mechanisms

By definition, discipline regulates everything. Discipline allows nothing to escape. Not only does it not allow things to run their course, its principle is that things, the smallest things, must not be abandoned to themselves. The smallest infraction of discipline must be taken up with all the more care for it being small.[35]

---

31 Foucault, *The Order of Things*, p. 141.
32 Foucault, *The Order of Things*, p. 142.
33 Foucault, *The Order of Things*, pp. 171-172.
34 Foucault, *The Order of Things*, p. 144.
35 Michel Foucault, '18 January 1978', in Senellart and Davidson (eds), *Security, Territory, Population*, pp. 29-54.

The list is a critical support technology of discipline in how it at once delimits and calls into question spaces of representation, and at the same time operates as a tool for caring for the minutiae of increasingly granular data. It is the web that does not let data slip through the cracks, forcing classification of the finer and finer elements of living beings, things, and events into discipline's enclosures. In this way, the list serves discipline in how it provides an underpinning structure for the materialization and visual inspection of whatever discipline might analyze, break down, prescribe and seek to control. Discipline lists, and once listed, components can be seen and prescriptions can be made for their ordering. In providing such visualization, lists as disciplinary mechanisms also present opportunities for modification, facilitating the classification of components according to other objectives, all the while continuing to serve their administrative, organizational and knowledge development roles. But as technologies of discipline, they also help establish sequences, or coordinations of people, actions, and things; how they are to be optimally assembled. Who is best suited to what? What is best suited to whom? How are actions, people, and things to be efficiently and effectively linked together? Lists provide answers to such questions for discipline, materializing prohibitions and prescriptions, and at the same time, exercising new force in the fracture of abnormal populations from normal ones for the purposes of control. As Foucault writes,

> Discipline fixes the processes of training ['*dressage*'] and permanent control, and finally, on the basis of this, it establishes the division between those considered unsuitable or incapable and the others. That is to say, on this basis it divides the normal from the abnormal.[36]

In this way, lists serve as a control function in what Foucault calls 'disciplinary normalization'[37] which consists of positing an optimal model and prescription for a certain 'normal' result, and then steering people, movements, and actions to conform to the optimal model. 'The normal being precisely that which can conform to this norm, and the abnormal that which is incapable of conforming to the norm.'[38] Indeed, for Foucault, it is not the normal and the abnormal that are of primary importance to disciplinary normalization; rather, it is the norm. It is the 'originally prescriptive character of the norm and the determination and the identification of the normal and the abnormal [that] becomes possible in relation to this posited norm'.[39] Foucault specifies that really we are not so concerned with normalization as we are with 'normation'.

> Due to the primacy of the norm in relation to the normal, to the fact that disciplinary normalization goes from the norm to the final division between the normal and the abnormal, I would rather say that what is involved in disciplinary techniques is a "normation" rather than normalization.[40]

A simple list of rules, like say, the Ten Commandments, can be used here to clarify how the list serves disciplinary 'normation' in systems of law. Out of the vast disorder that marked

---

36 Foucault, '25 January 1978', p. 57.
37 Foucault, '25 January 1978', p. 57.
38 Foucault, '25 January 1978', p. 57.
39 Foucault, '25 January 1978', p. 57.
40 Foucault, '25 January 1978', p. 57.

the world in biblical times, ten tenets were drafted that constituted a list of basic prohibitive and prescriptive norms of, and for, life in a milieu of high uncertainty. If we take any one of the most commonly referred to commandments, like say, 'thou shall not murder' or 'thou shall not steal', we can clearly see on a very simple level how the listed object – the prohibition of murder or theft – posits a norm from which we can identify populations who don't murder or steal as normal, and those who do murder or steal as abnormal. That these norms are materialized as a list of prohibitions, is at the simplest level how the list serves to enclose what discipline analyzes, breaks down, prescribes, and modifies. In this way, we can see how from one of the earliest systems of law, the Ten Commandments, and forward, lists have served disciplinary normation. Put differently, the materialization of discipline's prescriptions for 'good life' through the positing of a list of prohibitionary norms is the fundamental basis of systems of law.

> Order is what remains when everything that is prohibited has in fact been prevented. I think this negative thought and technique is typical of legal code.[41]

Indeed, there is a fundamental relationship between discipline and lists, and the law and the norm, in that 'every system of law is related to a system of norms',[42] but also in that everything system of norms functions on the critical support technology of lists in the visual materialization of laws. Where discipline delimits a space of rules and prescriptions, the basic function of law is to give greater definition to that which is prohibited through the materialization of written lists of norms. The history of the juridical-legal mechanism is nothing more than the increasingly complex materialization of prohibitions of lists of posited norms. In other words, order is established in systems of law through an increasingly subtle analysis of disorder, listing more and more prohibitions for disciplining the uncertainty of the world – for controlling and bringing order to it.

In basic or complex, religious or governmental, systems of law, everything that remains beyond the list of prohibitions for countering disorder becomes what is thus called order. In this way, we can say that disorder, in biblical law and times, was everything that remained beyond a list of rules that delimited a space where murdering, stealing, lying, coveting one's neighbor, etcetera are prohibited. In other words, disorder is what remains beyond discipline's ever-finer prescriptions and lists of rules, and at the same time, order itself is called into question by the delimiting and knowledge development effects of the critical support technology of lists functioning as juridical-disciplinary mechanisms themselves.

We can say that law, as a disciplinary mechanism that explicitly materializes lists of prohibitions, is a system that imagines the negative. Law as a disciplinary mechanism is understood as planning and working a space that is complementary to reality, a space to counter the reality that 'Man is wicked, bad, and has evil thoughts ... etcetera'[43]; a mirrored sphere of prohibitions intended to steer the bad to the good, where lists serve as critical support technologies. Law operates in the imaginary, since systems of law are based on the formulation

---

41 Foucault, '25 January 1978', p. 46.
42 Foucault, '25 January 1978', p. 56.
43 Foucault, '18 January 1978', p. 47.

and listing of 'all the things that could and must be done'[44] as imagined by a set of rules and prescriptions invoked by discipline and materialized as lists.

The List Serves: The Apparatuses of Security

In other words, the law prohibits and discipline prescribes, and the essential function of security, without preventing or prescribing, but possibly making use of some instruments of prescription and prohibition, is to respond to reality in such a way that this response cancels out the reality to which it responds – nullifies it, or limits, checks, or regulates it. I think this regulation within the element of reality is fundamental in apparatuses of security.[45]

The 1977-1978 lectures series that Michel Foucault delivered at the Collège de France marked the emergence of Foucault's conception of 'governmentality'. For Foucault governmentality begins to take shape in the eighteenth century, a period in which Western societies not only began to adopt the fundamental biological fact that human beings are a species, part of a broader 'truthful' natural history of everything, but also, wherein the apparatuses of security first emerged. Throughout these lectures, and indeed, throughout Foucault's work overall, he emphasizes time and again that the history of the emergence of juridical-legal mechanisms, disciplinary mechanisms, and mechanisms of security, are not marked by moments of rupture, but rather, by a deepening of the correlations between these mechanisms. For Foucault, relations of power reside in these correlations, associations, and representations, and it is precisely here that a strategic analysis must unloosen relational bonds. In other words, an analysis of technologies and their techniques is taken up here in order to detach them from relations of power, and then resituate all within the perspective of the constitution of fields, domains, and objects of knowledge.

So there is not a series of successive elements, the appearance of the new causing the earlier ones to disappear. There is not the legal age, the disciplinary age, and then the age of security. Mechanisms of security do not replace disciplinary mechanisms, which would have replaced juridical-legal mechanisms. In reality you have a series of complex edifices in which, of course, the techniques themselves change and are perfected, or anyway become more complicated, but in which what above all changes is the dominant characteristic, or more exactly, the system of correlation between juridical-legal mechanisms, disciplinary mechanisms, and mechanisms of security. In other words, there is a history of the actual techniques themselves.[46]

In turn, the list conceived of as a critical support technology of juridical-legal, disciplinary, and security mechanisms is not to be understood in isolation and as unchanging, but rather as an instrument, or more precisely a technology, with the dual role of delimiting and developing knowledge, whose techniques have been deployed, redeployed, and transformed since ancient times in different political formations of power. Indeed, there is a different treatment of space by juridical-legal mechanisms, disciplinary mechanisms, and what the apparatuses

---

44 Foucault, '18 January 1978', p. 48.
45 Foucault, '18 January 1978', p. 47.
46 Foucault, '11 January 1978', p. 8.

of security install, and as such, the list as a critical support technology is called upon to play a variety of roles and serve a variety of different functions within and between each.

The List Serves: Milieus of Circulation and Populations

In order to understand the shift from sovereignty to discipline, to the space of govern-mentality, Foucault explores the town in the seventeenth and eighteenth centuries, which for him, was marked overall by uncertainty and unpredictability regarding the indefinite series of events,[47] indefinite series of accumulating units,[48] and indefinite series of mobile elements,[49] whose circulation needed to be controlled day and night. In the eighteenth century what emerged for the town was a need to organize circulation, not to enclose and prohibit spaces as sovereignty had long done through juridical-legal and disciplinary mechanisms, but rather, to *let things happen,* to encourage 'good' circulation and discour-age 'bad'. In other words, governing towns in the seventeenth and eighteenth centuries began to concern itself with security, or more specifically, with the creation of a space or a milieu that neither permitted nor prohibited circulation, but took it as its maxim cal-culating populations and controlling their movement as a means of maximizing the good circulation of elements and nullifying the movement of the bad. In these arrangements, the finer the grains of data collected regarding populations, the more potential there is for controlling their circulation.

> I think the management of these series that, because they are open series can only be controlled by an estimate of probabilities, is pretty much the essential characteristic of the mechanism of security.[50]

Where sovereignty had capitalized territory through juridical-legal and disciplinary mecha-nisms, enclosing and structuring spaces through operations of prohibitionary delimitation and the hierarchical and functional distribution of elements, and thus raised location as the major problem of government, security began to attempt to install a milieu of circulation in which elements and events as well as *probable* elements and events are regulated 'within a multivalent and transformable framework' that raised probabilities and populations as the major problem of government. In this way, 'the space in which a series of uncertain elements unfold is, I think, roughly what one can call the milieu'.[51] In other words, the milieu is where the circulation of populations is controlled.

In short, the apparatuses of security of the eighteenth century worked, fabricated, organized, and planned a space that addressed the questions of uncertainty and unpredictability posed by the town, through the installment of a milieu of circulation; where good circulation was intended to be maximized and bad circulation was intended to be diminished and nullified

---

47 Plagues, famines, etc.
48 Homes, inhabitants, etc.
49 Carts, horses, people, etc.
50 Foucault, '11 January 1978', p. 20.
51 Foucault, '11 January 1978', p. 20.

through mathematical and statistical techniques involving calculations, probabilities, risk assessments, and the delimitation of 'populations'.

> The milieu appears as a field of intervention in which, instead of affecting individuals as a set of legal subjects capable of voluntary actions – which would be the case of sovereignty – and instead of affecting them as a multiplicity of organisms, of bodies capable of performances, and of required performances – as in discipline – one tries to affect precisely, a population. I mean a multiplicity of individuals who are and fundamentally and essentially only exist biologically bound to the materiality within which they live. What one tries to reach through this milieu, is precisely the conjunction of a series of events produced by these individuals, populations and groups, and quasi natural events which occur around them.[52]

Instead of a binary division between the prohibited and the permitted, the marker of sovereignty and discipline, the apparatuses of security install a milieu of circulation where on the one hand, an 'average' considered as 'optimal' is established, and on the other hand, 'a bandwidth of the acceptable'[53] is set to keep circulating elements in check. What takes shape within this milieu of circulation is a completely different distribution of people, things, and mechanisms that now take as their focus the normalization of populations, the realm of statistics, and its specific techniques of calculations, probabilities, predictions, and populations. With this shift to affecting populations, the spotlight of government is shifted from questions of individuals subjected to the rule of a sovereign, or bodies disciplined by the limits of performance, re-focusing on agglomerations of individuals as the primary unit of analysis: populations as the focus of governmentality.

'The more I have spoken of population, the more I have stopped saying "sovereign".'[54] For Foucault a crucial event in the emergence of this art of governmentality was how questions of food scarcity and epidemics began to be treated in the eighteenth century. Prior to the eighteenth century, these problems were countered by juridical-legal and disciplinary mechanisms involving regulating, permitting, and prohibiting the circulation of grain – the complete prevention of famine being the objective. But henceforth, solutions would begin to take as their focus ensuring circulation, not preventing, nor prohibiting famine or epidemics per se, but installing market mechanisms of security that would seek to ensure the free movement of 'grain' as a means of nullifying 'famine' and 'plague' movements. Random fluctuations in abundance/scarcity and dearness/cheapness would be allowed for, but countered by an analysis of populations with the aim of statistical normalization, rather than prevention and prohibition.

> The physiocrats and the economic theorists of the eighteenth century, tried to arrive at an apparatus ['*dispositif*'] for arranging things so that, by connecting up with the very reality of these fluctuations, and by establishing a series of connections with other

---

52 Foucault, '11 January 1978', p. 21.
53 Foucault, '11 January 1978', p. 21.
54 Foucault, '25 January 1978', p. 76.

elements of reality, the phenomenon is gradually compensated for, checked, finally limited, and the final degree canceled out, without it being prevented or losing any of its reality. In other words, by working with the reality of fluctuations between abundance/scarcity, dearness/cheapness, and not by trying to prevent it in advance, an apparatus is installed, which is, I think, precisely an apparatus of security and no longer a juridical-disciplinary system.[55]

What uniquely characterizes the apparatuses for arranging things – these market mechanisms of security – that are installed in the eighteenth century is the emergence of population as a primary unit of analysis, established through the operations of the statistical techniques of calculation, probability, and prediction of worth/risk in the 'securing' of milieus of circulation. 'This conception of market mechanisms is not just the analysis of what happens. It is at once an analysis of what happens and a program for what should happen.'[56] The event of food scarcity in the town led to a whole new way of 'conceiving' and 'programming' things; a way where curbing scarcity was countered 'by a sort of "*laisser-faire*", a certain "freedom of movement (*laisser-passer*)", a sort of "*laisser-aller*", in the sense of "letting things take their course"'.[57]

Where discipline is a centripetal force in how it concentrates, focuses, and encloses a space, the security mechanism that is installed to curb food scarcity in the eighteenth century is precisely the opposite; it 'lets things happen'.[58] In other words, where discipline circumscribes a space in which the mechanisms of power will 'function fully and without limit ... preventing everything, even and above all the detail',[59] the function of security is to provide a milieu of circulation that lets things happen, relying 'on details that are not valued as good or evil in themselves', a milieu that does not prohibit or prescribe, but rather, ensures the 'secure' circulation of elements in, between, and amongst populations. Indeed, data regarding details of elements circulating in the milieu installed by the apparatuses of security while 'necessary', 'inevitable', and 'natural processes' are not deemed 'good' or 'bad' in their own right, but only pertinent insofar as they situate matters in their function in establishing population and controlling circulation. 'The multiplicity of individuals is no longer pertinent, the population is.'[60]

The list as a technology of control is redeployed in two ways in these arrangements. As per the above, the list continues to serve its administrative, organizational, and knowledge development roles in the apparatuses of security through its redeployment as a critical support technology of juridical-disciplinary mechanisms. But at the same time, the list becomes a technology of security in and of itself in the apparatuses of security, one that takes as its focus the fracture of 'threatening populations' from 'general populations', serv-

55 Foucault, '18 January 1978', p. 37.
56 Foucault, '18 January 1978', p. 40.
57 Foucault, '18 January 1978', p. 41.
58 Foucault, '18 January 1978', p. 41.
59 Foucault, '18 January 1978', p. 41.
60 Foucault, '18 January 1978', p. 42.

ing the raw and practiced schisms of ongoing battles and struggles between populations – the caesuras of 'us' and 'them'.

As we will also see through the work of Giorgio Agamben,[61] Foucault engages the literary term 'caesura', meaning 'a break between words within a metrical foot', or 'a pause near the middle of a line', in a sense that extends the definition beyond the literary, to encompass breaks or fractures of and between bodies. From its Latin origins, *caes-* and *caed-* 'cut, hewn', and 'fell, slaughter, murder' respectively, as well as the Latin verb *caedere*, 'to fall', words like *cadaver* appeared in the sixteenth century. This etymology reveals a meaning for caesura as related to fractures of and between bodies in a biological sense.[62] The symbol for caesura ‖ will be deployed throughout this work to exemplify such breaks.

The List Serves: Risk Assessment

> The population as a political subject, as a new collective subject absolutely foreign to the juridical and political thought of earlier centuries is appearing here in its complexity, with its caesuras. You can already see it appearing as an object, that is to say as that on which and towards which mechanisms are directed in order to have a particular effect on it, as well as a subject, since it is called upon to conduct itself in such and such a fashion.[63]

In order to understand how the apparatuses of security relate to disciplinary normalization, Foucault invokes the example of the epidemic disease of smallpox in a town in the eighteenth century. What happened with the event of the epidemic was that the effects of the purely empirical techniques of statistics began to be applied to medical problems involving questions of circulation, in what would inevitably appear as a domain that concerned itself with 'medical policing'.[64] Thanks to the statistical instruments available, it was now possible to think through the phenomenon of epidemics in new terms; those of the 'calculus of probabilities', a field of empiricity previously not tied to medical science.[65] What was remarkable about this application of statistics and probabilities in the prevention of smallpox were the operations of variolization and vaccination, and more generally, of the application of techniques of populations and probabilities to diseases. In other words, the approach was not to

---

61 Giorgio Agamben, *Homo Sacer: Sovereign Power and Bare Life*, Stanford: Stanford University Press, 1998; Giorgio Agamben, *Remnants of Auschwitz: The Witness and the Archive*, New York: Zone Books, 2000; Giorgio Agamben, *State of Exception*, Chicago: University of Chicago Press, 2005.

62 Dictionary sources: 'caesura *noun*', *The Oxford Dictionary of English* (revised edition), ed. Catherine Soanes and Angus Stevenson, Oxford University Press, 2005; 'caes, caed, caedere', *The Pocket Oxford Latin Dictionary*, ed. James Morwood, Oxford University Press, 1994; 'cadaver *noun*', *The Oxford Dictionary of English*. All accessed with *Oxford Reference Online*, Oxford University Press, Concordia University Library, Montreal, 31 January 2008.

63 Foucault, '18 January 1978', p. 42.

64 Foucault, '8 February 1978 *Governmentality*', p. 59.

65 Foucault, '8 February 1978 *Governmentality*', p. 159.

... try to prevent smallpox so much as provoke it in inoculated individuals, but under conditions such that the nullification of the disease could take place at the same time as this vaccination. With the support of this kind of first small, artificially inoculated disease, one could prevent other possible attacks of smallpox. We have here a typical mechanism of security with the same morphology as that seen in the case of scarcity. There is a *double integration*, therefore, within different technologies of security, and within the rationalization of chance and probabilities.[66]

With the disease accessible at both the level of the group and at the level of each individual case, and thanks to statistics and its analysis of populations and distributions, physiocrats were now able to identify the risk for each individual within a group of contracting, succumbing, or being cured of a disease, and listing such populations as risks to circulation targeted for control. Where variolization provokes the threat by materializing the disease in the individual, vaccination seeks to nullify the threat and disease through the materialization of the disease that variolization itself provoked. In other words, the operations of variolization and vaccination can be understood as a double integration self-elaborating process, in that variolization calls the disease into reality and vaccination acts on this invoked reality, nullifying its effects, each authorizing and reinforcing the other. As with the mechanisms installed to counter scarcity; as with those aimed at countering epidemics; and as with the statistical technologies and techniques of rationalizing chance and probabilities; the list equally displays this 'double integration' effect.

Where the list materialized threats of 'Jews' and other 'abnormal populations' in the Nazi era, and 'communists' in the Cold War era, and 'terrorists' in contemporary times, it also acts as the key instrument for the nullification of the movement of the risks it delimits. In other words, the list invokes the category risk, calls it and its elements into reality, and then acts as the key instrument in the policing of the risks it itself invokes. Where list technologies delimit boundaries, they open up questions of the classes they constitute, now serving apparatuses of security that take as their aim the delimitation and policing of the movement of risks in milieus of circulation. As we will see in the next chapters, the list understood as a security technology exhibits this 'double integration'. On the one hand, it delimits a class of risk, carving out the fundamental caesura of 'us' || 'them', and on the other hand, the list serves as the primary instrument for the identification and control of the movement of the very risks it delimits; all the while self-elaborating itself as the purveyor of 'truth'.

A constant interplay between techniques of power and their object gradually carves out in reality, population and its specific phenomena. A whole series of objects were made visible for possible forms of knowledge on the basis of the constitution of the population as a correlate of techniques of power. In turn, because these forms of knowledge constantly carve out new objects, the population could be formed, continue, and remain as the privileged correlate of modern mechanisms of power.[67]

---

66 Foucault, '8 February 1978 *Governmentality*', p. 159.
67 Foucault, '8 February 1978 *Governmentality*', p. 79.

Like with statistics, the list serves to materialize populations, and at the same time, in materializing populations it provides a way of delimiting and policing the movement of risks, through disciplinary normalization. What Foucault provides with his articulation of the 'double integration' of security technologies – the delimitation, policing, and self-elaboration processes – is a way of unloosening the pivotal operations of risk management in the apparatuses of security. Risk is everywhere in the circulation of elements, but risks are never the same for everyone and everything, and vary according to condition, place, and milieu. Meaning that there are 'zones of higher' and 'zones of lower risk' and apparatuses of security concern themselves with the thresholds for identifying 'what is dangerous' within such milieus of circulation.[68] The explicit role that the list plays in identifying 'what is dangerous' and serving the apparatuses of security's management and policing of elements circulating in 'zones of higher and lower risk', is elaborated in depth in chapter 3 on 'Fear and No-fly Listing in Canada'.

For now, suffice it to say, the double integration effects of lists in the delimitation and policing of what they deem dangerous make them a political technology of security. At the same time, lists also serve the phenomenon of 'sudden worsening, acceleration, and increase' of threats, or what Foucault calls 'bolting', and 'the crisis' that appears within the milieus of circulation installed by the apparatuses of security: 'The crisis is the phenomenon of sudden, circular bolting that can only be checked either by a higher, natural mechanism, or by an artificial mechanism.'[69] As we shall see in chapter 4 on no-blank list culture, when terrorist alerts bolt or rather when a terrorist crisis is *seen* to be looming on the horizon, when risk alerts are heightened to code yellow, orange, and the dreaded red, more and more no-blank list technologies of security are deployed, in more and more zones of risk, listing more and more threatening populations and elements for management and policing (people, things, events, and knowledge).

The List Serves: Freedom of Circulation

An apparatus of security, in any case the one I have spoken about, cannot operate except on condition that it is given freedom, in the modern sense that it acquires in the eighteenth century: no longer the exemptions and privileges attached to a person, but the possibility of movement, change of place, and processes of circulation of both people and things. I think it is this freedom of circulation, in the broad sense of the term, it is in terms of this option of circulation, that we should understand the word freedom, and understand it as one of the facets, aspects, or dimensions of the deployment of apparatuses of security.[70]

For Foucault, 'the game of liberalism' hinges on the apparatuses of security ensuring 'freedom of circulation', 'lettings things happen', 'not interfering', 'allowing free movement', and 'letting things follow their course' – *laisser faire, passer et aller* – which 'basically and fundamentally means acting so that reality, develops, goes its way, and follows its own course

---

68 Foucault, '18 January 1978', p. 61.
69 Foucault, '25 January 1978', p. 61.
70 Foucault, '18 January 1978', p. 49.

according to the laws, principles, and mechanisms of reality itself'.[71] And it is precisely this *laisser faire milieu* that the apparatuses of security install, and that lists serve as technologies of security. In essence, encouraging favorable over unfavorable circulation through the self-elaborating double integration effects of interweaving population and probabilities in the nullification of the movement of circulating risks.

> So this problem of freedom ... can be considered and grasped in different ways. For sure, we can say – and I don't think it would be false, it cannot be false – that this ideology of freedom really was one of the conditions of development of modern or, if you like, capitalist forms of economy. This is undeniable ... this freedom, both ideology and technique of government, should in fact be understood within the mutations of and transformation of technologies of power.[72]

As we shall see in subsequent chapters, Foucault's tentative polemics bear out; freedom of circulation does not just characterize the space installed by the apparatuses of security in modern times, but equally in contemporary times. Moreover, the research presented here argues that the 'free' milieus of circulation installed by apparatuses of security are abetted by the redeployment of the list as a critical support technology of juridical-disciplinary mechanisms and as a technology of security in and of itself. In other words, the list continues to serve its historical role of administration, organization, and knowledge development in the apparatuses of security, but also emerges as a technology of security in its own right: one that serves the fracture of 'risky' populations from 'normal' populations, installing the caesura of 'us' ‖ 'them', and at the same time, taking on a new and critical self-elaborating role of managing, and controlling the circulation of the risks it delimits.

The List Serves: Governmentality

> First, by "governmentality" I understand the ensemble formed by institutions, procedures, analyses and reflections, calculations, and tactics that allow the exercise of this very specific, albeit, very complex, power that has the population as its target, political economy as its major form of knowledge, and apparatuses of security as its essential technical instrument.[73]

What we have seen thus far in this examination of how lists serve is that the essential issue of government in the eighteenth century was the introduction of 'economy' into 'political' practice. Where the word 'economy' in the sixteenth century designated a form of government, 'in the eighteenth century, through a series of complex processes that are absolutely crucial for our history, it will designate a level of reality and a field of intervention for government'.[74] So what Foucault argues we have from the eighteenth century forward is an economic mechanism that targets population, installing a field of intervention whose

71 Foucault, '18 January 1978', p. 48.
72 Foucault, '18 January 1978', p. 48.
73 Foucault, '18 January 1978', p. 108.
74 Foucault, '18 January 1978', p. 95.

politics is to let things happen as a means of governing all of the elements circulating in its milieu. In this milieu, the list serves a uniquely new role of fracturing risks from normal populations and, at the same time, serves as the primary instrument for the enforcement or the policing of the classes it constitutes.

> So we should not see things as the replacement of a society of sovereignty by a society of discipline, and then of a society of discipline by a society, say, of government. In fact we have a triangle: sovereignty, discipline and governmental management, which has population as its main target and apparatuses of security as its essential mechanism.[75]

Managing populations is not simply a task of controlling the overall movement of people, things, and events, all freely circulating, but rather, 'managing the population means managing it in depth, with all its finer points and detail'.[76] In other words, governmentality is not merely about controlling the circulation of populations, but is also inextricably intertwined with managing accumulations of data. In Foucault's conception of governmentality, the administration, organization, and knowledge development of the mundane minutiae that the list has served since ancient times continues to be critical, as it is redeployed in the apparatuses of security and their attendant juridical-disciplinary mechanisms. But governmentality means more than just the management of populations and the minutiae of elements that circulate in milieus of security, and lists too serve a different role in this art:

> And maybe, in a completely general, rough, and therefore inexact way, we could reconstruct the major forms, the major economies of power in the following way: first, the state of justice, born in the feudal type of territoriality and broadly corresponding to a society of customary and written law, with a whole interplay of commitments and litigation; second, the administrative state that corresponds to a society of regulations and disciplines; and finally, a state of government that is no longer essentially defined by its territoriality, by the surface occupied, but by a mass: the mass of the population, with its volume, its density, and, for sure, the territory it covers, but which is, in a way, only one of its components. This state of government, which essentially bears on the population and calls upon and employs economic knowledge as an instrument, would correspond to a society controlled by apparatuses of security.[77]

In this way, Foucault saw in governmentality a 'tendency', 'a line of force', that for a very long time, and particularly throughout the West, had constantly pushed its way into pre-eminence over other types of power, particularly over sovereignty and discipline, and this is the kind of power we call 'government'.[78] Indeed, government, as Foucault theorizes it, is a series of knowledges ('*savoirs*') coupled with the development of a series of governmental apparatuses ('*appareils*') that install an economic milieu of political circulation, and it is the space of movement that lists serve.

---

75 Foucault, '1 February 1978 *Governmentality*', p. 108.
76 Foucault, '1 February 1978 *Governmentality*', p. 107.
77 Foucault, '1 February 1978 *Governmentality*', pp. 109-110.
78 Foucault, '1 February 1978 *Governmentality*', p. 108.

Finally, by "governmentality" I think we should understand the process, or rather, the result of the process by which the state of justice of the Middle Ages became the administrative state in the fifteenth and sixteenth centuries and was gradually "governmentalized".[79]

Taking up Foucault's lines of force, blockages, and constrictions, this investigation into how the list serves, argues, at its core, that his assertion is one that fully bears out:

We live in the era of a governmentality discovered in the eighteenth century.[80]

In all these ways, *The List Serves* is not a technological history; rather, it is an examination of struggles over governmentality in modern and contemporary formations of power. It consists of unloosening the relational bonds of the apparatuses of security that have historically correlated the development of fields, domains, and objects of knowledge, and propelling them into a contemporary analysis. In order to achieve this unloosening and propulsion, this research presents a series of four events that highlight how the list has served, and continues to serve, modern and contemporary formations of power. This involves oscillating between analyzing the list as a technology of security, articulating the juridical-disciplinary mechanisms the list underpins in these events, and interrogating the kinds of knowledge/power formations it correlates, associates, and represents. How does the list contribute to greater ensembles of truth in these events? How does the list serve to fracture risky populations, and at the same time act as the primary instrument for their management and policing? The four events studied here each provide their own unique insights into how the list serves apparatuses of security and governmentality as such.

The problems of governmentality and the techniques of government have really become the only political stake and the only real space of political struggle and contestation.[81]

Like Foucault's interrogations of madness, incarceration, education, and sexuality,[82] this work focuses on the unfinished boundaries and borders of power/knowledge – the abutments that the list cements – and the forces that exert thrust and pressure on them – the bridges of people, things, knowledge, events, actions, associations, and representations they cantilever. Drawing on Foucault, I would like to suggest that *just as the list abuts power, power abuts the list*. Their boundaries are inseparable and intertwined, forced together and constituted in the differential tension of listing practices; on the one hand supporting disciplinary enclosures of power/knowledge – *of truth* – and on the other, operating as bridges to modifications, revealing new ways of doing the art of governmentality involving fracturing risky elements from populations, and managing and policing them in the interest of 'free' circulation.

---

79 Foucault, '1 February 1978 *Governmentality*', pp. 108-109.
80 Foucault, '1 February 1978 *Governmentality*', p. 109.
81 Foucault, '1 February 1978 *Governmentality*', p. 109.
82 Michel Foucault, *Madness and Civilization: A History of Insanity in the Age of Reason*, New York: Vintage Books, 1973; Michel Foucault, *The History of Sexuality*, New York: Pantheon Books, 1978; Michel Foucault, *Discipline and Punish: The Birth of the Prison*, New York: Vintage Books, 1995; Michel Foucault, *Archaeology of Knowledge*, New York: Routledge, 2002.

I wanted to ask how these divisions are effected. It's a method that seems to me to yield – I wouldn't say the maximum of possible illumination – at least a fairly fruitful kind of intelligibility.[83]

It is this middle-ground, this practiced space-in-between, where risks are called into existence and fractured from normal populations that is the focus of this work. Therefore, following Foucault's methodological approach rooted in discourse analysis,[84] rather than asking *what* in a given time is regarded as a list, I ask how divisions, boundaries, and borders are constituted through the technologies and techniques of the list. How does the list support juridical-disciplinary mechanisms and apparatuses of security? How does the list serve governmentality?

It is my overall contention that the list is a technology of security characterized by a 'double integration' effect – the hallmark of the self-elaborating art of governmentality's apparatuses of security. Where lists reveal a way of seeing, listing practices provide a way of doing, and this is brought to light in examination of a series of struggles over power/knowledge, with the ultimate aim of resituating them where they belong: in relations of power operating in the constitution of fields, domains, and objects of knowledge. Where Goody's *The Domestication of the Savage Mind* provides a natural temporal starting point for this research in analyzing the list as an 'intellectual technology' of ancient societies, I am far more compelled to begin this work by highlighting an event which marks the first conjuncture of listing practices with a powerful 'new' technological form: computers. Indeed, early information technologies, statistical techniques, and the accumulation of data articulated by the Nazis, made self-evident a very complex regime of listing practices, which resonate strongly today. By interrogating an early conjuncture of computers, data, statistical techniques, and list technologies, wherein a 'new' self-evidence regarding controlling populations was sutured, I hope to begin to exhume the list from our social woodwork, demonstrating how juridical-disciplinary mechanisms and apparatuses of security were installed by the Nazis during WWII, which reinforced a regime of truth where struggles over power/knowledge were firmly rooted in the establishment of caesuras between 'healthy' || 'diseased' populations.

---

83 Michel Foucault, 'Questions of Method', in Faubion (ed.), *Power*, p. 224.
84 Foucault, *Discipline and Punish*; Michel Foucault, 'Space, Knowledge, and Power', in Faubion (ed.), *Power*, pp. 349-364; Michel Foucault, 'Truth and Juridical Forms', in Faubion (ed.), *Power*, pp. 1-89; Michel Foucault and James D. Faubion, 'Power', in Faubion (ed.), *Power*, pp. xliii, 484; Michel Foucault and Colin Gordon, 'The Eye of Power', in *Power/Knowledge: Selected Interviews and Other Writings, 1972-1977*, New York: Pantheon Books, 1980, pp. 146-165.

CHAPTER 1. THE LIST SERVED: NAZI GOVERNMENTALITY

Introduction

> Mankind barely noticed when the concept of *massively organized information* quietly emerged to become a means of social control, a weapon of war, and a roadmap for group destruction. The unique igniting event was the most fateful day of the last century, January 30, 1933; the day Adolf Hitler came to power. Hitler and his hatred of the Jews was the ironic driving force behind this intellectual turning point.[1]

Through the ages, technologies for organizing people, things, and knowledge with aims towards governance have clearly evolved well beyond anything early papyrus and ink writers might have fathomed in their wildest administrative, organizational, and managerial dreams, capable of wrangling into focus endless amounts of data, and moreover, global populations. And yet despite the emergence of 'new technologies' like early computer punch card technologies in the 1930s, and their effects of installing massively organized information and data as a primary way of seeing and doing governance, one technological form and its attendant practices has continued to underpin such attempts at delimitation, and at the same time, to exercise new force: the list, an indispensable pivot of juridical-disciplinary mechanisms and the apparatuses of security ‖ the site of caesuric fracture in Nazi governmentality. Lists were not only the primary intellectual technologies for administering and organizing people and things, and developing knowledge in ancient times, but additionally, in the period following the emergence of governmentality Foucault describes,[2] lists begin to take on roles as critical security technologies in their own right, ones that exercise force in the delimitation and policing of the movement of risky elements circulating in uncertain milieus. And it is precisely these relations of power installed by Nazi governmentality that this chapter seeks to unloosen and propel into contemporary times.

Following on Foucault's analysis of the events in the eighteenth century which saw the historian's role transformed from raconteur to one who sees, names, classifies, and articulates the 'truthful' natural history of living beings and things – the interweaving of taxonomy and biology – and inspired by Jack Goody's 'intellectual technology'[3] conception of lists as fundamental to the administration and organization of people and things, and the development of knowledge, this chapter argues that with the event of Nazi governmentality lists continued to serve their age old 'intellectual' roles, but also, and further, in conjunction with the accumulation of massive data came to constitute a unique new way of seeing and doing in their own right: involving fracturing 'threatening populations' from 'healthy populations'. The list was at the heart of these schisms that marked modern Nazi governmentality – healthy ‖ diseased; Aryan ‖ Jew; us ‖ them – serving the delimitation and policing of abnormal cases in populations; installing caesuric social fractures.

---

1   Edwin Black, *IBM and the Holocaust: The Strategic Alliance Between Nazi Germany and America's Most Powerful Corporation*, New York: Crown Publishers, 2001, p. 7.
2   Foucault, '8 February 1978 *Governmentality*'.
3   Goody, *The Domestication of the Savage Mind*.

The work presented here argues that in the same way that lists brought administration, organization, and order to the management of people and things, and the development of knowledge for ancient cultures,[4] they equally played these roles in the milieu of circulation installed under Nazi governmentality, redeployed as critical support technologies of juridical-disciplinary mechanisms. At the same time, lists emerged under the Third Reich as critical to the delimiting, managing, and policing of 'diseased' elements of populations in their own right, becoming primary technologies of security in this biologically defined milieu of circulation. Lists brought contradiction to Nazi governmentality, calling into question the veracity of 'classes' they constituted; namely abnormal populations in relation to the *Volk*, beginning with undesirables, valueless loafers, and the physically and mentally 'deficient', and finally, culminating in the category and listing of 'Jews'.

In the apparatuses of security installed by Nazi governmentality, the list fully exhibits the double integration characteristic of security technologies, serving the dual role of delimiting and policing the very classes it constitutes, and at the same time self-elaborating its own operations, as well as those involving the accumulation of data, statistics, and computers as the ultimate fabricators of such 'truth'. We will see how lists were as divisive as scythes under Nazi governmentality, fundamentally securing caesuras of 'diseased' || 'healthy' populations, which turned on the severing, controlling, and policing of abnormal populations, ultimately divesting these populations of humanity.

Under Nazi governmentality, the contradictory but interwoven fabrics of microscopic examination and taxonomies as natural history took hold in apparatuses of security characterized by double integration technologies, including early computer technologies, the accumulation of data, statistical technologies, and list technologies, which served the delimitation and policing of the movement of fractured 'risks' in the Third Reich. In this way, the list served a Nazi milieu of circulation where the controlling and policing of abnormal populations, Jews and other, was installed as a way of seeing and doing a 'healthy' cultural body, in which elements circulate freely, but are distributed and regulated by apparatuses of security.

The concept of 'security' is employed here as per Foucault who in *Security, Territory, and Population* refines his earlier notions of sovereignty and discipline into a theory of governmentality that hinges on the apparatuses (*dispositifs*) of security where statistical techniques including probabilities, calculations, populations, and the prediction and limitation of 'bad' outcomes – risk assessments of the aleatory – rule the day. It is argued here that the centripetal force of juridical-legal and disciplinary mechanisms and apparatuses of security, which Foucault describes in his lectures, were further correlated under Nazi governmentality, and it is precisely the interweaving of these relations of power that this chapter aims to unloosen and resituate in the constitution of fields, domains, and objects of knowledge that the list served in this modern event.

---

4   Goody, *The Domestication of the Savage Mind*.

The List, Early Information Technology, and Nazi Governmentality

So, while it might strike one as odd that this research into modern and contemporary list technologies of security begins with a historical event not normally associated with the advent of 'new technologies', but rather, with the unprecedented and abhorrent mass genocide orchestrated by the Nazis in Europe throughout the rise and fall of the Third Reich[5]; there is clearly precedence for looking at the Shoah as a technological event. Surprisingly, it was only at the turn of the millennium, when Edwin Black's *IBM and the Holocaust*[6] was first published, that scholars and those touched by the Shoah in general began to even remotely consider the indispensable role that IBM – who made and owned Hollerith tabulators, sorters, and punch cards, all early information technologies – played in achieving the destruction of so many lives. Indeed, the 'early information technology' Black describes in *IBM and the Holocaust* helped, along with the accumulation of massive amounts of data and the deployment of statistics, underpin the installation of a milieu of circulation that pivoted on biological classi-fication, wherein the technology of lists continued to serve its administrative, organizational, and knowledge development role under Nazi governmentality, through their redeployment in juridical-disciplinary mechanisms. But the list also took on a new role, serving a new purpose in managing the delimitation and controlling of the movement of the risky elements it itself called into reality.[7]

> I was haunted by a question whose answer has long eluded historians. The Germans always had the lists of Jewish names. Suddenly a squadron of grim-faced SS would burst into a city square and post a notice demanding those listed assemble the next day at the train station for deportation to the East. But how did the Nazis get the lists?[8]

While the Holocaust has proven to be the most studied event in history, it is surprising to discover that before Black's publication, there had been virtually no mention of the under-pinning early information technologies that were crucial to and at the heart of the precise orchestration of mass human inventorying, classification, control, and extermination the Nazis conducted in waging their racial war across Europe. It is even more shocking that the lists, which hinged such endeavors, have neither been taken up as objects of research in their own right.

From Raul Hilberg's definitive and seminal three volume tome on *The Destruction of the European Jews*[9]; to precise studies on *The Order of Terror: The Concentration Camp*[10] and

---

5   Raul Hilberg, *The Destruction of the European Jews*, New York: Holmes & Meier, 1985.
6   Black, *IBM and the Holocaust*.
7   Black, *IBM and the Holocaust*.
8   Black, *IBM and the Holocaust*, p. 10.
9   Hilberg, *The Destruction of the European Jews*.
10 Wolfgang Sofsky, *The Order of Terror: The Concentration Camp*, Princeton: Princeton University, 1997.

The Roots of Nazi Psychology[11] to interrogations into the *Anatomy of the SS State*[12], and into *The Theory and Practice of Hell: The German Concentration Camps and the System Behind Them*[13]; there is quite literally no mention of the IBM developed Hollerith punch card technologies, and only passing references to the lists, while both were at the heart of the one question surrounding the Holocaust that was seemingly unanswerable: 'How did they know? How were they able to target, with such brutal accuracy, the homes of all people of Jewish decent?'[14]

Edwin Black's research, a decade in the making and involving the investigative efforts and expertise of over 200 people across the world, finally provided a partial answer: The Nazis achieved such brutal accuracy and precision – they got the lists – through the use of IBM technologies. Specifically, IBM's founder, Herman Hollerith's punch card tabulators and sorters that he developed while working for the US Census Bureau in the mid to late-nineteenth century.[15] And this revelation shocked Holocaust scholars and the world at large, at once answering the long-standing mystery of how the Nazis got the lists, and at the same time opening the door to a range of new lines of research around this 'technological' event, including this work, which owes a great debt to Black for his groundbreaking and highly illuminating historical investigation into the ties between one of America's most successful 'technology' corporations and a brutal totalitarian regime bent on seeing, naming, delimiting, risk assessing, managing, controlling, policing, and ultimately nullifying or exterminating undesirable and abnormal populations.

Where the Nazis' use of Hollerith punch card technology really began with the tabulating, sorting, and analysis of the 1933 census[16], the technology of punch cards, sorters, and tabulators had already been in existence for over fifty years in the United States.[17] In 1879, Herman Hollerith, at the behest of a Columbia professor, became an assistant in the US Census Bureau. At the time, the decennial census that was held in the US was really nothing more than a basic head count and the idea of gathering information pertaining to millions of individuals' occupations, ages, gender, or any other trait, while desirable, was seen as an insurmountable computational endeavor.[18]

11 Jay Y. Gonen, *The Roots of Nazi Psychology: Hitler's Utopian Barbarism*, Lexington: University Press of Kentucky, 2000.
12 Helmut Krausnick, Hans Bucheim, Martin Broszat, and Hans-Adolf Jacobsen, *Anatomy of the SS State*, London: Collins, 1968.
13 Eugen Kogon, *The Theory and Practice of Hell: The German Concentration Camps and the System Behind Them*, London: Secker & Warburg, 1950.
14 Ellen Rose, 'The War Machine: IBM and the Holocaust by Edwin Black', *The Antigonish Review* (2001): 91-95.
15 Emerson W. Pugh, *Building IBM: Shaping an Industry and Its Technology*, Cambridge: MIT Press, 1995.
16 Gèotz Aly, Karl Heinz Roth, Edwin Black, and Assenka Oksiloff, *The Nazi Census: Identification and Control in the Third Reich*, Philadelphia: Temple University Press, 2004.
17 Robert Sobel, *I.B.M., Colossus in Transition*, New York: Times Books, 1981.
18 Sobel, *I.B.M.*.

Inventive Hollerith began to think about a solution. French looms, simple music boxes, and player pianos used punched holes on rolls or cards to automate rote activity. About a year later, Hollerith was struck with his idea. He saw a train conductor punch tickets in a special pattern to record physical characteristics such as height, hair color, size of nose, and clothing – a sort of 'punched photograph'. Other conductors could read the code and then catch anyone re-using the ticket of the original passenger ... Hollerith's idea was a card with standardized holes, each representing a different trait: gender, nationality, occupation and so forth. The card would then be fed into a reader ... The machines could render the portrait of an entire population – or could pick out any group within that population. Indeed, one man could be identified from among millions if enough holes could be punched into a card and sorted enough times. Every punch card would become an informational storehouse limited only by the number of holes. It was nothing less than a nineteenth-century bar code for human beings.[19]

Hollerith invented his first sorters and tabulators – machines that used electromagnetic contact brushes to detect holes punched in cards – which were capable of counting people and things as they had never been counted before, with the unparalleled and seemingly magical ability to track, identify, and compute; almost instantly sorting elements and listing populations. 'Suddenly, the government could profile its own population.'[20] Because of their unprecedented speed in tabulating and sorting, Hollerith punch card systems revealed whole new dimensions of census and registration possibilities for government statisticians, and at the same time, unearthed whole new ranges of questions that could be asked of the US population.

Before long, IBM technology demonstrated it could do more than just count people or things. It could compute, that is, the technology could record data, process it, retrieve it, analyze it, and automatically answer pointed questions.[21]

Such pointed questions included those pertaining to the risks surrounding elements 'freely' circulating in milieus. As with all technologies that record data, process it, retrieve it, analyze it, the answers to pointed question are delivered in the form of outputted lists of people, things, or objects of knowledge – sorted lists of elements, at once profiles, and at the same time, sites of prescription. The world took notice of IBM's powerful 'double integration' technology, as it became a 'global' company in the early part of the twentieth century.[22] By 1933, in Nazi Germany, Hollerith technologies and IBM interests were represented by IBM Germany, or *Deutsche Hollerith Maschinen Gesellschaft*, simply known as *Dehomag*. Dehomag would eventually come to design, develop, supply, implement, and maintain the punch card systems that would prove to be indispensable to the Third Reich's ultimate aim: 'the automation of human destruction'.[23]

---

19 Black, *IBM and the Holocaust*, p. 25.
20 Black, *IBM and the Holocaust*, p. 24.
21 Black, *IBM and the Holocaust*, p. 24.
22 Pugh, *Building IBM*.
23 Black, *IBM and the Holocaust*, p. 7.

Parallel to the use of Hollerith machines by the Third Reich to delimit populations was the emergence of immense infrastructure, including card-sorting operations across Nazi Germany, factories which accumulated data and processed punch cards day and night, as more and more acts of 'biopolitical' classification and delimitation insidiously crept into every aspect of daily life in the Third Reich, and ultimately across all of Nazi-occupied Europe. From train platforms to factories and concentration camps, people, animals, and goods were increasingly and systematically tabulated, sorted, identified, catalogued, coded, divided, listed, and moved about with 'icy automation'[24] in a biopolitically charged milieu of circulation.

Statistics and the Volk: Constituting Aryan Natural History, or the Normal in Nazi Governmentality

It is first through the anonymizing statistical process that individuals are reduced to pieces in a conceptual puzzle, with a so-called "probability of fertility rate", "probability of divorce rate", "individual social behavior", and so on. In this way people are categorized according to character profiles – traits that can be multiplied into almost infinitely precise components and grouped arbitrarily. It is also through statistics that people can be divided into increasingly smaller groups by means of social and demographic policies. In this way it is possible to enact laws, regulations and guidelines targeting ever smaller groups of people, laws and regulations that to the individual subject are ever more opaque.[25]

In 1941, Friedrich Zahn, President of the German Statistical Society, declared that: 'In using statistics, the government has the road map to move from knowledge to deeds, from advice to action, in order to succeed in its enormous task of building society.'[26] In other words, the means to move from disordered data to the control of populations. Indeed, Friedrich Zahn was on the vanguard of a new approach to understanding statistics that hinged on a vision for planning and working society and all its parts as data, populations, probabilities, and distributions of cases. 'At first glance the term "individual statistic" seems to be an oxymoron. It appears that statistics is the polar opposite of individuality. However, a "new method" was appearing on the horizon.'[27] The 'new method' that was emerging through the work of statisticians like Zahn in the Third Reich involved the reduction of individuals to risk factors – to cases – statistical objects that could be held constant in populations, and then repeatedly observed over time. Prior to World War II, statisticians had for the most part contained their observations and analyses to collective statistical objects, in large part due to technological limitations, but Nazi statisticians, as well as their American counterparts, shifted the lens with their use of Hollerith tabulators and sorters, focusing on 'individual cases' within populations as statistical objects.[28]

---

24 Black, *IBM and the Holocaust*, p. 7.
25 Aly, Roth, Black, and Oksiloff, *The Nazi Census*, p. xii.
26 Zahn translated and quoted from 'Die Statistik im nationalsozialistischen Großdeutschland', *ASA* 29 (1939/40): 370.
27 Aly, Roth, Black, and Oksiloff, *The Nazi Census*, p. 65.
28 Aly, Roth, Black, and Oksiloff, *The Nazi Census*.

Instead of taking a ball out of the "urn of nature" from time to time and then retuning the ball to the urn with others, now those balls are marked before they are returned. After some time has elapsed, one can very carefully check to see how many of those marked balls are still there, how many have been destroyed in the mixing process, and how many have been added. One checks their weight increase and decrease, not just their color.[29]

Where statistics served much of Nazi planning and order, they were more than a means of merely doing, they were also a way of seeing – one that pivoted on the accumulation of data, the delimitation of populations, and the specific observation of cases within populations, repeatedly and continually monitored and surveilled *ad infinitum* according to factors of risk. In this way, statisticians were very much 'soldiers of science in the new Reich'[30] blurring the boundaries between people and things, which were both reduced to empirical statistical objects distributed in populations. Every invasion and conquest brought with it Nazi statisticians, who were always on the vanguard of the charge – at the tip of the spear – indexing, registering, tabulating, and sorting each and every population the Reich came to contain[31] and in turn, producing the statistically-derived racial roadmaps that would illuminate the way for the highest level of Nazi planners and organizers who could with more precision than ever generate the lists which would direct the storm troopers in their policing of risky elements.

> Raceology was enabled as never before. Statistician Zahn extolled the fact that "reg-istered persons can be observed continually, [through] the cooperation of statistical central offices ... [So] other statistical population matters can be settled and regulated," Zahn proposed a "single file for [the] entire population to make possible an ethnic biological diagnosis [to] turn today's theory into tomorrow's practice. Such a file would serve both practical considerations as well as science," he argued, adding, "Clarified pictures of the volume of genetic diseases within the population ... now gives science a new impetus to conduct research ... which should promote good instead of bad genetic stock."[32]

Good versus bad stock; pure versus impure genetics; Aryan versus Jewish bloodlines; healthy versus diseased populations: black and white categories and classifications of elements circulating in populations revolving around ascriptions of net-social-worth and risk through biological frames of reference were at the heart of Nazi governmentality spawning divisive caesuric practices everywhere across the Greater Reich. As data was increasingly accumu-lated, cases were increasingly risk assessed, and in turn lists generated, and populations controlled by them. With these increasing practices, more social policies emerged involving empirically reductive differentiation and enforcement. 'The Nazi functionaries understood all too well what kind of differentiation it should be. They separated the productive from the

---

29 Aly, Roth, Black, and Oksiloff, *The Nazi Census*, p. 65; Zahn translated and quoted from A. Schwarz 'Das Individuelle in der Statistik: Ein Beitrag zur statistisches methodenlehre', in *ASA*, 22 (1932): 321.
30 Chapter title in Aly, Roth, Black, and Oksiloff, *The Nazi Census*.
31 Black, *IBM and the Holocaust.*
32 Black, *IBM and the Holocaust*, p. 96.

unproductive, the useful from the useless.'[33] Indeed, Nazi raceologists and statisticians, and increasingly, all German nationals, came to see society through the lens of black and white categories, classifications, and social divisions – all of which functioned on the reduction of populations and cases to statistical distributions and measures of productivity and risk. 'As the egalitarian principle was systematically destroyed and as the population began to be categorized into superior and inferior, the power of statistics increased.'[34]

In *The Nazi Conscience*, Claudia Koonz[35] argues that Nazi pseudo-science interweaving both statistics and eugenics provided scientific and rational validation for engaging the deplorable kinds of social divisions that marked much of life under the Third Reich, playing a central role in assuaging the consciences of German nationals everywhere. Racial science coupled with statistics had provided seemingly scientific proof of the risk that Jews and undesirables posed to the *Volk*, ultimately justifying and validating the delimitation and control of the movement of these unproductive, and moreover, 'diseased elements' through their reduction to trackable statistical objects and risk assessed scores. For German nationals, the delimitation, policing, and eventual elimination of abnormal populations was increasingly seen as the cost for maintaining a healthy and productive *Volk*.

In his epistemological survey of statistical thinking in the eighteenth and nineteenth centuries Ian Hacking[36] argues that,

> Statistics has helped determine the forms of laws about society and the character of social facts. It has engendered concepts and classifications within the human sciences. Moreover the collection of statistics has created, at the least, a great bureaucratic machinery. It may think of itself as providing only information, but it is itself a part of the technology of power in a modern state.[37]

Hacking describes how with the advent of statistics in the eighteenth and nineteenth centuries determinism as a way of practicing government was increasingly eroded, as milieus of circulation – governed by market mechanisms, which did not prevent, prohibit, or prescribe, but let things happen based on probabilities and populations – were increasingly installed by the apparatuses of security. For Hacking, determinism was eroded precisely by the creation of these 'new places for freedom'[38] in which elements circulated freely, coming to be governed by what Hacking calls the 'taming of chance'.[39] 'In short, almost no domain of human enquiry is left untouched by the events that I call the avalanche of numbers, the erosion of determinism and the taming of chance.'[40] Moreover, most of the modern categories through

---

33 Aly, Roth, Black, and Oksiloff, *The Nazi Census*, p. 95.
34 Aly, Roth, Black, and Oksiloff, *The Nazi Census*, p. 24.
35 Claudia Koonz, *The Nazi Conscience*, Cambridge: Belknap Press, 2003.
36 Ian Hacking, 'How Should We Do the History of Statistics?', in Foucault, Burchell, Gordon, and Miller, *The Foucault Effect*, pp. 181-196.
37 Hacking, 'How Should We Do the History of Statistics?', p. 181.
38 Hacking, 'How Should We Do the History of Statistics?', p. 189.
39 Ian Hacking, *The Taming of Chance*, Cambridge, New York: Cambridge University Press, 1990.
40 Hacking, 'How Should We Do the History of Statistics?', p. 189.

which we think about people, things, activities, and the development of knowledge – this interweaving – are installed by our attempts to collect as much data as possible in the service of delimiting populations.[41] With the emergence of such statistical practice, different kinds of people came to be counted, as the categories installed by censuses and the creation of other statistical bureaucracies began to establish the form of 'class structure' in industrial societies.[42]

> The bureaucracy of statistics imposes not just by creating administrative rulings but by determining classifications within which people must think of themselves and of the actions that are open to them. The hallmark of indeterminism is that cliché, information and control. The less the determinism, the more the possibilities for constraint.[43]

Risk Assessment in the Third Reich

In a 1934 essay entitled 'On the Economic Value of a Human Being as an Object of Statistics', Friedrich Zahn wrote:

> The only value of a human being – and this is a direct object of statistics – is his economic value. In the money economy, this is the monetary worth of human labor productivity ... Statistics is thus in its essence related to the Nationalist Socialist idea [which] has as its goal the dividing and classifying of the whole. Categorizing through an organic mode of thinking puts the whole before the parts. Thus it is relatively easy for statistics to work for German life in its entirety as long as it values the individual as a part of the community.[44]

According to Zahn, the only pertinent measure of a human being was that of their productive economic relation to the greater population, the *Volk*, and as such, the value ascribed to cases in the Nazis' statistical 'organic mode of thinking'[45] was based on exactly the same principles and measures accorded by the insurance industry: 'We must consider age, health, occupational hazards, and expected life earnings,' Zahn wrote.[46] The ties between the insurance industry and the apparatuses of security are profound and longstanding. Francois Ewald[47] argues that one of the critical conditions that made possible the modern word 'sociopolitics' is the entry into governmental thought of a philosophy of risk. 'Risk, enterprise, progress and modernity are genealogically interdependent social ideas.'[48] In historicizing how the concepts

---

41   Ian Hacking, *The Emergence of Probability: A Philosophical Study of Early Ideas About Probability, Induction and Statistical Inference*, Cambridge, New York: Cambridge University Press, 2006.
42   Hacking, 'How Should We Do the History of Statistics?', pp. 181-196.
43   Hacking, 'How Should We Do the History of Statistics?', p. 194.
44   Aly, Roth, Black, and Oksiloff, *The Nazi Census*; from F. Zahn 'Vom Wirtschaftswert des Menschen als Gegenstand der Statistik', in *ASA*, 24 (1934-35): 461-64; *Allgemeines Statistisches Archiv* (General Archive of Statistics), Journal of the German Statitistical Society.
45   Aly, Roth, Black, and Oksiloff, *The Nazi Census*, p. 94.
46   Aly, Roth, Black, and Oksiloff, *The Nazi Census*, p. 94.
47   Francois Ewald, 'Insurance and Risk', in Foucault, Burchell, Gordon, and Miller, *The Foucault Effect*, pp. 197-210.
48   Colin Gordon, 'Governmental Rationality: An Introduction', in Foucault, Burchell, Gordon, and Miller, *The Foucault Effect*, p. 39.

of 'risk' and 'risk taking' are products of insurance techniques, wherein the insurer takes on the risk of a client or statistical object, which is 'freely' circulating in a distribution of cases or in a population and contained in a milieu of unpredictability, one of Ewald's critical insights is that 'risk is a capital, not a spirit of capitalism'.[49]

> Risk becomes in the nineteenth century ... a kind of omnivorous encyclopaedizing principle for the objectification of possible experience – not only in the hazards of personal life and private venture, but also of the common venture of society.[50]

This 'organic mode of thinking' – a vision of human value as a measure of actual and expected cost-productivity, or socio-economic value over time, or the probability of risk for elements circulating freely in milieus – was promulgated throughout the Third Reich, insidiously woven into the minutiae of everyday practices, increasingly seeking to reduce all aspects of life to data points: 'The reduction of men to points on a cost-productivity curve, to shaded segments of a statistical bar, and to cost-benefit analyses had become a standard feature of the high school curriculum.'[51] In this way, Nazi statisticians and eugenic pseudo-scientists advocated a belief system – a way of seeing – that depended on one crucial empirical reduction:

> "A man's right to live was determined by his net worth to Nazi society. Statistics is identical in character with the National Socialist idea." Zahn ... called for a "regis-tration of the various risks which threaten the value of productivity: illnesses, disa-bility, unemployment and non-accomplishment of occupational goals. Population engineering," he emphasized, "would rely upon extensive data analysis, including statistics from a gamut of health bureaus, disability and liability insurers, unem-ployment offices, and even academic testing data from schools".[52]

The Nazi way of seeing human beings as reducible to points on a cost-productivity curve – valuing and risk assessing human life as empirical scores distributed in pop-ulations – brought with it attendant ways of doing. 'Quickly, the notion of sterilizing the physically undesirable expanded to include *the socially undesirable.* So-called *anti-socials*, that is misfits who seemed to be unsuited for labor, became targets.' As the vision of 'human net value' was promulgated throughout the Third Reich, increas-ingly the German population became accustomed to and comfortable with delimitation and control practices revolving around suspending the movement, or the outright removing, of 'undesirable elements' from everyday society. Germans began to over-whelmingly see the need to put the whole of society before its individual parts; and in turn, undesirable elements were being weeded out, sterilized, and/or exterminated for the good of the *Volk*. For Zahn,

---

49 Gordon, 'Governmental Rationality: An Introduction'.
50 Gordon, 'Governmental Rationality: An Introduction'.
51 Aly, Roth, Black, and Oksiloff, *The Nazi Census*, p. 39.
52 Aly, Roth, Black, and Oksiloff, *The Nazi Census*, pp. 93-94.

... population politics, according to the principles of racial hygiene, has to focus on the propagation of valuable genetic stock, prevent the reproduction of inferior life, and be aware of genetic degeneration. In other words, population politics involves superior life selection, on the one hand, and the eradication of genetically unwanted stock on the other. An ethno-biological diagnosis is inevitable in order to carry out this task.[53]

By 1939, the Nazis' desire to significantly reduce 'genetically unwanted stock' in the Third Reich, including people with mental illnesses, loafers, and social misfits, was at its apex. Caesuric fractures had come to define almost all aspects of everyday life, as the Germans accumulated more data and tabulated, calculated, and organized society more and more through the double integration of statistical techniques – the delimitation of biological popula- tions and the calculation and control of the risky populations they contained – in a self-elab- orating process where statistics were increasingly seen as a 'natural' purveyor and fabricator of truth. Ethno-biological diagnoses and caesuric fractures were at a maximum in the Greater Reich, as lists were redeployed in juridical-disciplinary mechanisms and also operated as technologies of security in their own right for controlling the policing of abnormal populations.

Seeing the abnormal as unproductive economic elements of society that offered little or no return-on-investment brought with it new social research, programs, and policies that would redeploy lists in a variety of functions. In the fall of 1939, a program named 'Economically Based Survey of all Mental Institutions and Nursing Homes' was introduced by the Admin- istration of the Reich Interior Ministry and included a medical questionnaire.

> All patients who had been in these institutions for more than five years, who were incar- cerated as criminals, or who, according to their medical records, suffered from schiz- ophrenia, epilepsy, senility, feeble-mindedness, or "irreversible paralysis" and "did not work in institutional factories or were only able to perform mechanical tasks (e.g. plucking)" had to be reported ... The source of the individual's financial support was to be identified, as well as the "exact" productivity of the sick person ... [A] reduction program began in autumn of 1939 under the code word "Euthanasia". These "useless eaters", whose productivity was in the red anyway because of their health status, were singled out and exterminated.[54]

Seeing human beings as distributed and risk-assessed 'net-value' cases in populations, a view promulgated by Friedrich Zahn and the 'statistical soldiers of the Third Reich', not only enabled the widespread social acceptance of mandatory sterilization, but eventually came to assuage collective conscience[55] with regards to the extermination of undesirable elements in this biopolitical milieu of circulation. Statistically speaking, extermination equaled success for

53 Aly, Roth, Black, and Oksiloff, *The Nazi Census*, p. 105; Zahn quoted from H.W. Kranz and S. Koller's study *The Anti-Socials: Die Gemeinschaftsunfähigen – ein Beitrag zur wissenschaftlichen un praktischen Lösung des sogenannten 'Asozialenproblems'*, Teil I, II, and III, Gießen, 1939- 1941.
54 Aly, Roth, Black, and Oksiloff, *The Nazi Census*, p. 96.
55 Koonz, *The Nazi Conscience*.

the Nazis; the complete nullification of the abnormal, since any living and breathing human being whose productivity in society reduced to a negative number was seen as little more than 'economic dead weight' or even a threat to Aryanism itself.[56]

The National Socialist State elevated the statistical sciences to a role that went well beyond research involving pure numbers and general economic conditions. Behind the pomp of the blood and soil, hereditary man, and the dying-*Volk* rhetoric lurked a social politics that cloaked itself in claims of objectivity. The person becomes a case, an example, an index card.[57]

Moreover, as Claudia Koonz[58] argues, such cases, examples, and index cards exert minimum weight on human conscience when nullified, least of all when reduced to numbers and scores. By 1944, 'undesirables' in the Greater Reich were further reduced to one last statistical object – a 'talking number'; *ein sprechende zahl* – a concept introduced by Friedrich Zahn.

It would simplify matters if every inhabitant of the German Reich were to receive a particular identification number, a number that accompanied him from birth to death ... This number would not simply be a random one ... It would have to be a talking number [*sprechende Zahl*], a number that would convey basic information about the bearer; information that had already been used in identifying the person other than through his or her name, such as sex and place and date of birth. However, it would also have to be a simple number without any special markings and without fractions, a number that could appear alongside other numbers. This would be a number that could easily be a part of a list or index.[59]

By 1944, the transformation of individuals into listed or indexed cases, examples, and paper identities was increasingly seen as insufficient for the Nazis' extensive and highly orchestrated plans: '...a number was now necessary to freeze things in their tracks'.[60] Thus a final reduction of the human species was at hand, from cases in populations to worth/risk-assessed scores circulating freely in milieus, with 'dangerous' elements listed for policing. 'Even if these dreams of technocratic prowess were only realized on a small scale, the last eight months of the National Socialist regime saw a feverish push to create a general identification numbering system.'[61]

The most important component was the assignment of a numerically based code to each individual. If this "talking number" were to be integrated into a central filing system based on the punch card principle, then it would be possible to create links to other existing card files. Then the era of 'final accounting of humans' would be

56 Aly, Roth, Black, and Oksiloff, *The Nazi Census*, p. 98.
57 Aly, Roth, Black, and Oksiloff, *The Nazi Census*, pp. 22-23.
58 Koonz, *The Nazi Conscience*.
59 Aly, Roth, Black, and Oksiloff, *The Nazi Census*, p. 121.
60 Aly, Roth, Black, and Oksiloff, *The Nazi Census*, p. 122.
61 Aly, Roth, Black, and Oksiloff, *The Nazi Census*, p. 123.

ushered in, at which point individuals would not only be inventoried at certain levels, but on an individual and permanent basis. A site for central data collection, which the planners of the war so desperately needed in order to "move the right person to the right location", was in sight.[62]

In this 'final accounting of humans' which was seen as capable of distributing and regulating all elements of the *Volk* – the identification of individuals reduced to risk assessed numbers and subjected to circulatory control through massively organized data systems – paved the way for new revelations about the limitations of yearly, or bi-yearly census-taking practices, and the advantages of ongoing everyday registration of the populace. Increasingly, the Nazis dreamed of an everyday registration system that could track the social, political, financial, and biological meanderings of the entire populace of the Reich, enabling up-to-date data accumulation and thus delimitation and control of abnormal populations and the diseased cases they contained. In May of 1944, Dr. Friedrich Herbst, a director at the Accounting Office for the Third Reich, succinctly summarized the revelations as such,

> While there have been occasional censuses in the past, which were inventories for a particular date, there needs to be an accounting of the deployment and status of each individual person. In this way, up-to-date statistical data would always be available that could be used in decisions regarding individual deployment. It would also provide us with statistical information about movements within the populace. The basis for this accounting is the continuous registration of arrivals, departures, and changes, which would also ensure that the files stay current.[63]

In other words, the Nazis were in many ways masters of Foucault's governmentality, deploying statistical mechanisms to delimit populations and provide information about movements within them for control purposes. Had the Nazis prevailed it might have only been a matter of time before they would have designed and developed a daily automated registration system – a final accounting of humans – providing up-to-date tracking and regulating the distribution of the financial, social, political, and biological meanderings of cases across the Greater Reich. Nazi governmentality had arrived and total information awareness was really just around the corner; a hegemonic conjunction of computer technologies, the accumulation of massive data, divisive social practices, and juridical-disciplinary mechanisms that pivot on the delimitation and risk assessment of the movement of abnormal cases had been established and cemented; all policed through the technology of lists.

> In everyday language the term "risk" is understood as a synonym for danger or peril, for some unhappy event which may happen to someone; it designates an objective threat. In insurance the term designates neither an event nor a general kind of event occurring in reality, but a specific mode of treatment of certain events capable of happening to a group of individuals – or more exactly, to values or capitals possessed or represented

---

62 Aly, Roth, Black, and Oksiloff, *The Nazi Census*, p. 124.
63 Aly, Roth, Black, and Oksiloff, *The Nazi Census*, p. 133.

by a collectivity of individuals: that is to say, a population. Nothing is a risk in itself, there is no risk in reality. But on the other hand, anything can be a risk; it all depends on how one considers the danger, considers the event.[64]

For Robert Castel also, the 'new' strategies of risk assessment that emerge with the apparatuses of security, further erode the notion of a 'dangerous' individual subject and put in place a conjunction of factors, 'the factors of risk',[65] that delimit statistical objects. It is precisely through the techniques of risk assessment that the apparatuses of security establish and ensure flows of populations (people and things), and at the same time delimit dangers, based on the accumulation of data and the calculation of a range of abstract factors randomly deemed as liable to produce risk in the milieu of circulation. What is palpable here is the double integration effect of statistics and the techniques of risk assessment as technologies of security in policing assemblages. On the one hand, the apparatuses of security neither prohibit, nor prescribe, but simply install a space of free circulation for elements in milieus, established as populations, whose distribution and regulation is attended to by statistical worth/risk assessment techniques. But at the same time as installing a 'free' milieu of circulation, statistics become a key instrument in the control of elements and populations themselves, by materializing as risk a series of abstract factors that serve to enforce the normalization of the populations that statistics themselves calls into reality.

> Such a shift becomes possible as soon as *the notion of risk is made autonomous from that of danger.* A risk does not arise from the presence of particular precise danger embodied in a concrete individual or group. It is the effect of a combination of abstract *factors* which render more or less probable the occurrence of undesirable modes of behavior.[66]

Thus we can see how the preventive policies enabled by data accumulation, statistical technologies, and risk assessment techniques in apparatuses of security, in many ways promote a 'new mode of surveillance': that of 'systematic predetection'.[67] Castel describes the erosion of the individual subject and the emergence of the 'case of risk factors' through an examination of contemporary techniques for gauging abnormalities in children without actually observing the child in corporeal reality, but rather, through data accumulated through identity-based screening; a series of questions regarding factors of risk. In this regard, he argues that,

> To intervene no longer means, or at the least not to begin with, taking as one's target a given individual, in order to correct, punish or care for him or her ... There is, in fact, no longer a relation of immediacy with a subject *because there is no longer a subject.* What the new preventive policies primarily address is no longer individuals but fac-

---

64 Ewald, 'Insurance and Risk', p. 199.
65 Robert Castel, 'From Dangerousness to Risk', in Foucault, Burchell, Gordon, and Miller, *The Foucault Effect*, p. 281.
66 Castel, 'From Dangerousness to Risk', p. 291.
67 Castel, 'From Dangerousness to Risk', p. 288.

tors, statistical correlations of heterogeneous elements. They deconstruct the concrete subject of intervention, and reconstruct a combination of factors liable to produce risk. Their primary aim is not to confront a concrete dangerous situation, but to anticipate all the possible forms of irruption of danger.[68]

As Castel also reminds us, eugenic practices were widespread during the first third of the twentieth century, and even in a country like the United States, with its supposed liberty, special laws like those enacted in Missouri in 1923 imposed sterilization for a wide range of abnormal persons. Surely, it must be noted that it was not just the Jews, Gypsies, homosexuals, and 'undesirables' of the Third Reich who were delimited, policed, rounded-up, and interned during World War II through a conjunction of security technologies (early computers, data accumulation, statistics, and lists), through divisive social practices revolving around census and registration, and through discourses of public health, security, and well-being – this conjunction played a significant role in Allied war efforts, too.

In addition to the extensive use of Hollerith machines to crack enigma codes, IBM also developed powerful mobile Hollerith units for the United States military, which spawned IBM-trained military units[69] specializing in the deployment of IBM-made equipment.[70] 'It was an irony of the war that IBM equipment was used to encode and decode for both sides of the conflict',[71] as well as to delimit, control, and police populations not just in Nazi Germany but around the globe. IBM machines were not just used by Allied forces to wage war against the Nazis during World War II; they were also used to manage and control populations within and across nations. In addition to organizing millions of people for drafts and deployment, locating servicemen around the world, and automating military payments, Hollerith sorters, tabulators, and punch cards were also used extensively in analyzing the data derived from the US census held in 1940[72]; and as such risk assessing elements circulating in populations and identifying lists of dangerous cases in America, too.

In one radio address, First Lady Eleanor Roosevelt promoted the 1940 census as "the greatest assemblage of facts ever collected by any people about the things that affect their welfare". She acknowledged, "Much doubt has been raised as to the propriety of some of the questions." But she added, they were designed to yield "facts which will provide illuminating data on problems which have become particularly pressing".[73]

---

68 Castel, 'From Dangerousness to Risk', p. 288.
69 The so-called 'Machine Records Units'.
70 Black, *IBM and the Holocaust.*
71 Black, *IBM and the Holocaust*, p. 344.
72 Black, *IBM and the Holocaust.*
73 Black, *IBM and the Holocaust*, p. 345.

One of the 'pressing' problems confronted by President Roosevelt leading up to the United States' declaration of war in 1942 was the presence of threats within American borders. Thanks in large part to their use of Hollerith sorters, tabulators, and punch cards; the United States Census Bureau began to accumulate data on the racial ancestry of all American citizens beginning with the 1940 census. Indeed, immediately leading up to the US declaration of war, and in an eerily similar fashion to the Nazis, the United States began to leverage a conjunction of Hollerith technologies, census and registration practices, statistics, and lists as a practical means of delimiting, controlling, and policing the movement of risky populations.

> Using IBM applications, the Census Bureau had tracked the racial ancestry of Japanese Americans based on their responses to the 1940 census ... Census Director J.C. Capt confirmed, "we didn't wait for the [American] declaration of war. On Monday morning, we put our people to work on the Japanese thing." Since only 135,430 Japanese-Americans lived in the United States, the results were tabulated quickly. A single sort was necessary: race.[74]

Racial maps displaying Japanese population densities across the United States by the presence of dots – one for every ten Japanese-Americans – became a roadmap for identification and control in the United States. In this way, both 'American and Dutch [Nazi-occupied] census bureaus simultaneously used Hollerith systems in 1943 to create racial "dot maps" as a means of organizing transfers to concentration camps'.[75] Just as the fate of Jews and 'undesirables' across the Greater Reich was determined by a conjunction of Hollerith technological systems, the accumulation of large pools of data, statistics, and lists, combined with a population's acquiescence to and compliance with census and registration policies and practices with a view towards 'safe' and 'healthy' society, the fate of Japanese-Americans was assured in the US: delimitation, control, policing, and eventual internment in concentration camps.

'By February 19, 1942, President Roosevelt could confidently sign Executive Order 9066 authorizing the internment of Japanese Americans on the West Coast.'[76] Roosevelt's confidence stemmed from the knowledge that virtually no Japanese-American could escape the net cast by the conjunction of Hollerith punch card systems, statistics, and lists. But in addition to their reliance on IBM technology, what the Allies and the Third Reich also had in common was a need for extensive delimitation and policing of the movement of 'abnormal' cases within populations, which despite the use of Hollerith technologies, could never have been achieved without the adoption of ubiquitous census and registration policies and practices, and moreover, without the promulgation of a way of seeing humanity through a lens of data accumulation and the calculation of net-worth and risk. In other words, seeing groups of people as populations and individuals as risk assessed statistical objects controlled and policed through lists.

---

74   Black, *IBM and the Holocaust*, pp. 345-346.
75   Black, *IBM and the Holocaust*, p. 346.
76   Black, *IBM and the Holocaust*, p. 346.

Statistics and the Control and Policing of Dangerous Elements

> The modern ideologies of prevention are overarched by a grandiose technocratic rationalizing dream of absolute control of the accidental, understood as the irruption of the unpredictable. In the name of this myth of absolute eradication of risk, they construct a mass of new risks which constitute so many new targets for preventive intervention.[77]

In this conjuncture of the apparatuses of security installed by Nazi governmentality, interventionist technologies like statistics and their techniques of calculation, risk assessment, and prediction, as well as early information technology, the accumulation of massive data, and list technologies, 'make it possible to "guide" and "assign" individuals without having to assume their custody'.[78] As Castel argues, the policing that statistics enable, 'could well prove to be a decisive resource'.[79] For Foucault too, the instrument that guides, assigns, and integrates, and is common to both the military-diplomatic technique of balance and to policing, is statistics.[80] 'Statistics is the state's knowledge of state, both of itself and other states.'[81]

> Police makes statistics necessary, but police also makes statistics possible. For it is precisely the whole set of procedures set up to increase, combine, and develop forces, it is this whole administrative assemblage that makes it possible to identify what each state's forces comprise and their possibilities of development. Police and statistics mutually condition each other.[82]

Like all technologies of security, police and their attendant assemblages of techniques are characterized by double integration effects: technologies and techniques are deployed expressly to patrol the populations that statistics call into reality through the analysis of accumulated data, both internal and external to the state. In this way, assemblages of police concern themselves with the distribution, regulation, and control of elements circulating in populations and milieus, helping to ensure balance through the statistical operations of prediction, normalization, and steering of the movement of elements that other technologies of security like computers, statistics, and lists materialize and call into reality. In this way, we can say that in 'securing' the 'freedom of movement' that governmentality takes as its maxim, computers, the accumulation of data, statistics, lists, and control and policing all mutually condition and self-elaborate each other.

---

77 Castel, 'From Dangerousness to Risk', p. 289.
78 Castel, 'From Dangerousness to Risk', p. 295.
79 Castel, 'From Dangerousness to Risk', p. 295.
80 Michel Foucault, '29 March 1978', in Senellart and Davidson (eds), *Security, Territory, Population*, pp. 311-332.
81 Foucault, '29 March 1978', p. 315.
82 Foucault, '29 March 1978', p. 315.

What is characteristic of a police state is its interest in what men do; it is interested in their activity, in their "occupation". The objective of police is therefore control of and responsibility for men's activity insofar as this activity constitutes a differential element in the development of the state's forces.[83]

It is precisely for these reasons that statisticians like Friedrich Zahn derived their notions of 'talking numbers' as a means and ends to delimiting, controlling, policing, and normalizing the movement of risky abnormal cases. For if one was to manage the overall 'health' of the cultural organs of the *Volk*, policing would take as its concrete task to provide itself with whatever resources are necessary and sufficient for efficiently and effectively assigning, guiding, and integrating the activity of people into the state's objectives, thus ensuring that the state, 'in turn, can stimulate, determine, and orientate this activity in such a way that it is in fact useful to the state'.[84] And as statisticians like Zahn advocated, this form of policing was most efficiently practiced and expressed as a single risk-based 'talking' number.

In this way, double integration technologies of security, like statistics, computers, and lists, and their attendant techniques, hinge the apparatuses of security's assemblage of police, wherein the list is redeployed as a disciplinary mechanism which concerns itself with the administration, organization, control, and regulation of the distribution and circulation of people and things. But lists are also technologies of security in and of themselves in this portrait of policing, ones which serve this assemblage in a unique way: instruments for both calling into reality the fruits of accumulated data and for efficiently and effectively assigning, guiding, integrating, and policing modern and contemporary caesuras of 'us' ‖ 'them'.

According to Foucault, assemblages of police concern themselves with numbers and populations[85], wanting to know how many elements are circulating in order to ensure that necessary and sufficient distributions of elements are present in populations to best meet the objectives of the state. When the apparatuses of security identify that necessary elements are not well distributed, lists are deployed in assemblages of police to administer, manage, and organize the necessary distribution of resources. Indeed, when the apparatuses of security identify that there is a redundancy of elements in populations and milieus, and moreover, when elements are predicted to be risks to the 'free' movement of 'normal' populations, lists are equally deployed in assemblages of police, operationalized to delimit and control the movement of 'dangerous' elements, and in turn, secure 'free' circulation; the chief objective of governmentality.

In this way, in the operations of policing milieus of circulation, the list continues to serve the administrative, organizational, and knowledge development roles it has historically played. But, at the same time, it also becomes an instrument for policing the whole material network that the apparatuses of security install: milieus that allow not only for the 'free' circulation of people, things, and knowledge, but also for circulating the concept of this kind of 'circulation'

83 Foucault, '29 March 1978', p. 322.
84 Foucault, '29 March 1978', pp. 322-323.
85 Foucault, '29 March 1978', p. 323.

and 'policing' itself. That is to say, the whole self-elaborating set of constraints and blockages, including assemblages of police, that neither prohibit nor prescribe but let things happen over and above any perceived notion of territory.

> Generally speaking, what police has to govern, its fundamental object, is all the forms of, let's say, men's coexistence with each other. I mean by this that police must ensure that men live, and live in large numbers; it must ensure that they have the wherewithal to live and so do not die in excessive numbers, but at the same time, it must also ensure that everything in their activity that may go beyond this pure and simple sub-sistence will in fact be produced, distributed, divided up, and put in circulation in such a way that the state really can draw its strength from it.[86]

Early information technologies, the accumulation of massive data, statistics, and list tech-nologies are the hinges of the technological assemblage of police, and indeed these further correlations of power of the state – the redeployment of juridical-disciplinary mechanisms in the installation of milieus of circulation – are what allowed assemblages of police, like the Nazi *Gestapo*, to ensure that the forces and resources of the state – populations and their distributed elements – were put to good use in the protection and evolution of the *Volk* under Nazi governmentality.

Now that we have seen how early information technologies, the accumulation of massive data, statistics, risk assessment, assemblages of police, and lists served Nazi governmentality, let us turn our attention to how juridical-disciplinary mechanisms underpinned by list tech-nologies were redeployed in this modern art of governmentality, characterized by practices surrounding census and registration.

Juridical-legal and Disciplinary Mechanisms in Nazi Governmentality

> Precisely in the light of historical experience, censuses, with their seemingly objective data and usefulness for policymaking, constitute an assault on the social imagination. Humanity is in danger of being run over by a steamroller of data. The continuous counting and singling out of the weakest and those who are isolated by sociological constellations only serves to deepen inequality and break up social existence, render-ing it into splinters and particles.[87]

Germany had a long history of census-taking prior to the decisive 1933 census including early counts in states like Prussia all the way back to 1816. It was the Imperial Office of Statistics that conducted the first general, all-German census in 1871, and subsequently censuses were held in 1875 and for every five years up until 1915. Like the ones held in the United States in this era, these censuses were little more than basic head counts. Such counts were conducted in Germany during and post-WWI, in 1916, 1917, and 1919, all specifically geared toward the maintenance of post-war society, focusing on basic questions of food rations and vocational

---

86 Foucault, '29 March 1978', p. 326.
87 Aly, Roth, Black, and Oksiloff, *The Nazi Census*, p. 7.

and business registration.[88] Another census was held in 1925 with a focus on 'economic and social-statistical evaluation' of populations in Germany.[89] But due to financial objections by various states, the Weimar Republic's last government postponed the census planned for 1930 repeatedly. However, immediately upon seizing power in January 1933, Hitler ignored any objections and made the census one of his government's first priorities, calling it into law on April 12, 1933 with a decree for counting on June 16, 1933.[90]

A series of seemingly banal, but highly exclusionary laws were put into effect in April 1933, which ultimately paved the way for intense registration in Nazi Germany and the emergence of caesuric social fractures. Carrying innocuous names such as 'The law for the re-estab-lishment of the career civil service',[91] and 'The law for preventing overcrowding in German schools',[92] these decrees served as the basis for the dismantling and splintering of the German *Volk* starting with the delimitation of Jewish and 'diseased' populations.[93] These laws were the precursor to justify the accumulation of data, and the subsequent intense delimitation, control, and policing of abnormal populations that would come to mark almost every aspect of daily life in Nazi Germany.

As with the 1925 census, 'household lists' served as the basis for registration for the 1933 census.[94] But the 1933 census proved to be different than those that had been held prior, constituting a critical turning point in Nazi Germany. The 1933 census revealed two important implications for future registration and census taking.[95] Firstly, it clearly demonstrated that a mere head count was insufficient; not all Jews and 'diseased elements' could be delimited through such basic census taking measures alone, as more complex statistical operations would be required to trace genetic bloodlines and lineage. More granular and precise data had to be accumulated. What this massively organized data revealed was that while the 1933 census identified nearly half a million Jews, these were only the visible layer of Jews – the practicing Jews – and if all Jews were to be identified, including those that had been assimilated through generations, more data would need to be gathered and new statistical practices involving delimitation and risk assessment would have to be developed in order to police these abnormal and risky elements.

Between 1933 and 1939, The Reich Office of Statistics doubled its personnel to approxi-mately 5,000 civil servants and employees.[96] During these years, the accumulation of data through registration practices and the ensuing delimitation of populations quickly became the bureaucratic cornerstone of the Third Reich's power. Where the 1933 census aimed to list all Jews in the Reich, it only managed to capture the so-called 'practicing Jews', and as

---

88 See, Aly, Roth, Black, and Oksiloff, *The Nazi Census*.
89 Aly, Roth, Black, and Oksiloff, *The Nazi Census*, p. 16.
90 Aly, Roth, Black, and Oksiloff, *The Nazi Census*, p. 16.
91 7 April 1933.
92 25 April 1933.
93 Aly, Roth, Black, and Oksiloff, *The Nazi Census*, p. 16.
94 Aly, Roth, Black, and Oksiloff, *The Nazi Census*, p. 16.
95 See, Black, *IBM and the Holocaust*.
96 See, Aly, Roth, Black, and Oksiloff, *The Nazi Census*.

a result had the consequence of also raising questions as to what constituted a Jew in this first place; and further, how to efficiently and effectively go about more precisely identifying, controlling, and policing this population. Nazi race theory coupled with statistical technologies sought to categorize 'Jewishness' more broadly than as a function of religious practice, namely through bloodline, and subsequent to the 1933 census a fierce debate raged amongst Nazi theoreticians as to how far back to look. 'Nazi theoreticians debated tracing parentage. Some looked at grandparents. Some suggested searching back four generations. Still others focused on the year 1800, before Jewish emancipation, before assimilation into German society.'[97] Indeed, subsequent to the 1933 census, Nazi race scientists began to devise

> ... bizarre pseudo-mathematical formula[e] that grouped ancestral Jews into a series of grades, such as *fully-Jewish, half-Jewish,* and *quarter-Jewish*, depending upon how many Jewish parents and grandparents could be calculated from their past ... Linguistics played a dynamic role. Words such as *public health and medicine, nationality, foreigners, family,* and *family genealogy, hereditary,* and even the word *German*, took on a special anti-Semitic implications. Jews were foreigners, and in many cases thought to be disease carriers. Racial impurity was a public health issue. Only Aryans could be Germans. The word *German* became exclusionary.[98]

Everyone in Nazi Germany was being forced to confront his or her racial ancestry. At the center of these debates was the *Reichssippenamt,* or Reich Family Office, a section of the Reich Interior Ministry that ultimately had the final authority in ascribing Jewish or Aryan status.[99] The second implication of the 1933 census was how the census itself morphed; no longer was it to be just about evaluating current and future population trends, it became something more akin to racial road-mapping; a means of not only delimiting the disease-ridden organs of the *Volk*, namely Jews and undesirables, but also a '...vehicle for calculating the expected number of births by "biologically valuable" women in the years to come'.[100] In other words, a new way of seeing and doing the distribution of necessary and sufficient elements that would ensure the 'healthy' evolution of the *Volk*. Where the results of earlier censuses provided very limited snapshots of populations, the Nazis came to see that the census could effectively provide a platform for complete control of the milieu of circulation. In this arrangement, the list as a technology of control would be deployed extensively to secure the preservation of Aryan lineage itself. This way of seeing censuses, data accumulation, registration, statistics, punch card computing technologies, and lists as ways of doing 'racial roadmaps' laid the groundwork and paved the way for even more juridical-legal and disciplinary mechanisms aimed at promoting a 'healthy' *Volk*.

97 Aly, Roth, Black, and Oksiloff, *The Nazi Census*, p. 89.
98 Aly, Roth, Black, and Oksiloff, *The Nazi Census*, p. 90.
99 Black, *IBM and the Holocaust.*
100 Aly, Roth, Black, and Oksiloff, *The Nazi Census*, p. 17.

Starting in 1933 special loans for married couple were offered as an incentive for promoting marriage. These loans could be paid off by having offspring: Nazi-demo-graphic politicians raised the monetary incentives by offering cash payments for each child born to a couple. The sum increased substantially with the fourth child. However, families could only claim these payments if the wife (if possible) stopped working, if the applicant was Aryan and a German citizen, and if the "applicant" was "free from any hereditary diseases".[101]

In practice, what these two implications of the 1933 census had in common – calling into question what constituted a Jew and the promotion of healthy Aryan stock through the effec-tive use of racial roadmaps – was the fostering of what Foucault[102] and also Giorgio Agam-ben[103] refer to as 'caesuras'; biopolitical fractures that culminated in Nazi governmentality with the establishment of strict divisions between Germans and Jews and equally functioning to install schisms between all 'undesirables' and the German *Volk*. The registration and accu-mulation of data related to biological bodies through strict and utterly divisive juridical-legal mechanisms were thus seen as paramount to the survival of Aryan lineage itself, and essential to the protection of Aryan hereditary stock were lists of risks.

Indeed, 'after 1933 National Socialism was publicized as "the biological will of the German people", and as "political biology",'[104] census and registration practices and data accumula-tion in Nazi Germany were inextricably tied to the statistical derivation of eugenic and racial pseudo-scientific imaginings, paving the way for the invocation of numerous divisive laws from 1933 through 1945, with their attendant caesuric practices aimed at diagnosing, controlling, policing, and ultimately cleansing German society of its diseased elements. In late June of 1933, Interior Minister Wilhelm Frick detailed an extensive program aimed at evaluating the *Volkskörper*, or '..."ethnic body politic", according to "genetic value" as a crucial dimension of a comprehensive moral revolution that would revive communal values'.[105]

> On July 14, 1933 ... the law for the "prevention and continuance of hereditary disease" was promulgated, stipulating that "those afflicted with a hereditary disease may be steri-lized by a surgical operation if there is medical evidence to suggest that their descendants will most likely be afflicted by serious hereditary disorders of the body or the mind".[106]

Such juridical-legal mechanisms pivoted on a eugenic 'natural history' that imagined and classified Jewishness as a hereditary disease, and thus as a risk to the 'biological' milieu of circulation Nazi governmentality sought to install. And such 'hereditary disease' would be identified through statistical practices of mining massive data to produce lists that would serve to control, police, and ultimately exterminate populations. On October 18, 1933, legislation was extended to marriage through the 'Law for the protection of the hereditary health of the

101 Aly, Roth, Black, and Oksiloff, *The Nazi Census*, p. 18.
102 Foucault, '1 February 1978 *Governmentality*'.
103 Agamben, *Homo Sacer*.
104 Krausnick, Bucheim, Broszat, and Jacobsen, *Anatomy of the SS State*.
105 Koonz, *The Nazi Conscience*, p. 103.
106 Agamben, *Homo Sacer*, pp. 148-149.

German people'.[107] In 1934, the 'Law for simplification of the health system' required doctors and other clinicians to fill out detailed forms constituting intense racial profiling, to file them first with local Health Offices, and eventually up to the Reich Statistical Office in Berlin.[108] The 'Law for the prevention of genetically sick offspring' was also invoked in 1934, involving the determination of bloodlines based on the statistical probability of 'endowing defective genes'. Sterilization was initially specified for individuals deemed insane, retarded, epileptic, or manic-depressive, but ultimately came to contain 'anti-socials' in general, including *loafers* – those who routinely missed or were late for work – and of course Jews.[109]

> What is decisive is that for the Nazis these laws had an immediately political character. As such, they are inseparable from the Nuremberg laws on "citizenship in the Reich" and on the "protection of German blood and honor", which transformed Jews into second-class citizens, forbidding among other things, marriage between Jews and full citizens ... The laws authorizing discrimination against Jews have almost completely monopolized scholarly interest in the racial politics of the Third Reich. And yet the laws concerning the Jews can only be fully understood if they are brought back to the general context of National Socialism's legislation and biopolitics. This legislation and this praxis are not simply reducible to the Nuremberg laws, to the deportations to the camps, or even to the "Final Solution": these decisive events of our century have their foundation in the unconditional assumption of a biopolitical task in which life and politics become one.[110]

Revelations garnered from the lists of 'diseased elements' generated by the 1933 census, coupled with the invocation of subsequent registration decrees and laws, compounded by the widespread acceptance of the pseudo-science of Nazi raceology and eugenics, coalesced as biopolitical praxis in Nazi Germany, an art of governmentality involving the redeployment of juridical-disciplinary mechanisms, wherein registration, delimitation, and the policing of divisive social caesuras through lists came to increasingly mark all facets of daily life. Moreover, citizens of the Greater Reich became accustomed to and comfortable with a form of governmentality based on the functional installation of caesuras and the increasing delimitation of all risky people, things, and knowledge. And at the hub of it all were lists, whose double integration effects wielded the greatest force in the gloved-hand of an SS Security Officer.

As such, registration laws proliferated like wildfire under Nazi governmentality: *The Labor Book,* requiring all Germans to register by occupation, was enacted in 1935; *The Health Pedigree Book* was a national registry focusing on isolating genetic deficiencies amongst the entire populace, also enacted in 1935; the *Duty to Register* invoked in 1938 was a precursor to the 1939 census, a legally decreed registry intended to yield a comprehensive and alphabetized listing of the entire populace, or *Volkskartei* (people's registry).

---

107 Agamben, *Homo Sacer*, p. 149.
108 Koonz, *The Nazi Conscience*.
109 Koonz, *The Nazi Conscience*.
110 Agamben, *Homo Sacer*, p. 149.

Lists were everywhere. Non-Germanic Registries were maintained in police stations, employment bureaus, professional associations, church organization, local Nazi departments, and the SS Security Office.[111]

The series of registration laws, decrees, and juridical-legal mechanisms invoked between 1933 and 1939, paved the way for a bureaucratic foundation on which the intense delimitation, control, and policing of the movement of 'diseased elements' or rather their eradication could be enacted.

Lists were distributed, exchanged and updated continuously, often in a haphazard fashion. To cope with the growing bureaucratic fascination with punch-card records, senior Interior Ministry officials reviewed one fanciful proposal for a twenty-five-floor circular tower of data to centralize all personal information. The proposal was rejected because it would take years to build and stock. But the futuristic concept opened the eyes of Reich planners. Each of the twenty-five floors in the imagined tower would be comprised of 12 circular rooms representing one birth year. Every circular room would contain 31 cabinets, one for each day of the month. Each cabinet would in turn contain 7,000 names. Registrations and updates would feed in from census bureaus. All 60 million Germans could then be organized and cross-indexed in a single location regardless of change of residence. Data could be retrieved by some 1,500 couriers running from room to room like so many magnetic impulses fetching files.[112]

The prescience of this vision is clearly undeniable: how the conjunction of massive modern computing and lists could serve the control of populations and the exercise of power. On September 15, 1935, *The Reich Citizenship Act* was brought into law, stipulating unequivocally that, 'No Jew can be a Reich citizen. The right to vote on political questions is not extended to him and he may not be appointed to any office of State.'[113] Jews were on their way to being not only fully delimited, but also fully denationalized in the Third Reich; in many ways, it was the first test case of the powerful conjunction of modern computing and lists applied as a technology of population control.

In order to fully enforce all of these biopolitical laws, the Nazis needed comprehensive listings of the Jews. Beginning in 1936, the Gestapo and Criminal Police became increasingly involved and active in registration processes.[114] Politics and policing became increasingly indistinguishable, doubly integrated in this assemblage of security.[115] Indeed, after 1938, whenever the Nazis invaded a foreign country, the frontline consisted of Security Services (*Sicherheitspolizei*)[116] who would immediately register, count, and separate whole populations. 'Residential registers, church books, Jewish books, and files of any kind were the primary items

---

111 Black, *IBM and the Holocaust*, p. 92.
112 Black, *IBM and the Holocaust*, pp. 91-92.
113 Aly, Roth, Black, and Oksiloff, *The Nazi Census*, p. 32.
114 Aly, Roth, Black, and Oksiloff, *The Nazi Census*.
115 Foucault, '1 February 1978 *Governmentality*'.
116 Gestapo and Criminal Police.

of interest for the German occupation commissioners.'[117] And the more the Nazis registered and delimited populations, the more they trapped Jews and undesirables in a conjunctive net from which there was no escape.

> The Reich Registration Order of January 6, 1938, accustomed the German people – up through May 8, 1945 – to police surveillance of their comings and goings, a control that was hitherto unknown in most states and regions ... This was invoked for "the protection of the people against criminals and the Security Police's fight against those criminals".[118]

For these were no ordinary criminals; they were racial criminals, whose very lives were risks to the German *Volk's* biological existence and natural history, and the disease that such cases represented would be contained by the assemblage of early computers, statistics, and lists as a mechanism of police. By May 1939 the Nazis could identify with almost one hundred percent precision every 'practicing Jew' in the Reich; but still this was insufficient.

> The 1939 census was to be different. [Friedrich] Burgdörfer [Director of the Office of Statistics] wrote, "I hope that we will now approach the goal of the total registration of all Jews and mixed Jews in the old Reich and in Austria with the help of a general and far-reaching registration of family trees."[119]

The 1939 census had a far more elaborate agenda than those held prior: to delimit, police, and ultimately, nullify the so-called 'racial Jews' across the Reich, those that had been assimilating since the 1800s. At the same time the 1939 census intended to also classify all 'racial Jews' from the new, expanded Reich;[120] delimiting populations of Jews everywhere across Nazi-occupied Europe and locating each specific case, all as a precursor to the necessary and effective re-distribution of such diseased elements of the *Volk* into ghettoes, concentration camps, and ultimately gas chambers.

> It was the Reich Office for Statistics, rather than any quasi-official Nazi organizations, that perfected the registration process on a step-by-step basis. The 1939 census was the cornerstone in the ongoing registration of Jews. Artur Kääb, the organizer of the *Volkskartei*, formulated the goal publicly: The Jews will be identified through the processing of their cards in part for present considerations and in part in preparation for future plans. It is absolutely clear that we must have an overview that includes information on residential address. The communities, state police administrators, and county counselors must have an overview of whether any Jews live in their districts and, if so, where.[121]

---

117 Black, *IBM and the Holocaust*, pp. 84-85.
118 Aly, Roth, Black, and Oksiloff, *The Nazi Census*, pp. 38-39.
119 Aly, Roth, Black, and Oksiloff, *The Nazi Census*, pp. 51-52.
120 Black, *IBM and the Holocaust*.
121 Black, *IBM and the Holocaust*, p. 84.

A special envelope containing a Supplemental Card[122] was created expressly for the 1939 census, and these punch cards carried but a single column, coded for descent – a column that had been designed into the card prototype long before the census was engaged.[123] This Supplemental Card, containing the crucial bloodline data, would ultimately produce the lists that would operate as the pivot for the delimitation and extermination of Jews and undesirables across the Third Reich. The data assembled from the 1939 census, and specifically the Supplemental Card, provided the Nazis with a crucial component of the 'Final Solution': a single national register of the entire Third Reich, a comprehensive listing of all Jews and 'diseased elements' of the *Volk*. By the end of 1939 all populations and cases in the Greater Reich that had been classified in any way as Jewish – whether full-Jewish, half-Jewish, or married Jews – were delimited and listed many times over and readied for eradication.

> Racial purity was not just a catchphrase for the Nazis, it was an obsession. Germany wanted more than a society of Aryans, it wanted a master race: tall, strong, blond, and blue-eyed, intellectually and physically dominant. Eugenics became an elite cult. Nazis sought to weed out the weaker elements of its population, regardless of parentage – even from among their own people. The mentally ill, diseased, handicapped, homosexual individuals, and certainly Jews, Gypsies, and a group of misfits termed "anti-social" were not to be part of Germany's future.[124]

By 1939, stringent delimitation and policing of 'undesirables' across the Greater Reich became accepted practices, and in many ways, became a modus operandi of everyday life for all German nationals. And all of this had been achieved through increasingly ubiquitous registration practices and the resulting accumulation of data. Ultimately, for most, there would be no escaping their registration, and the coded numerical reductions that came to mark lives in the Greater Reich.

> A few hours before Eichmann's execution, his Israeli prison warden asked him to respond, as an "expert", to the following question: What should the Jews have done? How could the Jews have resisted, in your view? *Eichmann*: By disappearing. We would have been at a loss if they had disappeared before being registered and concentrated. The number of our commandos was very small, and even if local police had helped us with all they had, their chances would have been at least fifty-fifty. A mass flight would have been disastrous for us.[125]

---

122 Hollerith punch card.
123 Black, *IBM and the Holocaust*.
124 Black, *IBM and the Holocaust*, p. 93.
125 Aly, Roth, Black, and Oksiloff, *The Nazi Census*, p. 93; translated and quoted from H. Kipphardt, *Bruder Eichmann*, Rowohlt, p. 114

The Biopolitical Milieu of Circulation: Managing the Volk's Cultural Organs

> The relation between the individual and the collective, between the totality of the social body and its elementary fragments, is made to function in a completely different way: it will function differently in what we call population. The government of populations is, I think, completely different from the exercise of sovereignty over the fine grain of individual behaviors.[126]

To speak of caesuras, list technologies, and Nazi governmentality is to speak of a conjuncture of technologies of security that installed a milieu of circulation wherein the categorization, classification, naming, and securing of risky biological populations was valued above all else – a way of seeing and doing the human species as an empirical and ordered reduction where probabilities, populations, and the intermingling of natural history and biology ruled the day. In leveraging early punch card computing technologies, massive data, statistics, and lists, Nazi governmentality took the fracture of 'abnormal' populations from 'normal' populations to a new extreme; infusing biopolitics into the classification and ordering of the human species to the point of using metaphors of disease to describe the fundamental caesuras that were at once the hallmark and pivot of Nazi governmentality: Aryan ll Jew.

This is no better evidenced than in a speech delivered at the opening of a 'new' IBM facility in Berlin on January 8, 1934 by Willy Heidinger:[127]

> The physician examines the human body and determines whether all organs are work-ing to the benefit of the entire organism ... We [Dehomag] are very much like the physician, in that we dissect, cell by cell, the German cultural body. We report every individual characteristic on a little card. These are not dead cards, quite the contrary, they prove later on that they come to life when the cards are sorted at a rate of 25,000 per hour according to certain characteristics. These characteristics are grouped like the organs of our cultural body, and they will be calculated and determined with the help of our tabulating machine. We are proud that we may assist in such task, a task that provides our nation's physician [Adolf Hitler] with the material he needs for his examinations. Our Physician can then determine whether the calculated values are in harmony with the health of our people. It also means that if such is not the case, our Physician can take corrective procedures to correct the sick circumstances. Our characteristics are deeply rooted in our race. Therefore we must cherish them like a holy shrine which we will – and must – keep pure. We have the deepest trust in our Physician and will follow his instructions in blind faith, because we know that he will lead our people to a great future. Hail to our German people and *der Führer*.[128]

---

126 Foucault, '25 January 1978', p. 56.
127 An IBM salesman who in 1910 founded *Dehomag* – IBM Germany – and was its major share-holder in 1934.
128 Translated and quoted from *Denkschrift zur Einweihung der neuen Arbeitstätte der Deutschen Hollerith Maschinen Gesellschaft m.b.H. in Berlin-Lichterfelde*, 8 January 1934, United States

What we can clearly glean from this speech is how a way of *seeing* and *doing* built on the double integration of microscopic statistical science – the dissection, cell by cell, data point by data point, of the German cultural body, revealing all of its 'healthy' and 'diseased' organs – and the pseudo-science of Nazi eugenics and race theory was fundamental to Nazi governmentality. This cemented a powerful regime of truth that legitimized the extermination of risky elements in populations. In other words, a way of seeing and doing that took as its primary metaphor the need to calculate, delimit, examine, determine, police, and exterminate 'diseased cultural organs' and all of their circulating elements; populations and their individual cases.

> It is not the division between those who are sick and those who are not. It takes all who are sick and all who are not as a whole, that is to say, in short, the population, and it identifies the coefficient of probable morbidity, or probable mortality, in this population, that is to say the normal expectation in the population of being affected by the disease and death linked to the disease.[129]

When quantitative analyses are made of 'cultural organs' or populations, like they were under Nazi governmentality, the result is that the notion of 'disease' is unloosened from its relationship with individual human bodies and is seen as a statistical problem of distribution. Different possibilities for 'contamination' were calculated and determined, and risky elements were targeted for normalization. In such a milieu of circulation that privileged the policing of 'natural biological' classifications, the 'double integration' effect of the apparatuses (*dispositifs*) of security was clearly exhibited, wherein Nazi governmentality policed the biological classifications that it itself called into reality. Just like with Foucault's epidemics of the eighteenth century, the apparatuses of security that were installed under Nazi governmentality were clearly about populations, probabilities and the normalization of risky elements.

The more the Nazis registered, gathered data, tabulated, named, sorted, categorized, and divided society through conjunctions of juridical-disciplinary mechanisms and technologies of security like the list, the more social policies and practices emerged that revolved around ascribing and predicting quantifiable net-worth values to elements in populations in the interest of securing a 'healthy', or normal *Volk*. With each sort of data by a Hollerith system, human beings in the Third Reich were increasingly constituted as listed elements—identifiable, trackable and risk assessed elements of populations. Like with epidemics and food insufficiency, the apparatuses of security under Nazi governmentality installed a milieu of circulation that was fundamentally marked by population and probability and the need to ensure the free circulation of necessary and sufficient elements and the policing of risky elements.

In this way, where IBM-developed punch card technologies did ultimately provide a crucial means of orchestrating mass extermination and genocide, as Black argues, these technologies did not by any means emerge in a vacuum. Juridical-legal and disciplinary mechanisms involving strict social policies surrounding census, registration, and the frac-

---

Holocaust Memorial Museum Library, p. 23. Translated in Black, *IBM and the Holocaust*, pp. 50-51.
129 Foucault, '25 January 1978', p. 62.

ture of populations were developments both prior and parallel to the Third Reich's adoption of IBM's Hollerith punch card technology and the installation of Nazi governmentality.

How such early information technology served to materialize fractured risky elements in Nazi governmentality did not begin with IBM's Hollerith technologies, but rather with census and registration processes. These juridical-disciplinary mechanisms had been effect in Germany for almost fifty years by 1930, and had laid the groundwork for a form of governmentality that would hinge on seeing, naming, predicting, limiting, and neutralizing the effects of risks to a population called the Aryan *Volk*.

And while it was quite clearly IBM's Hollerith tabulators and sorters, used to decipher the 1933 German census,[130] that helped crystallize this intermingling of classification and biology under Nazi governmentality, Herman Hollerith, the father of IBM, had been making this a reality since the late 1870s in the United States, from the time he was brought on as a clerk in the US Census Bureau and began applying his early ideas in information technology to questions of social statistics and populations.[131] But ultimately, it was under Nazi governmentality that a conjunction of juridical-disciplinary mechanisms, redeployed in apparatuses of security, coalesced as a governmentality that sought to delimit, police, and nullify risky elements to an extreme; and it is in this moment and in these conditions that Nazi governmentality deployed the list as a security technology for identifying and policing threats in a wide variety of milieus of circulation. In this way, the list would emerge as the pivot of an everyday existence marked at every turn by the caesura of 'Aryan' II 'other' – at once a way of seeing and naming, for calling 'risks' into reality, and at the same time providing a practical means for nullifying them.

So while the work presented here is inspired and informed by Black's illuminating revelations, beginning with an investigation into the moments leading up to the Nazis' integration of IBM's Hollerith punch card technology with social practices surrounding census, registration, and selection, it is intended to extend this history to an articulation of the modern art of governmentality. This work contends that the Nazi conjunction of juridical-legal and disciplinary mechanisms and technologies of security, and specifically the way the list served the policing and enforcement of caesuras, represents a crucial event in the governmentality, wherein through their interweaving with early 'computer' systems and statistical technologies, lists began to serve the delimitation, policing, and nullification of risky, abnormal, and undesirable elements circulating in populations.

Thanks to their installation of this unique conjunction of security technologies, the Third Reich, in its quest for racial supremacy, came to see that virtually all aspects of life could be automated and organized; from military personnel to individual citizens; from the largest industries to the smallest grocers and dry-goods stores; from the biologically desirable to the Jews and anti-socials. 'Just as people would be categorized and regimented down to the least characteristic, so would all of German business be analyzed to the smallest

---

130 Black, *IBM and the Holocaust.*
131 Pugh, *Building IBM.*

detail – and then subjected to Nazi discipline.'[132] In this way, in the Third Reich, the list was much more than a functional means of administering and organizing people and things and developing knowledge, it also represented a whole new way of seeing populations marked by fractured risky biological elements and the need to police and nullify them. IBM's Dehomag explicitly embraced its critical role in the Nazi apparatuses of security and governmentality, producing a publicity poster (circa 1934) that depicts an all-encompassing, omnipresent eye floating in the sky, its gaze directed downwards, in the form of a punch card subsuming a city skyline. The text simply reads, 'See everything with Hollerith punch cards',[133] but as this research argues, it could also read 'See everything with statistics', or, 'See everything with lists'; as early computer systems, statistics, and list technologies would all come to critically serve Nazi governmentality and its apparatuses of security.

The List Served: 'Seeing Everything' Through Nazi Apparatuses of Security

> Unless we understand how the Nazis acquired the names, more lists will be compiled against more people.[134]

Seeing everything under Nazi governmentality started with seeing Jews. As the security technologies (statistics, computers, and lists) became more refined in Nazi governmentality; as the sorting, cross-indexing, classifying, and predicting routines became more sophisticated, statistical race researchers were able to probe deeper and deeper into Jewish bloodlines and lineage, and produce more and more lists of diseased elements and cases for policing. Indeed, as the Nazi apparatuses of security were installed across larger swaths of Europe, Jews and those sorted as 'anti-social' increasingly found nowhere to hide from the endless punch cards clattering through Hollerith machines and from their statistically-derived lists of risky elements: '…comparing names across generations, address changes across regions, family trees and personal data across unending registries'.[135] By 1944, life in Nazi-occupied Europe was unequivocally marked by such delimitation, policing, and nullification.

But not only were people tabulated, sorted, and delimited; they were coded, and '…it was the code that branded the individual and sealed his destiny. Each code was a brick in an inescapable wall of data.'[136] Everywhere throughout the Greater Reich, the human species was being valued and reduced to risk and net-worth scores, and subdivided as such. With each and every conquest, the art of governmentality the Nazis were perfecting was being installed further and further, enmeshing unlimited territory in an apparatus of security designed to trap Jews and 'undesirables' of all kinds in a fiery hell where one's code and score would very much come to determine one's fate.

---

132 Black, *IBM and the Holocaust*, pp. 86-87.
133 Black, *IBM and the Holocaust*, p. 104.
134 Black, *IBM and the Holocaust*, p. 7.
135 Black, *IBM and the Holocaust*, p. 107.
136 Black, *IBM and the Holocaust*, p. 365.

Hollerith tracking worked so well that the SS Economic Administration was able to authoritatively challenge the slave labor reports they were receiving on any given day. For instance, at one point in the latter part of 1943, the central office asked for the number of Auschwitz Jews fit for reassignment to an armaments plant. On August 29, Auschwitz replied that only 3,581 were available. Senior SS Economics Administration Officer Gerhard Maurer knew from [their own] Hollerith sorts that fully 25,000 Jews were available for work transfers. Four days later, Maurer dispatched a brash rejoinder to Auschwitz Camp Commandant Rudolf Höss himself. "What are the remaining 21,500 Jews doing?" Maurer demanded. "Something's amiss here! Please again scrutinize this process and give a report".[137]

Critical to 'seeing everything' in Nazi Germany was the highly complex administration, organization and orchestration of millions of elements in motion across Nazi-occupied Europe, an increasingly large milieu of circulation. A key industry that was radically transformed by Nazi governmentality was the railway industry. Prior to the deployment of Nazi apparatuses of security to railroads, tracking trains and their contents was an odious affair for railway companies, requiring weeks to manually identify and locate boxcars. But Nazi governmentality now made it possible to efficiently and effectively schedule, locate, and deploy trains, stock, and boxcars within 48 hours.

During the war years, IBM supplied elaborate Hollerith systems to nearly all the railways of Nazi-dominated Europe. Knowing how many freight cars and locomotives to schedule on any given day in any given location, anywhere across the map of Europe, required the computational capabilities of Hollerith. Punch card systems identified the exact location of each freight car, how much cargo it could accept, and what schedule it could adhere to for maximum efficiency. In fact, the main method of tracking freight cars was a network of Hollerith systems installed at railroad junctions across Europe.[138]

The Nazis relied heavily on Hollerith technologies, to track their trains and schedule delivery of the 'desirable' and 'undesirable' cargo their boxcars contained. 'Trains were Himmler's most valuable tool – and railroads were among IBM's most lucrative clients in Europe.'[139] Indeed, it was not only Hollerith identification and control that provided unmatchable efficiency and effectiveness in railway and boxcar tracking, satisfying the Nazis' highly-complex and fully-integrated scheduling needs, managing the flow of millions of bodies and tons more cargo across their occupied lands, it was the whole agglomeration of the apparatuses of security and their technologies, including the list which continued to serve its historical 'intellectual technology' role, but also now served to delimit, manage, and police the fundamental caesuras that marked day to day life.

---

137 Black, *IBM and the Holocaust*, p. 355.
138 Black, *IBM and the Holocaust*, p. 265.
139 Black, *IBM and the Holocaust*, p. 357.

Now it seems to me that through the obviously very partial phenomena that I have tried to pick out we see the emergence of a completely different problem that is no longer of fixing and demarcating the territory, but of allowing circulations to take place, of controlling them, sifting the good and the bad, ensuring that things are always in movement, constantly moving around, continually going from one point to another, but in such a ways that the inherent dangers of this circulation are canceled out.[140]

By January 1944, this art of governmentality, of accumulating data to control and secure the circulation of living beings and things, had become so prevalent and ubiquitous across Nazi-occupied Europe that a special 'central' statistics bureau was established by Hitler to sort, tabulate, analyze, and coordinate all of the information that flowed in from the many Hollerith operations across the Third Reich. While there is little that is known about this highly secret centralized card sorting facility, the *Zentral Institut*[141] as it was known, served as a clearinghouse for '...all new registrations, death lists, daily strength reports and transfers from site to site'.[142] The *Zentral Institut* was the pivot for railway and concentration camp coordination and scheduling – tabulating, sorting, analyzing, and tracking with cold mechanized automation and precision the extent of destruction the Nazis were waging across Europe.

It was enough to inform *Zentral Institut* that the people had boarded a train. Hence the machines only tabulated the evacuations. No more was necessary. From these trains, there was no escape, no need for tracking, no further utility, and no further cost would be expended. At this point, the Jews were no longer worth a bullet, nor the price of a single punch card ... Only at the moment of extermination did the Jews of Europe finally break free from Hitler's Holleriths.[143]

But for those who had yet to break free, who were still in the concentration camps, there was no way of escaping their branded code.

Every hell has its hierarchy. Each Hollerith code carried consequences. In the concentration camps, the level of inhumanity, pain, and torture were not the happenstance of incarceration as much as a destiny assured by Hollerith coding. It was impossible to shirk one's Hollerith code.[144]

Almost every concentration camp opened and operated a Hollerith facility, known as a *Hollerith Abteilung*,[145] and at these facilities all prisoner cards and labor transfer rosters were processed. These operations yielded a constant flow of traffic, primarily consisting of lists including departure lists, transfer lists, and work assignment lists. Lists were the primary output of the *Hollerith Abteilung*, which assembled the detailed information contained on

---

140 Foucault, '25 January 1978', p. 65.
141 Central Institute.
142 Black, *IBM and the Holocaust*, p. 360.
143 Black, *IBM and the Holocaust*, p. 372.
144 Black, *IBM and the Holocaust*, p. 362.
145 Black, *IBM and the Holocaust*, p. 351.

punch cards, outputting daily lists that came to regiment every aspect of prisoner existence including exterminations.[146] Punch cards for camp prisoners detailed everything; date of birth, marital status, number of children, nationality, physical characteristics, work skills, and even, at the Mauthausen concentration camp in Austria, the kinds of torture and punishment the prisoner had been subjected to. '*Hollerith erfasst*, or "Hollerith registered". That designation was stamped in large letters on hundreds of thousands of processed Personal Inmate Cards at camps all across Europe.'[147]

Critical to existence in the concentration camps were sixteen categories, classifications, or scores that were established for the reason for incarceration, and the code that was punched on one's card in this category most assuredly determined one's fate. Among the codes, homo-sexuals were given the number 3, anti-socials were coded with the number 9, and Gypsies with the number 12; but the code that was reserved for the biggest risk and ultimately ensured the most violent torture and treatment was for the Jews, the number 8.

> As horrific as camps were for all, Jews coded by number experienced an additional nightmare of unspeakable dimension. Because Jews were instantly recognizable by their patches, they could be denounced at every turn as "Jewish swine" or "Jewish muck" with the attendant physical abuse. One could never escape his code.[148]

Among the most ominous codes that appeared on prisoner punch cards were those contained in column 34, which was labeled 'Reason for Departure'.

> Code 2 simply meant transferred to another camp for continuing labor. Natural death was coded 3. Execution was coded 4. Suicide was coded 5. The ominous code 6 des-ignated "special handling", the term commonly understood as extermination, either in a gas chamber, by hanging or by gunshot.[149]

The column 34 code was the last code, the last hole punched, the last bit of humanity reduced and divested; a final dehumanizing number assigned in a column on a punch card, in a process that began with divisive and caesuric practices, and ended with extermination. By 1944 millions of human beings had been identified, sorted, assigned, guided, integrated, and transported in this way, by means of an apparatus of security, which tracked them mercilessly along their journeys; from their homes to the ghettos, to the train platforms, boxcars, camps, and ultimately, gas chambers. Not surprisingly, 'to obliterate all evidence of the mass murders documented by Hollerith records, Himmler ordered all camp card indices destroyed before the Allies arrived'.[150] But not everything was destroyed at the camps; evidence remained of the apparatuses of security.

---

146 Black, *IBM and the Holocaust*, p. 351.
147 Black, *IBM and the Holocaust*, p. 353.
148 Black, *IBM and the Holocaust*, p. 363.
149 Black, *IBM and the Holocaust*, p. 11.
150 Black, *IBM and the Holocaust*, p. 359.

At Mauthausen "Departure Lists" were fundamentally roll calls of the dead. A typical handwritten "Departure List" ran on for many pages. No names were used, just the inmate's five- or six-digit Hollerith identity, listed on the left in numerical order for efficient punching into column 22 of the Dehomag cards printed for camp death tallying.[151]

Columns and numbers appearing on seemingly innocuous punch cards had killed millions of people and ironically, numbers were all that remained of them – outputted on lists – ready as ever to be punched, tabulated, sorted, and analyzed in an endless mechanized cycle that began with fracturing caesuras, and ultimately turned on a population's compliance with and acquiescence to stringent governmental registration policies that sought to dismantle and secure society through the delimitation, policing, and nullification of listed 'risks'.

The List Serves: Governmentality or Bare Life?

For millennia, man remained what he was for Aristotle: a living animal with the additional capacity for a political existence; modern man is an animal whose politics places his existence as a living being in question. – Michel Foucault[152]

The correct question to pose concerning the horrors committed in the camps is, therefore, not the hypocritical one of how crimes of such atrocity could be committed against human beings. It would be more honest, and above all more useful, to investigate carefully the juridical procedures and deployments of power by which human beings could be so completely deprived of their rights and prerogatives that no act committed against them could appear any longer a crime. – Giorgio Agamben[153]

Thus far this has been an attempt to critically address the 'juridical procedures and deployments of power' that Agamben points to; an examination of how Nazi governmentality came to reduce human beings to statistical objects, risk assessed numbers on lists. Moreover, we have seen how such complex bureaucratic laws, policies, procedures, and practices would ultimately so fracture a people, the *Volk*, and so dehumanize individuals as 'diseased cases' that an entire nation's collective conscience would barely stir while with cold efficiency its government delimited, policed, and ultimately exterminated 'undesirable' elements in the bio-political milieu of circulation that was the hallmark of Nazi governmentality. The interweaving of Nazi 'raceology' and eugenics provided a veneer of pseudo-scientific validation to a vision of social control that depended on the accumulation of data and the reduction of the human being to net-values of worth and risk. This in turn legitimated the ongoing ethno-biological diagnoses of a 'disease-ridden' *Volk*, and these diagnoses involved splintering and fracturing the *Volk* in the interest of isolating the cancerous elements within. From there, the prescription was clear: delimit, police, and exterminate.

---

151 Black, *IBM and the Holocaust*, p. 359.
152 Foucault, *The History of Sexuality*.
153 Agamben, *Homo Sacer*.

At the hub of this 'biopolitical' praxis were the minutiae of bureaucratic practices that Hannah Arendt[154] first pointed to in *Eichmann in Jerusalem*. But where Arendt illuminated how banal, everyday practices in Nazi Germany contained within them the incunabula for profound evil, absent in her analysis is precisely this biopolitical element; specifically an interrogation of how caesuric practices in the Third Reich came to provide a means of ordering and organizing society, and at the same time served to divest individuals of their humanity. Indeed, no juridical-legal mechanisms and practices of discipline were as pivotal to Nazi governmentality as those involving census and registration; and Götz Aly and Karl Roth's *The Nazi Census: Identification and Control in the Third Reich* has significantly helped us to see their profound implications in Nazi Germany. The book was originally published in 1983 '...in connection with a political and legal conflict surrounding the planned census, which was later called off by the German Federal Constitutional Court'.[155] Not surprisingly, the book contains a foreword by Edwin Black, who in addition to having sponsored its English translation hails Aly and Roth's work as pioneering, asserting that,

> Aly and Roth correctly comprehended and documented that registration in all its forms
> – from primitive paper and pencil records to the use of high-speed Hollerith machines
> – was the first step in Hitler's war against the Jews and other enemies. The types of
> registration covered all modalities, from massive censuses to ongoing population regis-
> trations, labor pools, and human numbering systems.[156]

Nazi governmentality hinged on census and registration practices, and the precise march of death the Nazi apparatuses of security orchestrated could never have been achieved had the groundwork for delimitation, policing, and extermination not been laid with the 1933 census, followed up with extensive registration policies and practices and all culminating in the 1939 census which effectively registered by name all German Jews and 'Jewish half-breeds' in the Third Reich. But where census and registration practices, the data accumulated from them, and statistical techniques, clearly played a key role in delimitation, policing, and extermination in Nazi Germany, surprisingly, like IBM's Hollerith technology and list technologies, scant Holocaust research has treated these questions. 'In fact, the crucial minutiae of registration are barely mentioned in any of the thousands of books on the Third Reich.'[157] And it is the crucial minutiae of registration practices – redeployed in apparatuses of security – that serve as the bureaucratic basis around which caesuric divisions are brought into reality and enacted, and how risky elements of living beings are culled and listed.

A politics that calls into question the existence and categorization of living beings is the quintessential essence of the biopolitics that Giorgio Agamben asserts.[158] When Agamben argues that, 'There is no clearer way to say that the first foundation of political life is a life

---

154 Hannah Arendt, *Eichmann in Jerusalem: A Report on the Banality of Evil,* New York: Penguin
     Books, 1994.
155 Aly, Roth, Black, and Oksiloff, *The Nazi Census*, p. xi.
156 Aly, Roth, Black, and Oksiloff, *The Nazi Census*, pp. viii-ix.
157 Black, *IBM and the Holocaust*, p. xi.
158 Agamben, *Homo Sacer*; Agamben, *Remnants of Auschwitz*; Agamben, *State of Exception*.

that may be killed, which is politicized through its very capacity to be killed'[159] he is striking a biopolitical stance, arguing that 'bare life' is the fundamental political unit around which sovereignty is practiced. But therein, it is a biopolitical stance that is decidedly different from the one associated with Michel Foucault's governmentality.

> One of the most persistent features of Foucault's work is its decisive abandonment of the traditional approach to the problem of power, which is based in juridico-institutional model (the definition of sovereignty, the theory of the State) in favor of an unprejudiced analysis of the concrete way in which power penetrates subjects' very bodies and forms of life ... In his final years Foucault seemed to orient this analysis according to two distinct directives for research: on the one hand, the study of the *political techniques* with which the State assumes and integrates the care of the natural life of individuals into its very center; on the other hand, the examination of the *technologies of the self* by which processes of subjectivization bring the individual to bind himself to his own identity and consciousness and, at the same time, to power.[160]

As the work presented here has demonstrated, Foucault never 'decisively abandoned' 'juridico-institutional models', but rather refined his conception from sovereignty to discipline and to governmentality; in fact, arguing in his later years, that juridical-legal, institutional, and disciplinary mechanisms are far from abandoned in modern and contemporary forms of government, but rather are redeployed within apparatuses of security that seek to regulate and distribute elements in the milieus of circulation, to meet the objectives of the state.

> The population is not, then, a collection of juridical subjects in an individual or collective relationship with a sovereign will. It is a set of elements in which we can note constants and regularities even in accidents, in which we can identify the universal of desire regularly producing the benefit of all, and with regard to which we can identify a number of modifiable variable on which it depends. Taking the effects specific to population into consideration, making them pertinent if you like, is, I think, a very important phenomenon: the entry of a "nature" in to the field of techniques of power, of a nature that is not something on which, above which, or against which the sovereign must impose just laws. We have a population whose nature is such that the sovereign must deploy reflected procedures of government within this nature, with the help of it, and with regard to it.[161]

Where for Foucault technologies of sovereignty are redeployed in the apparatuses of security with the aim of specifically effecting populations – the reflected procedures of government –Agamben argues that modern and contemporary existence continues to constitute 'political life' as a simultaneous inclusion and exclusion of what Aristotle called natural life, or 'bare life', from 'good life'. Drawing on Aristotle's fundamental ideas surrounding the sovereign politics of man, Agamben argues that humans are animals born to life, the Greek *zoe*, which

---

159 Agamben, *Homo Sacer*, p. 89.
160 Agamben, *Homo Sacer*, p. 5.
161 Foucault, '29 March 1978', pp. 74-75.

expresses the basic 'fact of living common to all living beings'[162], giving them *name*. But at the same time, this simple fact of living (*to z n*) is set in opposition to a politically qualified life (*to eu z n*), or the Greek *bios*, which indicates the form or way of living proper to an individual group. In Aristotle's ancient way of understanding and conceiving political sovereign existence, 'bare life', or *zoe*, is that which is transformed via the State into a representation of 'good life', *bios*, as we are 'born with regard to life, but existing essentially with regard to the good life'.[163] In this way, 'bare life' is understood as all that is excluded from the higher aims of the state, yet is included precisely so that it may be transformed into a regard for 'good life'. According to Agamben, this biopower, which takes the bare lives of individual citizens into political calculations from birth, imprinting a sovereignty of rights onto the bodies of babies in birth, has essentially existed since ancient times, as per Aristotle. And for Agamben, this structure of exception is essential to the core concept of contemporary Western sovereignty, and 'bare life' is thus the fundamental political unit around which power pivots.

So, where Foucault sees the juridical-legal mechanisms of sovereignty as redeployed along with disciplinary mechanisms in the apparatuses of security that install populations and milieus of circulation through the art of governmentality, Agamben looks to questions of individual rights, will, and agency, reinvigorating concepts of docile and revolting bodies in contemporary power formations. But, as we have seen through the work of Foucault, these issues are far more complicated than such models of sovereignty can contain. There has clearly been a shift from sovereignty to discipline and to governmentality, involving the installation of milieus of circulation, market mechanisms, statistics, probabilities, and populations in modern and contemporary formations of power that Agamben's articulation of 'bare life' decisively ignores. Indeed, so says Foucault of the juridical-legal mechanisms of sovereignty that are redeployed in the apparatuses of security,

> They do not attempt, at least not primarily or in a fundamental way, to make use of a relationship of obedience between a higher will, of the sovereign, and the will of those subjected to his will. In other words, the mechanism of security does not function on the axis of the sovereign-subjects relationship, ensuring the total and as it were passive obedience of individuals to their sovereign. They are connected to what the physiocrats called physical processes, which could be called natural processes, and which we could also call elements of reality. These mechanisms do not tend to a nullification of phenomena in the form of prohibition, "you will do this", nor even "this will not happen", but in the form of a progressive self-cancellation of phenomena by the phenomena themselves. In a way, they involve the delimitation of phenomena within acceptable limits, rather than the imposition of a law that says no to them. So mechanisms of security are not put to work on the sovereign-subject axis or in the form of prohibition.[164]

So where Foucault takes as his focus milieus of circulation, populations, and their indeterminacy, Agamben attends to sovereignty's disciplinary enclosures, and specifically the clearly

162 Agamben, *Homo Sacer*, p. 1.
163 Agamben, *Homo Sacer*, p. 2.
164 Foucault, '29 March 1978', p. 66.

delimited space of the concentration camp, where he argues that identification and control of human life – biopolitical order – is at its extreme. It is precisely in the concentration camp that Agamben articulates 'bare life', meaning life that no longer deserves to live, but cannot be martyred; life that cannot be sacrificed, yet may be killed; the last vestige of the body that violence is wholly permitted against; corporeal, passive-flesh utterly exorcised of humanity; the pivot of modern and contemporary biopolitical order. The space of the concentration camp is characterized by what Agamben calls the originary nomos – with the strongest hand comes order and power – a realm wherein violence and law, policing and politics become indistinguishable. At the extreme of this order, and unique to this indeterminate space, is the production of the Muselmann, the emergence of the last biopolitical caesura ‖ the final transformation of the prisoner into one indivisible entity ‖ the last layer of the onion peeled ‖ a body that no longer carries any markers of humanity ‖ a body that can be exterminated without conscience.

But where Agamben's 'passive flesh' conception of docile bodies – stripped of their rights by sovereigns, layer by layer, in closed disciplinary milieus of circulation like concentration camps, where sovereign policing is unconditional and brutal – serves as a way of remembering a violence and power that has historically been imposed downwards by sovereigns onto the bodies of subjects, this somewhat deterministic way of seeing power does not bear out in modern and contemporary formations of power, particularly given the complications of political economic milieus of circulation that Foucault has elaborated more deeply. Where Agamben provides us with a description of the atrocities of concentrating populations in disciplinary enclosures, stripping them of their fundamental rights and exposing bare life, the camp as such is not emblematic of governmentality, which we have seen is a space of circulation that is characterized as letting things happen. In this way, where Agamben argues that:

> Fascism and Nazism are, above all, redefinitions of the relations between man and citizen, and become fully intelligible only when situated – no matter how paradoxical it may seem – in the biopolitical context inaugurated by national sovereignty and declarations of rights.[165]

The research presented here, into how the list served Nazi governmentality, is in some ways at odds with Agamben's conclusion. It is argued here that the redefinition of the relations between people that Nazism represented were not about the rights and wills of individual bodies in relation to disciplinary enclosures of sovereignty, but were in fact the polar opposite. Nazism, or Nazi governmentality, installed apparatuses of security, wherein juridical-disciplinary mechanisms were redeployed in the installation of a milieu of circulation that let things happen, neither prohibiting nor prescribing rights on individual subjects, but assessing individuals as statistical factors of worth and risk circulating in uncertain milieus. As we will see in chapter 4, it is in the redeployment of juridical-legal mechanisms by the apparatuses of security to police global milieus of circulation that Agamben's 'bare life' and Foucault's 'governmentality' may just be reconcilable. But for now, rather than an enclosed space of legal rights, we have seen how Nazi governmentality installed a milieu of circulation that did not

---

165 Agamben, *Homo Sacer*, p. 130.

prevent, nor prohibit, nor impose power downwards, from sovereigns to subjects, but rather flattened the playing field, ensuring the efficient and effective circulation of necessary and sufficient elements in a milieu where the delimitation, policing, nullification, and extermination of risky biopolitical elements was at a maxim.

Conclusion

In the same way that lists brought contradiction to questions of who constituted a Jew or an undesirable in Nazi biopolitical order, today, they bring contradiction to questions of who constitutes a contemporary terrorist. But who are the terrorists? And how can they be identified and controlled most efficiently? What caesuric social practices are required? What are the most effective technologies for such operations? While the answers remain fluid and elusive, such questions are the eerie remnants of Nazi governmentality. And where Nazi governmentality dreamed of an everyday registration system that through the accumulation of massive data could track, organize, and order the political, social, physical and financial meanderings of massive populations on an up-to-the-minute basis, it is only in the last years, with the widespread global adoption of the internet and networked technologies in general that such dreams have taken shape as reality. No longer are houses the markers of residence, nor the focus of registration. Registration is now everywhere, as increasingly all facets of our lives are logged, tracked, and mirrored in our networked milieus of circulation. The tabulation, sorting, analysis, and coding of human beings as worth/risk elements, is now ubiquitous, receding further and further into the fabric of everyday culture.

In this way, where Hitler and the Third Reich lost, Nazi governmentality prevailed; as the conjunction of computer technologies, statistics, and list technologies assembled by the Nazi apparatuses of security continued to serve modern and contemporary formations of power. The Nazi dream of daily registration is now a reality. In this way, Nazi governmentality correlated a way of seeing and doing revolving around a conjunction of technologies of security – computers, the accumulation of data, statistics, and lists – where the installation of caesuras was at a maxim, and that continues to haunt us today. As such, the emergence of Nazi governmentality in fact represents the first correlation of the apparatuses of security as a massive computerized 'biofeedback system' that would inevitably come to serve the purpose of delimiting and policing global threats to social order. Indeed, it is with the emergence and widespread adoption of systems theory in the 1940s and 1950s, as well as with attendant evolutions in computing technologies that the form of governmentality installed through the apparatuses of security went well beyond global.

CHAPTER 2. THE LIST SERVES: ENTROPY AND GOVERNMENTALITY

Introduction

Contemplate now for a moment the great movement of Western science since the days of Galileo Galilei, its pioneer and quite properly its hero. The subsequent centuries may be viewed metaphorically as a journey of discovery and exploration, away from the medieval world, the personal and subjective, the moral, the theological, and the political, and into an objective, empirical, public reality in which measurements fit into abstract mathematical patterns with a claim to universality and the human observer is eliminated. The eye-opening insights of a Newton, a Gauss, an Einstein are among the great treasures discovered on the journey ... It was part of the same journey of Western civilization to create machinery of many kinds: elaborate tools, weapons, methods of mass production and complex organization, magical and diverse gadgets – in short modern technology. And this civilization, drunk with the power of this amazing technology and the benefits it seemed to bring, so forgot itself that it lost all perspective. It let its mode of existence be determined by science and technology. The Nazi gas chambers which came out of that civilization and nuclear bombs, its latest high technology, were like a shot of cold water in the face, awaking us to the discovery, once we had seen past the dazzling treasure, that our journey hadn't taken us as far as we had imagined. It was a familiar landscape because what dominated it, after all, was people – play and affections, politics and passions, pleasures and pains.[1]

Despite the Nazi gas chambers and nuclear bombs seemingly being 'a shot of cold water in the face' of civilization, the fundamental ironies of progress Steve J. Heims points to in his historical account and cultural interrogation of the meaning of the lives of John Von Neumann and Norbert Wiener, continue even today. Have we really been awakened to these modern discoveries, as he suggests? Have we now seen past the dazzling treasures of contemporary computer networked technologies and their underpinning statistical and list technologies or have we yet to see that this modern conjunction of computer, statistical, and list technologies is critical to the constitution and policing of contemporary fields, domains, and objects of knowledge, and as such, is critical to the association, representation, and correlation of contemporary power?

As we will see in this chapter, the assemblage of technologies and techniques of power that emerged with Nazi governmentality, would exert equal force in the development of the 'political technology' of modern and contemporary computers and network infrastructures. Moreover, the emergence of the modern computer – this event in the journey of civilization – would come to install milieus of circulation of many kinds, increasingly elaborate integrations of technologies and techniques for the administration, organization, and development

---

1   Steve J. Heims, *John von Neumann and Norbert Wiener: From Mathematics to the Technologies of Life and Death*, Cambridge: MIT Press, 1980, p. 414.

of living beings, things, and knowledge; and equally for the delimitation and policing of the movement of 'risky' circulating elements in unpredictable and ever-expanding entropic milieus. Lastly, as we shall see, the emergence of the 'modern computer' in the 1940s and 1950s, would also serve to install a new classification for the human species – as cyborgs: a further suffusing of taxonomy and biology, wherein the 'computer' and 'brains' and 'bodies' of living beings and things would be inextricably linked in their classification and subdivision as natural 'digital' elements; circulating, distributed, and steered in 'global classification infrastructures' the world over. Indeed, in these ever-expanding and highly unpredictable milieus, circulating elements are increasingly assigned values of worth/risk at every turn.

In short, this chapter argues that the emergence of modern computer technology in the 1940s and 1950s, underpinned by statistical and list technologies, served to further correlate a series of disciplinary and security mechanisms that would ultimately install a massive, unpredictable, and ever-expanding classification milieu of circulation in which risky elements would be delimited and policed on a global scale. As Heims[2] argues, the emergence of computer technology did in fact eliminate the human observer, automating decision-making at almost every level of life, but it also increasingly rendered the boundaries between people, things, and knowledge even blurrier.[3] Moreover, the emergence of the modern computer in the 1940s and 1950s also represents a moment when the 'double integration' effects of technologies like statistics and lists – the hallmark characteristic of the apparatuses of security – would help install a self-elaborating milieu of circulation, which would once and forever transcend any preconceived or perceived territorial boundaries, opening spaces as expansive, disordered, and never-ending as the globe and even the universe at large. Spaces that despite their indefiniteness could be probed for regularities and patterns through statistical mechanisms, and further, acted upon through circular causal feedback operations. Through the installation of such a massive playing field, a battle or game as immense as the 'space race' could be waged. Beginning in the 1940s and 1950s, the delimitation and policing of the movement of 'risky' elements from 'normal' populations would also be elevated to epic proportions, in this endless, indefinite, and highly unpredictable – entropic – milieu of circulation that would be installed by the apparatuses of security: 'the free world' versus 'the communist threat'.

In this way, the interweaving of computers, data, statistical, and list technologies, as they operate in assemblages of policing and apparatuses of security that install milieus dominated by probabilities and predictions, as well as practices involving the necessary and sufficient regulation and distribution of 'risky' and 'worthwhile' elements circulating in populations, continues to be a central trope of this chapter. Picking up on how the apparatuses of security served the delimitation and policing of 'risky' elements circulating

---

2   Heims, *John von Neumann and Norbert Wiener*; Steve J. Heims, *Constructing a Social Science for Postwar America: The Cybernetics Group, 1946-1953*, Cambridge: MIT Press, 1993.
3   See also Donna J. Haraway, *Simians, Cyborgs, and Women: The Reinvention of Nature*, New York: Routledge, 1991; Donna J. Haraway, *Modest Witness@Second_Millenium, Femaleman©_ Meets_Oncomouse™: Feminism and Technoscience*, New York: Routledge, 1997.

in populations under Nazi governmentality, this assemblage of security continued to evolve, grow, and be redeployed in the Cold War era, which post-World War II was marked at every political turn by eerily similar 'us' vs. 'them' discourses and divisive social practices revolving around the quantification and classification of living beings. Indeed, the delimiting, assigning, managing, listing, policing, steering, and nullification of 'abnormal' elements distributed in populations, installed under Nazi governmentality – these biopolitics – are clearly also implicated in the emergence of the modern computer.

Between the First World War and the present, biology has been transformed from a science centred on the organism, understood in functionalist terms, to a science studying automated technological devices, understood in terms of cybernetic systems. Organic form ... gave way to systems theory with its control schemes based on communication networks and a logical technology in which human beings become potentially outmoded symbol-using devices.[4]

In the same spirit as Foucault's conceptualization of the event of 'natural history',[5] for Donna Haraway the fusing of biology to functionalist automated technologies in the 1940s and 1950s also served to further render the organic form of living beings increasingly irrelevant, producing the 'natural' classification *cyborg*. In this spirit, this chapter builds on research that has interrogated cybernetics, game, and systems theories post-World War II, and the emergence of massive computing technologies as a critical event in the history of communication and cultural research.[6] Specifically examining the leveling of

4 Haraway, *Simians, Cyborgs, and Women*, p. 45.
5 Foucault, *The Order of Things*; Foucault, Senellart, and Davidson, *Security, Territory, Population*.
6 Geoffrey C. Bowker, 'How to Be Universal: Some Cybernetic Strategies', *Social Studies of Science* 23 (1993): 107-127; Geoffrey C. Bowker and Susan Leigh Star, *Sorting Things Out: Classification and its Consequences*, Cambridge: MIT Press, 1999; Umberto Eco, *The Open Work*, London: Hutchinson Radius, 1989; Paul N. Edwards, *The Closed World: Computers and the Politics of Discourse in Cold War America*, Cambridge: MIT Press, 1996; Sheryl N. Hamilton, 'Interrogating the Cybernetic Imaginary, or, Control and Communication in the Human and the Machine', Communication Studies, Montreal, Concordia University, 1999; Donna J. Haraway, 'Manifesto for Cyborgs: Science, Technology, and Socialist Feminism in the 1980s', *Socialist Review* 80 (1985): 65-108; Haraway, *Simians, Cyborgs, and Women*; Haraway, *Modest Witness@Second_Millenium*; Heims, *John von Neumann and Norbert Wiener*; Heims, *Constructing a Social Science for Postwar America*; Christopher Simpson, *Science of Coercion: Communication Research and Psychological Warfare, 1945-1960*, New York: Oxford University Press, 1994; Sherry Turkle, *The Second Self: Computers and the Human Spirit*, New York: Simon and Schuster, 1984; Sherry Turkle, *Life on the Screen: Identity in the Age of the Internet*, New York: Simon & Schuster, 1995; M. Mitchell Waldrop, *The Dream Machine: J.C.R. Licklider and the Revolution that Made Computing Personal*, New York: Viking, 2001; Joseph Weizenbaum, *Computer Power and Human Reason: From Judgment to Calculation*, San Francisco: W.H. Freeman, 1976; Norbert Wiener, *Cybernetics or, Control and Communication in the Animal and the Machine*, New York: M.I.T. Press, 1948; Norbert Wiener, *The Human Use of Human Beings; Cybernetics and Society*, Boston: Houghton Mifflin, 1950; Norbert Wiener, *The Human Use of Human Beings; Cybernetics and Society*, Garden City, New York: Doubleday, 1954; Norbert Wiener, *I Am a Mathematician, the Later Life of a Prodigy; An Autobiographical Account of the Mature Years and Career of Norbert Wiener and a Continuation of the Account of His Childhood in Ex-Prodigy*, Garden City: Doubleday, 1956.

living beings and things in the constitution of fields, domains, and objects of knowledge, this chapter will ultimately establish the intersection of computer technologies, mathematical classification, and listing techniques stemming from the transformation of statistical practices in cybernetics, game, and systems theory, and the widespread circulation of myths about the battles between 'us' and 'them' in the post-World War II or Cold War era, as installing a milieu of circulation characterized by expansion, disorder, and unpredictability; or rather, entropy.

As such, this chapter, and this work as a whole, can also be positioned as part of a stream of discursive counter-histories of computer technology, which includes Edwards,[7] Simpson,[8] Heims,[9] Black,[10] Haraway,[11] and Poster;[12] who all aim to set the history of intersections of people and machines, and questions of technoscience in general, into new and uncharted waters and directions. By exploring not the instrumental history of computer technology, but a discursive history, constructed around the fictions, fantasies, and myths that circulate around computers, statistics, and lists as critical supports of modern and contemporary governmentality, this work is part of a research movement that attempts to shift the focus of historical inquiry from the scientific power associated with technologies like the computer to their meanings in terms of contemporary social practices and political and cultural divisions and struggles. In this way, this work resituates computer technologies in the constitution of contemporary fields, domains, and objects of knowledge correlated by relations of power. As such, it can also be understood as a call for paying attention to competition and collaboration amongst discourses; how they operate as economies that are centrally motivated by the correlation of power, and unequivocally situated in human struggle.

In a society such as ours, but basically in any society, there are manifold relations of power which permeate, characterize, and constitute the social body, and these relations of power cannot themselves be established, consolidated nor implemented without the production, accumulation, circulation and functioning of a discourse. There can be no possible exercise of power without a certain economy of discourses of truth, which operates through and on the basis of this association.[13]

7   Edwards, *The Closed World*.
8   Simpson, *Science of Coercion*.
9   Heims, *John von Neumann and Norbert Wiener*, 1980; Heims, *Constructing a Social Science for Postwar America*.
10 Black, *IBM and the Holocaust*.
11 Haraway, 'Manifesto for Cyborgs'; Haraway, *Simians, Cyborgs, and Women*; Haraway, *Modest Witness@Second_Millenium*.
12 Mark Poster, *The Mode of Information: Poststructuralism and Social Context*, Chicago: University of Chicago Press, 1990; Mark Poster, *The Second Media Age*, Cambridge: Polity Press, 1995; Mark Poster, *What's the Matter with the Internet?*, Minneapolis: University of Minnesota Press, 2001; Mark Poster, *Information Please: Culture and Politics in the Age of Digital Machines*, Durham: Duke University Press, 2006.
13 Foucault and Gordon, 'The Eye of Power', p. 34.

In this way, Foucault's discursive economies, and those presented here, are constantly chang-ing and created ad-hoc. They are understood as collections of fragments of knowledge, interconnected around a support or supports, in this case computers, statistics, and list technologies.

> A discourse, then, is a way of knowledge, a background of assumptions and agree-ments about how reality is to be interpreted and expressed, supported by paradigmatic metaphors, techniques and technologies, and potentially embodied social institutions.[14]

Computers, data, population control, and lists are understood here as such an ever-changing and self-elaborating ensemble of heterogeneous elements, which combines other tech-nologies, techniques, institutions, metaphors, language, practices, fictions, fantasies, and fragments of competing and collaborating discourses, to form an assemblage of policing that is a critical support in the 'securing' of entropic milieus of circulation installed under modern and contemporary governmentality. For Foucault,[15] technological supports are the objects that are at once studied and at the same time invented by the discourses surrounding them, and this is the precise role computer, statistics, and lists play in the work presented here. Recognizing that 'a tool is also a model for its own reproduction and a script for the reenact-ment of the skill it symbolizes',[16] this chapter rests in many ways on the theoretical assertion of double integration outlined in the proceeding chapters: that just as the conjuncture of computers, statistics, and lists have shaped modern governmentality, contemporary govern-mentality continues to be shaped, authorized, and self-elaborated through this assemblage for policing disordered, chaotic, and ever-expanding – entropic – milieus of circulation. In this way, the calculation, prediction, delimitation, and policing of the movement of risky ele-ments distributed in populations not only continues to serve governmentality with the event of the emergence of the modern computer, but also serves as further proof of its power to reproduce its own praxis, delimiting evermore particularized populations, and predicting evermore risks for policing in ever-expanding milieus. The entropic milieus of circulation that the conjunction of computers, statistics, and lists installed post-World War II, not only dramatically altered how living beings, things, and knowledge would be classified, but also radically changed how people would come to see themselves as digital elements distributed in 'global classification infrastructures';[17] 'new' entropic milieus that would not only come to govern how we live, but also the possibilities and limitations we see for life from within such disordered and unpredictable but 'secured' spaces.

Picking up on the historical trajectory established in the first chapter, we now find ourselves in post-World-War II America, a cultural landscape which was increasingly fascinated by and in awe of the circulating myths and stories surrounding cybernetics, or what Hamilton[18] has called the 'cybernetic imaginary'; how conjunctions of humans and machines could

---

14 Edwards, *The Closed World*, p. 34.
15 Foucault, '1 February 1978 *Governmentality*'.
16 Weizenbaum, *Computer Power and Human Reason*, p. 25.
17 Bowker and Star, *Sorting Things Out*.
18 Hamilton, 'Interrogating the Cybernetic Imaginary'.

operate in tandem to protect and secure the American nation and defeat the arch-enemy Communist forces. In the tradition of Foucault, and specifically Edwards,[19] Heims[20] and Haraway,[21] it is argued here that we can make sense of how computers, statistics, and lists serve apparatuses of security, assemblages of policing, and contemporary governmentality, only when we understand the history of this modern technological conjuncture as critical to post-World-War-II and Cold War science, politics, and culture. The language and discourses this security conjuncture authorized, reinforced, and self-elaborated laid down the foundations for a global cultural politics that would increasingly be articulated through automated regimes of truth marked by divisive 'us' vs. 'them' fractures. Characterized by what Edwards[22] has called 'open-world' and 'closed-world' discourses, it is argued here that the emergence of modern computer technology and the assemblage of global policing it installed, continued to serve the authorization and self-elaboration of fractures of 'us' versus 'them' as a preeminent way of doing and seeing the necessary and sufficient management and distribution of elements circulating in entropic milieus the world over.

Computers, Data, Statistics, and Lists Serve: Entropic Milieus of Circulation

> Certain organisms such as man tend for a time to maintain and often even to increase the level of organization, as a local enclave, in the general stream of increasing entropy, of increasing chaos and de-differentiation. Life is an island here and now in a dying world.[23]

To characterize the milieus of circulation installed by the apparatuses of security underpinned by computer, statistical, and list technologies in the 1940s and 1950s and further, to propel this conjuncture into an analysis of contemporary governmentality, this work engages the term 'entropy', redeployed here as Norbert Wiener,[24] the father of cybernetics, intended it: as characterizing the milieu of circulation in which the governing of complex interactions between 'men [sic] and things' takes place. Entropy is a fundamental physical law on which physics, cybernetics, game, and systems theories are based, yet remains a seldom-explored language and theoretical construct for investigating technological, social and cultural phenomena. This work seeks to reinvigorate entropy as an analytical construct for techno-cultural investigation.

Rehashing the theoretical insights first gleaned by Norbert Wiener in his seminal book, *Cybernetics: Control and Communication in the Animal and Machine*, this section exam-

19 Edwards, *The Closed World*.
20 Heims, *John von Neumann and Norbert Wiener*; Heims, *Constructing a Social Science for Postwar America*.
21 Haraway, 'Manifesto for Cyborgs'; Haraway, *Simians, Cyborgs, and Women*; Haraway, *Modest Witness@Second_Millenium*.
22 Edwards, *The Closed World*.
23 Wiener, *The Human Use of Human Beings*, 1950, p. 95.
24 Wiener, *Cybernetics*; Wiener, *The Human Use of Human Beings*, 1950; Wiener, *The Human Use of Human Beings*, 1954; Wiener, *I Am a Mathematician*; Norbert Wiener, *Invention: The Care and Feeding of Ideas*, Cambridge: MIT Press, 1993.

ines and highlights Wiener's social model of cybernetics, investigating how entropy is not merely to be understood from the perspective of the hard sciences as the *Second Law of Thermodynamics*, but is also very much constitutive of social, cultural, and human existence; both as a way of doing and seeing living beings, things, and knowledge. The lens of cybernetics can be focused from the universe to the sky and all the way down to the molecule and the atom, seeing spaces as disordered and expanding – entropic – milieus of circulation, susceptible to systematic and automated probing, calculation, and prediction for regularities and patterns that factor the worth and/or risk of the movement and distribution of circulating elements.

What is Entropy, and Why are We Sailing in a Sea of It?

> Consider ... the chaotic effect (resulting from a sudden imposition of uniformity) of a strong wind on the innumerable grains of sand that compose a beach: amid this confusion, the action of a human foot on the surface of the beach constitutes a complex interaction of events that leads to the statistically improbable configuration of a footprint. The organization of events that has produced this configuration, this *form,* is only temporary: the footprint will soon be swept away by the wind. In other words, a deviation from the general entropy curve (consisting of a decrease in entropy and the establishment of *improbable order*) will generally tend to be reabsorbed into the universal curve of increasing entropy. And yet, for a moment, the elemental chaos of this system has made room for the appearance of an order, based on the relationship of cause and effect: the cause being the series of events interacting with the grains of sand (in this case, the human foot), and the effect of being the organization resulting from it (in this case, the footprint).[25]

In the same way that Umberto Eco sketches out the fleeting appearance of order in footprints left in the sand as a semblance of cause/effect relationships that mark temporary moments of decreasing entropy, we can also begin to see how entropy plays a pivotal role in the milieus of circulation installed under contemporary governmentality. In Eco's case of the footprint in the sand, cause is attributed to the interaction of a series of living beings, things, and activities, which produce the fleeting effect of order. But like with any act where order is established, such as when laws or prohibitions are invoked that posit a series of norms for good life out of the great disorder of human interaction (thou shall not steal, murder, etcetera), or when computer code is listed, compiled, and executed as a program; the semblance of order produced, is almost instantly swept right back up into the general curve of entropy, like footprints in the sand. In these processes, the double integration effect of technologies like lists, statistics, computers, or any juridical-disciplinary mechanism that administers, organizes, and develops knowledge out of chaos and disorder, leads to an inevitable avalanche of more questions – to more missing information and to more possibilities for delimitation, prediction, re-configuration, re-assembling, and re-listing.

---

25 Eco, *The Open Work.*

In Eco's example of the footprint, there is missing information as to the veracity of the classification of the footprint itself, is it in fact a human footprint or that of some other species? Also questions arise as to its precise origins specifically: whose footprint is it? And further, as to the endless series of things and events that led up to the 'foot' being there in the first place. We must investigate further. For each answer to our list of questions, will surely and inevitably generate infinitely more lists of questions in a self-elaborating process of knowledge development.

In order to extrapolate Eco's insights into an analysis of contemporary governmentality, let us briefly consider web-based 'cookies' and how they not only 'automate the process of demographic solicitation' and offer the possibility for surveillance,[26] but also, it is argued here, produce the effects of endlessly new questions of all sorts, highlighting all kinds of missing information in the vast sea of entropy.

> When a user visits a Web site, the site sends a small identifying piece of information, or "cookie", to a personal computer within a hypertext transfer protocol (HTTP) header. When users stop to view certain Web sites and pages, therefore, they receive text, graphics, streaming media, and so forth on their screens, but they also receive a small packet of information that is stored in the browser's memory and then stored in their own hard drives when the browser is closed.[27]

Like Eco's footprint in the sand, the 'cookie' produces the effect of a semblance of stability, or order, wherein a trace of the user is left behind that can be used to not only decipher their past movements, but also to materialize, predict, and reassemble future interactions between them, other users, and website owners. But like Eco's footprints in the sand, the semblance of order that cookies fleetingly delimit, are swept right back up into the general curve of entropy, leading to an avalanche of even more questions, missing information, and the self-elaborating need for more cookies, 'spiders', 'intelligent agents', 'web-bots', etcetera. Is this footprint, this cookie, really reflective of the registered user of the computer? If not, who surfed to the site, and how did they get there? How can we further identify who left the trace? What other kinds of information can the cookie gather that would be useful to predicting the future movements of the user on the web and beyond? How can the user be more efficiently and effectively steered to desired and optimal norms in this highly uncertain and ever-expanding milieu?

In *The Dream Machine* Michael Waldrop sketches out the history of information theory and its direct ties to physicists' understanding of entropy, recounting an anecdote about John von Neumann's insistence to Claude Shannon, the father of 'Information Theory', that information and entropy were quite simply one and the same concept. The story has it that von Neumann in a heated debate with Shannon insisted that 'Information' in his 'Theory' be re-named 'Entropy'. Firstly, because '...[Shannon's] formula for the information content of a message

---

26 Greg Elmer, *Profiling Machines: Mapping the Personal Information Economy*, Cambridge, Mass.: MIT Press, 2004, p. 26.
27 Elmer, *Profiling Machines*, p. 117.

[was] mathematically identical to the physicist's formula for entropy', but more importantly, because 'most people don't know what entropy really is, and if you use the word *entropy* in an argument, you will win every time!'[28]

Despite such stuffy offhandedness, von Neumann's point was valid and Shannon considered it as such: in physics, entropy is understood as an indicator of the randomness of molecules in an isolated or closed system; and randomness, according to the second law of thermodynamics, always increases, never decreases. In other words, an isolated or closed system, or a milieu of circulation, will always tend towards maximum disorder – the greatest heterogeneity known – unless acted upon. The larger the organism, population, or milieu of circulation, the more random it will be at the molecular level, and thus the 'less information' we will have about the arrangement of the molecules, digital elements, or individual people. Information, from von Neumann's perspective and from the perspective of physics in general, is merely the observation of patterns or regularities within an isolated or closed system. And for any physicist, the presence of entropy would always far outweigh that of information in 'closed' systems; for entropy in physics means 'missing information', an expression of the natural tendency of molecules in isolated systems to tend towards maximum disorder.

Building on such lines, one could argue that since ancient times and earlier, we have been engaged in a never-ending battle to manage never-ebbing flows of entropy. The earliest writings were lists of debits and credits owed, lists of events, and lexical lists of concepts,[29] which seemingly represent very early attempts at bringing order to and decreasing the entropy of life through isolated or closed systems and mechanized processes aimed at organizing living beings, things, and knowledge into materialized, classified milieus of circulation, establishing kinships between all kinds of things and equally questioning such classifications and relations, all on an ongoing basis. And as we have seen, where list technologies have proven to be tremendously efficient and effective in the management of living beings, things, and knowledge as such, they also produce the effects of endlessly new questions of all kinds. Moreover, when probed for regularities and patterns, disordered milieus of circulation can highlight all kinds of 'missing information' for those who wield the technologies for assessing worth and risk; ultimately subjecting elements circulating in populations to increasingly invasive forms of delimitation and policing through lists.

It is the overall argument of this work that contemporary governmentality pivots on the reduction of human beings to net-worth and risk-assessed scores; distributed digital elements derived from the observation of regularities and patterns within entropic milieus of circulation, like the internet and networked technologies today, which self-elaborate a state and milieu of pervasive and ubiquitous policing by assemblages of computers, statistics, and lists. As we shall see in the next chapters on contemporary no-fly lists and no-blank lists, such apparatuses of security are the legacy of the global milieus of circulation installed with the emergence of modern computer technologies.

---

28 Waldrop, *The Dream Machine*, p. 81.
29 Goody, *The Domestication of the Savage Mind*.

No one, I argue, understood *entropy* and its critical tie to governmentality better than Norbert Wiener, the father of cybernetics, and this despite him never having encountered Michel Foucault (a fact of which I am almost quite sure!). Wiener was first and foremost a self-professed patriotic American, an MIT professor, who applied his tremendous intellect to questions of artillery and ballistics during WWI, and ultimately solved the greatest impediment to the defeat of the Axis powers in WWII; namely, how to track and target a moving airplane in the sky so as to shoot it down before it has a chance to strike. It was in such a climate of uncertainty and dire consequence, where unlocking the key to identification and control in the wide-open skies was preeminent, that Norbert Wiener came to apply cybernetics and notions of feedback in isolated or closed systems to military-based problems.[30]

Despite the seemingly wide-open nature of the sky, Wiener recognized that, like the universe, the sky or more specifically a pilot in symbiosis with their plane in the sky, could be seen as isolated or closed systems – a milieu of circulation that despite tending towards maximum disorder could through mechanized processes be probed for recognizable and predictable patterns: the basis of identification, control, and communication in animals and machines. Wiener came to see that where isolated or closed systems, like anything from the universe down to the atom, do by nature tend towards maximum expansion and disorder – entropy – they can nonetheless be controlled by uncovering and honing in on regularities and patterns, which can be observed and subsequently manipulated through feedback operations. And his cybernetic theory and its language of 'causal-circular feedback loops' in 'closed-systems' proved to be invaluable to scientists and the US government, and ultimately helped found the military-industrial complex; providing a series of underlying mathematical operations that solved a wide variety of identification and control issues in weapons, security, and surveillance design and development throughout the end of WWII, into the Cold War era, and also in today's techno-cultural landscape.[31]

Where there is order, optimism, and progress to be found in cybernetic conjunctions of humans and machines that probe entropic closed systems, or entropic milieus of circulation, for regularities and patterns as Wiener imagined, such couplings also have the inherent capacity to pose grave risks to human survival, rights, and liberties when applied as large-scale social systems. In respect of this, Wiener penned the first edition of *The Human Use of Human Beings* in 1950, in which he invests significant time in considering and warning against the social consequences and the possible de-humanizing effects of mass adoption of mechanized feedback systems as social order, arguing that the 'mechanization of man' through 'isolated systems' is the simplest and easiest path to power. Recognizing that isolated systems applied as social order allow people with ambitions for power to craft social organizations where orders come from the top and go down unquestioned, Wiener wrote *The Human Use of Human Beings* as a protest and warning against the dehumanizing possibilities inherent in such practice and the dire implications to human survival of identification and control in isolated systems. For Wiener, enveloping a country, the world, or

---

30 Wiener, *Cybernetics*.
31 Heims, *John von Neumann and Norbert Wiener*; Heims, *Constructing a Social Science for Postwar America*; Edwards, *The Closed World*; Simpson, *Science of Coercion*.

all of humanity in an isolated, mechanized feedback system could provide the incunabula for a new global totalitarianism, where the tendency is maximum disorder, but for those who wield the technologies to observe regularities and patterns, and act on the molecules distributed in closed systems.

In a world and universe marked by unpredictability and expansion, Wiener conceived of cybernetics as a theory for decreasing entropy through the application of 'circular causal feedback' systems for the 'good of man'.[32] The Latin root *cyber*, in *cybernetics*, was expressly engaged by Wiener to denote the *steering* (decision-making) potential inherent in conjunctions of humans and machines to navigate the endless expansion of maximum disorder that marks organic life – entropy. Like a ship in rough, stormy, and unpredictable waters, Wiener imagined 'man' as a 'helmsmen', engaging the ship's integrated technologies and techniques to right and balance the boat and steer the vessel towards homeostasis. For Wiener, this was the preeminent metaphor for cybernetics, if not human existence and survival as a whole in the face of maximum disorder and expansion or entropy.

In his social model of cybernetics, 'homeostatic mechanisms' are extremely valuable, as human beings navigating precarious and rough seas need to receive accurate and precise information about the unpredictable entropic environments that surround them, in order to achieve balance, both in themselves and in the small, interactive, physical communities in which their lives take place. In his conception, machines, or homeostatic mechanisms, are engaged by humans in decision-making. Functioning as instruments that observe patterns and regularities, indicating changes in milieus of circulation like the high seas, homeostatic mechanisms serve the administration and organization of people and things and equally, predicting precarious dangers, such as the risks of ramming approaching icebergs or colliding with treacherous reefs, or succumbing to rocks in shallow-lying waters. Onboard Wiener's ships, the achievement of homeostasis or the normalization of unpredictable things circulating in the boat's milieu supersedes the goal of destination. The primary objective of the helmsmen is to keep the ship afloat and right, making decisions, steering, and assigning elements, with the preeminent aim of ensuring the security and well being of all passengers and cargo onboard.

For Foucault the very essence of government is also clearly wrapped up in the metaphor of righting and balancing the ship in the unpredictable but tamable, vast, stormy seas of disorder that fundamentally mark human existence:

> That government is concerned with things understood in this way as the intrication of men and things is readily confirmed by the inevitable metaphor of the ship that is always invoked in these treatises on government. What is it to govern a ship? It involves, of course, being responsible for the sailors, but also taking care of the vessel and the cargo; governing a ship also involves taking winds, reefs, storms, and bad weather into account. What characterizes government of a ship is the practice of establishing

---

32 Wiener, *Cybernetics*.

relations between the sailors, the vessel, which must be safeguarded, the cargo, which must be brought to port, and their relations with all those eventualities like winds, reefs, storms and so on.[33]

In this way, Wiener's 'social model of cybernetics', the topic he takes up at length in the *Human Use of Human Beings* is strikingly similar to the governmentality to which Foucault focused his lens, but with a moral and political spin, and polemic that Foucault was hesitant to elaborate. For both, the essential and main element of control or government is the complex integration of people and things, their delimitation and regulation in unpredictable environments, so to serve the 'best' or 'good' interests of the overall 'state' of balance. In this way, in both Foucault's governmentality and Wiener's 'social model of cybernetics', territory, property, and cargo (animate and inanimate) are considered as variables in milieus of circulation where concern is with the complex administration, organization, and distribution of elements.

But where Wiener's social model of cybernetics placed the moral and ethical imperative of decision-making firmly in the hands of human beings, in the ability of individuals in small, interactive, physical communities to achieve homeostasis, such is not the case with all systems theory that emerged from the 1940s onwards, and in this way, the legacy of Wiener's cybernetics and its technoscientific language cannot be separated from its theoretical and mathematical twin, John von Neumann's game theory.[34] Game theory contributed to the critical paradigm shift that the emergence of systems approaches to the hard and soft sciences ultimately represented post-World War II.[35] Where Wiener's social model of cybernetics emphasized human decision-making, extolled the merits of small interactive, physical communities, and shunned any concentration of administrative, economic, and political power, von Neumann's game theory advocated probability-based, automated decision-making, lending itself to global approaches to governance, administration, economics, and the concentration of political power that were rippling through the US post-World War II.

Von Neumann's 'Winners' and 'Losers'

Statistical techniques involving the delimiting of populations, reduction of individuals to cases, and 'numerical estimations of utility', played a pivotal role in von Neumann's *Theory of Games and Economic Behavior*.[36] In his theory, questions of 'good' and 'bad' are removed from the decision-making capacities of Wiener's helmsmen through their automated reduction to the 'mixed strategies' of statistical mechanisms, which not only express through distributions a 'picture' of the distance of the 'bad' from the 'good', but also prescribe a means for the normalization or nullification of abnormal elements. In other words, von Neumann, in his own way, embraced the 'double integration' effects of statistics in his

---

33 Foucault, '1 February 1978 *Governmentality*', p. 97.
34 John von Neumann, *Theory of Games and Economic Behavior*, New York: Science Editions J. Wiley, 1964; John von Neumann and Arthur W. Burks, *Theory of Self-Reproducing Automata*, Urbana: University of Illinois Press, 1966; John von Neumann and Oskar Morgenstern, *Theory of Games and Economic Behavior*, Princeton: Princeton University Press, 1953.
35 Heims, *John von Neumann and Norbert Wiener*.
36 Von Neumann and Morgenstern, *Theory of Games and Economic Behavior*, p. 12.

positing of a theory of games, which could at once automate the delimitation of populations and also serve the dual role of prescribing mechanisms for the normalization of mistakes or identified risks in the delimited populations. Among von Neumann's elaborate writings of mathematical formulae, we find section 17.10.1, on 'Mistakes and Their Consequences: Permanent Optimality':

> We want to express the distance from 'goodness' for those strategies which are not good; and obtain some picture of the consequences of a mistake – i.e. of the use of a strategy which is not good. However, we shall not attempt to exhaust this subject, which has many intriguing ramifications.[37]

Unlike Wiener who took the 'dangers' inherent in conjunctions of people, math, and machines very seriously, and wrote extensively about his fear of subsuming life in such conjunctive apparatuses, particularly in *The Human Use of Human Beings*,[38] von Neumann, despite his extensive contributions to the RAND corporation and the US Department of Defense during the Cold War,[39] never published many detailed thoughts on the social implications of his theories, preferring to nest his writings for the most part in the field of applied mathematics to computers and economics, and later to the biology of the human brain in *The Computer and the Brain*.[40]

It is essential to realize that economists can expect no easier fate than that which befell scientists in other disciplines. It seems reasonable to expect that they will have to take up first problems contained in the very simplest facts of economic life and try to establish theories which explain them and which really conform to rigorous scientific standards. We can have enough confidence that from then on the science of economics will grow further, gradually comprising matters of more vital importance than those to which one has to begin.[41]

In the footnote to this text in the 1964 edition of *Theory of Games* (originally published in 1953), von Neumann notes:

> The beginning is actually of a certain significance, because the forms of exchange between a few individuals are the same as those observed on some of the most important markets of modern industry, or in the case of barter exchange between states in international trade.[42]

As von Neumann's later research into *The Computer and the Brain*, and his *Theory of Self-Reproducing Automata* reveal, von Neumann saw his *Theory of Games and Economic*

---

37 Von Neumann and Morgenstern, *Theory of Games and Economic Behavior*, p. 162.
38 Wiener, *The Human Use of Human Beings*, 1950; Wiener, *The Human Use of Human Beings*, 1954.
39 Heims, *John von Neumann and Norbert Wiener*.
40 Von Neumann, John, The computer and the brain, New Haven: Yale University Press, 1964.
41 Von Neumann and Morgenstern, *Theory of Games and Economic Behavior*, p. 7.
42 Von Neumann and Morgenstern, *Theory of Games and Economic Behavior*, p. 7.

Behavior as providing a mathematical platform on which not only global economic life, but the life of all living beings could be approached from the standpoint of the 'zero-sum game', which took at its maxim the statistical delimitation, policing, and nullification of opponents in metaphorical battles involving exchanges. As the games got larger, von Neumann mathematically transformed the zero-sum game into what he called the constant-sum game. 'We are widening the domain of games which we consider, by passing from the *zero-sum games* to the *constant-sum games*. At the same time, we widen the concept of strategic equivalence introduced [earlier]...'[43] But regardless of how the concept was mathematically widened, the functional results were the same: the clear delimitation of winners and losers engaged in games of exchange.

In order to express these 'new' complexities of modern economics his game theory introduced in metaphorical terms, von Neumann drew on the story of *Robinson Crusoe*, stranded on a deserted island with a cast of subjects, and how it relates to questions of managing populations. In the 'Introduction' to *Theory of Games* he describes the operations and enclosures of sovereignty's juridical-disciplinary mechanisms, wherein Crusoe the sovereign faces what von Neumann calls a 'maximum problem' in satisfying the needs and desires of his set of subjects, the other deserted island dwellers.

> Crusoe is given certain physical data (wants and commodities) and his task is to combine and apply them in such a fashion as to obtain a maximum resulting satisfaction. There can be no doubt that he controls exclusively all the variables upon which this result depends – say the allotting of resources, the determination of the uses of the same commodities for different wants, etc.[44]

We see with Crusoe the same kinds of maximum problems faced by the sovereign in managing subjects, who, to solve such conundrums, leveraged the enclosing spaces of discipline in the administration, organization, and development of living beings and things, a space that technologies like statistics and probability techniques could serve. In the footnote to the preceding text, von Neumann notes:

> Sometimes uncontrollable factors also intervene, e.g. the weather in agriculture. These however are purely statistical phenomena. Consequently they can be eliminated by the known procedures of the calculus of probabilities: i.e., by determining the probabilities of the various alternatives and by introduction of the notion of "mathematical expectation".[45]

But for von Neumann, probabilities or 'mathematical expectations' alone, could never serve the 'social exchange economy' of this irruptive modern economic order, where the complexities of populations of elements in various exchanges introduced problems of an entirely different nature. For in such 'games' in social exchange economies, each participant is attempting to obtain not a prescribed result, but rather an optimum result.

43 Von Neumann, *Theory of Games and Economic Behavior*, pp. 347-348.
44 Von Neumann and Morgenstern, *Theory of Games and Economic Behavior*, p. 10.
45 Von Neumann and Morgenstern, *Theory of Games and Economic Behavior*, p. 10.

Unlike in the case of Crusoe's sovereign deserted island, where Crusoe administered and organized living beings and things from the top down, exchanges in 'social economies' occur in an unpredictable milieu of circulation where no participant controls all the variables – a space where the calculation of 'optimums' and 'risks', and the vanquishing of players, rules the day.

> Thus each participant attempts to maximize a function (his above mentioned [optimum] "result") of which he does not control all variables. This is certainly no maximum problem [like in the case of Crusoe], but a peculiar and disconcerting mixture of several conflicting maximum problems. Every participant is guided by another principle and neither determines all variables which affect his interest.[46]

Von Neumann's milieus of disconcerting or irruptive economic circulation are spaces where 'all maxima are desired at once – by various participants',[47] and it is precisely this milieu of circulation that his theory of games was devised to meet, constructing 'individuals' as probability-based statistical elements, 'numerical estimations of utility'[48] that provide 'mathematically complete principles which define "rational behavior" for the participants in a social economy, and to derive from them the general characteristics of that behavior'.[49] Herein, we can also see how the economic techniques of von Neumann's 'game theory' are characterized by the 'double integration' effects of disciplinary normalization, in the calculation of 'optimums' and 'risks', or norms for rational behavior from out of the great disorder of entropy, which serve as the basis for the articulation of the relational abnormal. In von Neumann's theory of games, complete normalization, or nullification of the opponent, is the primary objective and goal. In other words, the economic techniques of von Neumann's game theory installed a mechanism for declaring unequivocal winners and losers in a highly uncertain and ever-expanding milieu of global circulation.

So, where Wiener's humane 'social model of cybernetics' emphasized the intermingling of humans and machines to serve small, interactive, physical milieus of circulation, as a strategy for navigating the entropy that marks organic life – the privileging and achievement of cooperation and homeostasis within and between people as the primary means to the humane deployment of 'security' technologies; von Neumann's game theory in contrast emphasized competition between individuals and collectives, stressing the statistical nullification of opponents. In such games, the prize for winners is the absolute delimitation, policing, and nullification of losers, in milieus that themselves further reinforce and self-elaborate such never-ending games. Game theory was therefore laced with biases for Wiener, forcing humanity into a black and white procrustean bed of 'winners' and 'losers', of 'us' and 'them':

---

46 Von Neumann and Morgenstern, *Theory of Games and Economic Behavior*, p. 11.
47 Von Neumann and Morgenstern, *Theory of Games and Economic Behavior*, p. 11.
48 Von Neumann and Morgenstern, *Theory of Games and Economic Behavior*, p. 12.
49 Von Neumann and Morgenstern, *Theory of Games and Economic Behavior*, p. 31.

In many cases, where there are three players, and in the overwhelming majority of cases, when the number of players is large, the result is one of extreme indeterminacy and instability. The individual players are compelled by their own cupidity to form coalitions; but these coalitions do not generally establish themselves in any single, determinate way, and usually terminate in a welter of betrayal, turncoatism, and deception, which is only too true a picture of the higher business life, or the closely related lives of politics, diplomacy, and war. In the long run, even the most brilliant and unprincipled hucksters become tired of this, and agree to live in peace with one another, and the great rewards are reserved for the one who watches for an opportune time to break his agreement and betray his companion. There is no homeostasis whatsoever. We are involved here in the business cycles of boom and failure, in the successions of dictatorship and revolution, in the wars which everyone loses, which are so real a feature of modern times.[50]

Wiener's social model of cybernetics and von Neumann's game theory are positioned here as two competing and collaborating discourses, open-human and closed-world discourses respectively, operating in conjunction with computer, statistical, and list technologies in modern and contemporary formations of power. Through an analysis of these discourses, we will now see how conjunctions of computer technologies and statistical mechanisms revolving around the probing of milieus of circulation for regularities and patterns throughout the Cold War and beyond served to further reduce living beings and things to classes, increasingly identifying them on lists of all kinds, and ultimately subjecting them to more invasive and complex forms of computerized statistical delimitation, policing, and nullification; all in power struggles over knowledge and the constitution of truthful and factual classifications of human beings.

Open-human Discourse: Islands in a Sea of Entropy

Our view of society differs from the ideal of society, which is held by many Fascists, Strong Men in Business, and Government. Similar men of ambition for power are not entirely unknown in scientific and educational institutions. Such people prefer an organization in which all orders come from above and none return. The human beings under them have been reduced to the level of effectors for a supposedly higher nervous organism. I wish to devote this book to a protest against this inhuman use of human beings; for in my mind, any use of human beings in which less is demanded of him than his full status is a degradation and a waste. It is a degradation to chain a human being to an oar and use him as a source of power.[51]

Critical to Wiener's warning against enveloping human life in isolated or closed automated feedback systems is the relationship between progress and entropy; between the openness of human beings and the isolation of machines that probe milieus for patterns and regularities. For Wiener, it is only in the 'non-isolated parts of isolated systems' that optimism

50 Wiener, *Cybernetics*, pp. 185-186.
51 Wiener, *The Human Use of Human Beings*, 1950, p. 15.

is to be found: namely and exclusively in human beings, who are inherently and uniquely *open*, existing as islands in a vast but isolated sea of entropy, the ever-expanding universe; and who defy this greatest of all chaos and disorder by displaying unique instincts, traits, and tendencies towards order, optimism, and progress – *openness towards each other*. But where openness towards each other is Wiener's hallmark for 'order', 'optimism', and 'progress', and *is* the strict realm of humanity, it is not a given, as 'disorder', 'pessimism', and 'isolation' are equally preeminent characteristics of entropy and the predisposition of molecules in closed systems such as the universe, the world, religions, nations, universities, and corporations, to name but a few of the isolated social systems enclosing life Wiener cautioned against.

> Those who suffer from a power complex find the mechanization of man a simple way to realize their ambitions. I say, that this easy path to power is in fact not only a rejection of everything that I consider to be of moral worth in the human race, but also a rejection of our now very tenuous opportunities for a considerable period of human survival.[52]

For it is precisely the potential for closed/isolated systems to reduce people to effectors in machines, to quantifiable cogs in a wheel or to molecules circulating in an organism and susceptible to probing for patterns and regularities, that makes the second law of thermodynamics more than a cornerstone of physical science, but also a dire warning that life can be isolated and subjected to intense identification and control (delimitation and policing), despite an everyday existence that most experience as disorder and entropy. For Wiener, the danger of closed/isolated systems applied as social systems is an obfuscation of the wide-open possibilities and light inherent in human beings, who despite existing in a miasma of ever-expanding entropy find optimism, progress, and order in an openness to each other. In this way, human beings are the only inherently open systems, and the danger is that the closed/isolated systems in which we live (from the universe to the internet and to science in general) have a natural propensity to move us towards maximum disorder, highlighting more and more 'missing information', and thus making it difficult to see our openness and humanity through the dense closed isolation of cybernetic systems and machines.[53] It is precisely for these reasons that Wiener insists that homeostatic mechanisms serve small, interactive, physical communities, and that the adoption of any larger social mechanisms should be approached with extreme caution and trepidation.

> The question of whether to interpret the second law of thermodynamics pessimistically or without gloomy consequence depends on the importance we give to the universe at large, on the one hand, and to the islands of locally decreasing entropy we find in it, on the other. Remember that we ourselves constitute such an island of decreasing entropy, and that we live among other such islands.[54]

---

52 Wiener, *The Human Use of Human Beings*, pp. 15-16.
53 Kenneth C. Werbin, 'Sometimes a Great Notion: A Reflection on Cybernetics, Isolated Systems, and Open Beings', in Lipika Bansal, Paul Keller, and Geert Lovink (eds), *In the Shade of the Commons: Towards a Culture of Open Networks*, Amsterdam: Waag Society, 2006.
54 Wiener, *The Human Use of Human Beings*, p. 25.

Although we are embedded in closed/isolated systems where communication and informa-tion flow freely and endlessly towards entropy, we are nonetheless in constant feedback with those around us; capable of critiquing, making decisions, imagining other possibilities, acting, learning, and growing together. Far from being isolated automatons or circulating elements in populations and milieus, it is our continual and critical interaction with our environment and those around us, and the optimism, order, and progress we find in each other, that makes us open.[55] But that is not to say that openness, progress, and optimism are a given. Placing the weight of our beliefs in humanity over and above our isolated mechanized systems is a choice, and such practices and fundamental beliefs must be fostered and maintained, and their demise must be guarded against vigilantly – at least for Norbert Wiener.[56]

The more life is mechanized, the more we must place the weight of our belief in the non-iso-lated parts of isolated systems: in each other's openness. This was Wiener's warning and message in *The Human Use of Human Beings* with respect to viewing life as enclosed in entropic milieus of circulation. But where his warnings were dire, few picked up on his line of thinking, as cybernetic milieus of circulation supported by and supporting the computer, statistics, and list technologies were increasingly installed in endless fields and domains, and were further subsumed in the collective imaginary and social woodwork, eventually becoming a part of taken for granted everyday life.

> The real power of new technologies does not appear during their mythic period, when they are hailed for their ability to bring world peace, renew communities, or end scar-city, history, geography, or politics; rather their social impact is greatest when technol-ogies become banal – when they literally (as in the case of electricity) or figuratively withdraw into the woodwork.[57]

For Vincent Mosco in *The Digital Sublime,* new technologies embody and drive the utopian myths of their times. Whether the myths are about the telegraph, radio, television, modern computer, or cyberspace today, Mosco suggests that continuity rests in the utopian visions people engage around the advent of these technologies, how through the use of 'new' tech-nologies, people will '...experience an epochal transformation in human experience that [will] transcend time (the end of history), space (the end of geography), and power (the end of politics)'.[58] In this way, he argues that myth is 'congealed common sense', that although the taken-for-granted is 'continually transforming itself, enriching itself with scientific ideas and with philosophical opinions that have entered ordinary life', there are nonetheless 'powerful philosophical currents' that leave behind 'sedimented common sense' about 'new' techno-logical forms, establishing 'folklores of the future' that require interrogation.[59]

55 Werbin, 'Sometimes a Great Notion'.
56 Wiener, *The Human Use of Human Beings*, 1950; Wiener, *The Human Use of Human Beings*, 1954.
57 Vincent Mosco, *The Digital Sublime: Myth, Power, and Cyberspace*, Cambridge: MIT Press, 2004, p. 19.
58 Mosco, *The Digital Sublime*, pp. 2-3.
59 Mosco, *The Digital Sublime*, p. 29.

With the publication of Wiener's *Cybernetics* in 1948, the language, ideas, metaphors, and myths of human-machine couplings began to increasingly circulate and be absorbed throughout the United States and beyond.[60] The more communication and computer technologies became familiar everyday objects in people's lives, the more they produced an unique and new 'cybernetic imaginary'[61] filled with awe and wonder over computers, in which life was increasingly being understood as the 'transmission of information' and as 'programmed', and wherein society was increasingly seen as one large 'system' or 'organism'.

> Feedback has come to mean information about the outcome of any process or activity. No single word for the general idea seems to have existed in the English language before feedback was introduced in the context of cybernetics, and the analogy filled a gap. The ubiquity of feedback meant interaction is everywhere. It shifted attention from an individualism that had highlighted noncircular cause-and-effect and from the individual person – as if he or she could be independent of others and even independent of chance events occurring in the environment. Still, the word betrays its mechanical origins and encourages ignoring much that happens between people.[62]

With the emergence of cybernetics and the unique language of systems theory it brought forth, a whole new way of seeing and doing life was invoked, increasingly understood in analogy to computers. This in turn introduced an one-sidedness in our understanding of our societies and ourselves as large systems of computerized programs in which humans are increasingly positioned as transmittable bits of information or information processors in their own right, as distributed digital elements in programmable populations.

> In all, the language of cybernetics, like any system of concepts and their associated metaphors, illuminates one fact of our world and experience at the price of masking others.[63]

So, it is not surprising that Wiener's warnings were barely heard, as the language of cybernetic systems and the cyborgs it produced, circulated pervasively throughout American popular culture at the beginning of the Cold War. In turn his theoretical ideas and attendant mathematical practices began to be pervasively applied in more and more diverse research contexts, fields, and domains of knowledge.[64] And where many writers and intellectual luminaries in Wiener's time, such as von Neumann, began to use the concepts of cybernetics and systems theory as a language to promote the centralization of social, economic, and political power, Wiener went out of his way to 'argue passionately against the concentration of political and administrative power, and to extol the merits of small interactive communities'.[65] Wiener, true to his idea of people being the only open entities in a vast and isolated sea of entropy, privileged their values and decision-making over and above the cold programmed automated

---

60 Bowker, 'How to Be Universal: Some Cybernetic Strategies'; Hamilton, 'Interrogating the Cybernetic Imaginary'; Heims, *Constructing a Social Science for Postwar America*.
61 Hamilton, 'Interrogating the Cybernetic Imaginary'.
62 Heims, *Constructing a Social Science for Postwar America*, pp. 271-272.
63 Heims, *Constructing a Social Science for Postwar America*, p. 272.
64 Bowker, 'How to Be Universal: Some Cybernetic Strategies'.
65 Heims, *John von Neumann and Norbert Wiener*, p. 312.

decision-making of machines, for he understood that values are deeply embodied in patterns of communication and control, and the 'power elite' being unscrupulous would always favor 'instrumental rationality' in the service of 'maximizing power'.[66]

For these reasons, in his writings beginning with *Cybernetics* and moving forward to *The Human Use of Human Beings*, and later in *I Am a Mathematician*, Wiener argues for the privileging of small, interactive, physical, local communities. Deep in *Cybernetics*, we can find Wiener speaking passionately to the corporately controlled mass media, about the concentration of economic and political power such behemoths contained even in 1940s, cautioning against the limitations of how people experience community when messages are transmitted from such vast seas of entropy. He goes out of his way to warn that 'of all of these anti-homeostatic factors in society, the control of the means of communication is the most effective and most important',[67] adding,

> In a society too large for the direct contact of its members, these means are the press, both as it concerns books ... and newspapers, the radio, the telephone system, the telegraph, the posts, the theater, the movies, the schools, and the church. On all sides we have a triple-constriction of the means of communication: the elimination of the less-profitable means in favor of the more profitable; the fact that these means are in the hands of the very limited class of wealthy men, and thus naturally express the opinions of that class; and the further fact that, as one of the chief avenues to political and personal power, they attract above all ambitions for such power. That system which more than all others should contribute to social homeostasis is thrown directly into the hands of those most concerned in the game of power and money, which we have already seen to be one of the chief anti-homeostatic elements in the community. It is no wonder then that the larger communities, subject to their disruptive influence, contain far less communally available information than the smaller communities, to say nothing of the human elements of which all communities are built up.[68]

This not only attests to Wiener's insistence on privileging small, local, physical, interactive communities, but also is emblematic of his highly democratic, and perhaps utopian outlook in terms of communal practice; a testament to his unwavering belief in human beings to make the right choices and do the right things. Openness and community, for Wiener, are uniquely human values and traits, and according to his analysis, any society which privileges and places its highest values on competition for and concentration of money and power is anti-homeostatic to community, limiting and precluding individual open-human possibilities. In this way, Wiener found any large-scale society, whether communist or capitalist, to be anti-homeostatic, and instead advocated small communities in which people have direct contact with each other; for these were the only communities which Norbert Wiener believed could support the true open-nature of human beings.

---

66 Wiener, *The Human Use of Human Beings*, 1950, p. 160.
67 Wiener, *The Human Use of Human Beings*, 1950, p. 160.
68 Wiener, *The Human Use of Human Beings*, 1950, pp. 161-162.

Closed-world Discourse: Game Theory à la von Neumann

The story of Wiener and von Neumann can be brought to bear on present concerns and options, even though circumstances have changed considerably since their day. The dimensions relevant to technology and the available options can be viewed abstractly and thus propelled out of the realm of history.[69]

Where Wiener's social model of cybernetics positioned people as the only truly open entities, who require deep and careful critical engagement with their integration with new technologies, this was not the legacy that the cybernetic systems thinking revolution would leave behind – indeed, quite the contrary. It was game theory that would provide the underlying theoretical orientation of closed-world global governance discourses, which would ultimately come to dominate questions of social and global order and power in the Cold War era and into today – games with clear winners and losers, marked by epic battles between 'us' and 'them', and self-elaborated through computer technologies themselves. Moreover, game theory's closed-world conception of opponents in exchange battles would achieve near-hegemonic status as the preeminent force in the development of computers, networks, and social and military systems of control.[70]

With its disciplinary emphasis on the convergence and concentration of economic and political power, closed world discourse would also come to define the globe as reducible to a system of capital competition, wherein forces of good and evil – of us and them – are positioned in a constant struggle to liberate and inhibit the forces and enclosures of market economies. As early as 1948, Wiener accepted his own culpability for the emergence and widespread circulation of such closed techno-scientific, dehumanizing approaches to social control, which inevitably would come to underpin bilateral positions of good vs. evil between the 'free world' and the 'communists':

> Those of us who have contributed to the new science of cybernetics stand in a moral position which is, to say the least, not very comfortable. We have contributed to the initiation of a new science, which, as I have said, embraces technical developments with great possibilities for good and for evil.[71]

The eminent psychologist Gregory Bateson later provided substance to these concerns in a personal communication with Wiener in 1952, which is held in the MIT archives and published in Heims,[72] particularly regarding the widespread application of game theory. Bateson wrote,

> What applications of the theory of games do, is to reinforce the players' acceptance of the rules and competitive premises, and therefore make it more and more difficult for the players to conceive that there might be other ways of meeting and dealing with

---

69 Heims, *John von Neumann and Norbert Wiener*, p. 408.
70 Edwards, *The Closed World*.
71 Wiener, *Cybernetics*, p. 38.
72 Heims, *Constructing a Social Science for Postwar America*.

each other ... The theory may be "static" within itself, but its use propagates changes, and I suspect that the long-term changes so propagated are in paranoidal direction and odious. I am thinking not only of the propagation of the premises of distrust which are built into the von Neumann model *ex hypothesi,* but also of the more abstract premise that nature is unchangeable. This premise is the reflection or corollary of the fact that the original theory was set up only to describe the games in which the rules are unchanging and the psychological characters of the players are fixed *ex hypothesi.* I know as an anthropologist that the "rules" of the cultural game are not constant; that the psychology of the players is not fixed; and even that the psychology at times can be out of step with the rules.[73]

Where Wiener never saw the post-World War II situation, or understood people in terms of the caesura of us II them or as players in exchange competition, but rather concerned himself with the inhuman use of human beings as the primary enemy, John von Neumann, in contrast, concerned himself with the Russians and Communism as the primary enemy in the Cold War landscape.[74] Indeed, von Neumann would pay no mind to the hazards Wiener cautioned against, including highly centralized, technocratic governments, in which 'political leaders may attempt to control their populations through political techniques as narrow and indifferent to human possibility as if they had, in fact, been conceived mechanically'.[75] Quite the contrary really, for von Neumann's game theory took as its fundamental premise competition through optimum or mistake-driven 'statistical strategies'[76] in which life and political contexts were analyzed exclusively as mathematical games of chance – a tradition which Eco in *The Open Work* as well as Hacking in *The Taming of Chance* and *The Emergence of Probability* trace back to Hieronimo Cardano (1501-1576), who first articulated a set of mathematical procedures for making wise decisions while gambling, in effect founding a theory of games and probability.

Galileo Galilei's (1564-1642) subsequent elevation and sophistication of analyses of games to social and political contexts saw such approaches begin to encompass more complex interpersonal and political decision-making well beyond their 16th century applications in gambling.[77] In this way, the traditions of probability and statistical decision theory on which von Neumann's game theory were based, had always ignored other aspects of human decision-making including how people conceptualize themselves in the world at large, how they take into account paradox and irony, how multiple objectives are achieved by people simultaneously, and how they know when to take action or sit back and gather data.[78]

In game theory's worldview of statistical nullification such human considerations were merely factors of probabilities and populations, and the deployment of 'optimum statistical strategies'

---

73 Heims, *Constructing a Social Science for Postwar America*, pp. 307-308.
74 Heims, *John von Neumann and Norbert Wiener.*
75 Wiener, *The Human Use of Human Beings*, 1954, p. 181.
76 Von Neumann and Morgenstern, *Theory of Games and Economic Behavior.*
77 Eco, *The Open Work.*
78 Eco, *The Open Work.*

were engaged precisely to counter such 'aleatory' effects – the worst possible outcomes. In this way, like with Foucault's conception of the apparatuses of security 'letting things take their course', [79] von Neumann's theory embraced a statistical model for reacting to reality in a way that allows for a 'freedom of movement' of players, but at the same time involves predicting, limiting, and neutralizing random or aleatory effects. Indeed, the game is won through the engagement and application of statistical strategies involving delimiting and predicting, calculating odds, risks, and optimums that provide both a picture of reality and also a roadmap for victory.

> The formulae above make clear how much of a loss a player risks – relative to the value of a play for him – by using this particular strategy. We mean here "risk" in the sense of the worst that can happen under the given conditions.[80]

The emergence of game theory represented a whole new way of seeing and doing, where any number of players (*n*-players) are assigned measures of utility and risk in gaming milieus that extend upwards in their applications, from the most basic organisms, to simple one-on-one economic barters, to modern complex milieus of economic circulation, to the vanquishing of global opponents of war and all of their constituent populations.

> This was the era of the rise of a new style of thinker in military and world affairs, the "strategic analyst"; in particular, von Neumann's mathematical game theory became part of the arsenal of conceptual tools of American strategic thinking. At a time when social scientists were becoming increasingly disillusioned with the usefulness of game theory, the military strategists were becoming more and more enthusiastic about it. The Rand Corporation became the world center for studies in and promotion of game theory, and retained von Neumann as a consultant ... von Neumann was not only a consultant to the Rand Corporation but an active and respected participant in the making of government weapons policies.[81]

This new style of 'strategic analyst' in social, military, and worldly affairs, epitomized by von Neumann and his theory of games, became so highly coveted, precisely because they effectively connected questions of technology, strategy (practices), and culture and contained them in a disciplinary closed-world discourse, a quintessentially semiotic space of game theory in which there were clear protagonists and enemies: the free world and communist forces respectively.[82] The installation of such global automated 'semiotic spaces' completely removed any culpability for decision-making from individuals, as the onus for mistakes in the administration, organization, and management of 'risks' could be turned back on the machines themselves, thus insulating those in power from faults in policy.

---

79 Foucault, '1 February 1978 *Governmentality*'.
80 Von Neumann and Morgenstern, *Theory of Games and Economic Behavior*, p. 163.
81 Heims, *John von Neumann and Norbert Wiener*, pp. 313-315.
82 Edwards, *The Closed World*.

As we have seen repeatedly in popular culture, in classic films like Stanley Kubrick's 1964 *Dr. Strangelove or: How I Learned to Stop Worrying and Love the Bomb*, as well as in Sidney Lumet's 1964 *Fail-Safe*, and also in contemporary television shows like Fox's *24*, and Hollywood blockbusters like the 2002 film *The Sum of All Fears*, as well in lesser seen B-movies like *Deterrence* from 1999; the US President's insertion and turning of the key in the 'nuclear suitcase', this apocalyptic decision, is based exclusively on the nation's automated predetection systems, whose operations self-elaborate the 'natural' decision to obliterate the planet through the use of atomic mechanisms and devices that have themselves called the possibilities and predictions for this reality into effect.

In this sense, the technological embodiment of computers as tools for fighting atomic battles and defeating Communist foes allowed game theory to proliferate, entwine, and self-elaborate itself into other discourses, whereby 'systems analysis formalized this discursive connection between technology, strategy, and culture. It generated what Foucault called a "regime of truth", a set of implicit conventions about what could count as facts and reasons and who was authorized to elucidate them.'[83] Edwards clearly recognizes the integration and interplay of Foucault's disciplinary and security mechanisms, which involve the ongoing correlation of power through the further integration of such mechanisms in the constitution of fields, domains, and objects of knowledge. In this way he uses the phrase

> ..."closed-world-discourse" to describe the language, technologies, and practices that together supported the visions of centrally controlled, automated global power at the heart of American Cold War politics. Computers helped create and sustain this discourse in two ways. First, they allowed the practical construction of central real-time military control systems on a gigantic scale. Second, they facilitated the metaphorical understanding of world politics as a sort of system subject to technological management. Closed-world discourse, through metaphors, techniques, and fictions as well as equipment and salient experiences, linked the globalist, hegemonic aims of post-World War II American foreign policy with a high-technology military strategy, an ideology of apocalyptic struggle, and a language of integrated systems.[84]

Contrary to Wiener's conception of a humane social model of cybernetics, such closed-world discourse frames the global social and economic environment of the Cold War in terms of players – heroes and enemies, winners and losers – all defined by cost-benefit, net-worth, risk analyses, and the efficient and effective management of populations. In this way, game theory and closed-world discourse were very useful to the US government because they paralleled and reinforced the epic tale of good and evil that was beginning to unfold on the world stage, between the free world and communist forces. On the efficient and effective role that game theory played in post-war American mythology of the 1940s, Heims writes:

---

83 Edwards, *The Closed World*, p. 120.
84 Edwards, *The Closed World*, pp. 7-8.

It favored thinking in terms of "them and us"; was as mechanical and impersonal as possible; had a simplistic model of purposes and a simple, one dimensional, quantitative view of human nature; emphasized efficaciousness; and was conservative and uncritical of existing institutions.[85]

Although books like Schelling's *The Strategy of Conflict*,[86] and Rapoport's *Strategy and Conscience* and *Two-Person Game Theory: The Essential Ideas*[87] reveal that game theory as a tool or social analysis can be engaged in imaginative and depthful ways, we also have seen, as Wiener has argued, that game theory's tendency to reduce complex social problems to black and white players, where the parties are understood to be in total and complete opposition, makes it extremely fallible as a social model when anything more complex or realistic involving more than two players enters the equation; and this despite von Neumann's mathematical transformations from 'zero-sum games' to 'constant-sum games' in 1953. Yet still, closed-world discourse authorized and reinforced by game theory drove American foreign and domestic policy throughout the Cold War, and in many ways continues to today, precisely because it supports fantasies, fictions, and metaphors that depict a contained but highly uncertain world in an epic and eternal struggle of good and evil that can be efficiently and effectively managed through conjunctions of computer technologies, statistics, probabilities and the management of populations through instruments like lists. Game theory as a global approach came to dominate US foreign and domestic policy during the Cold War because 'the game' was perfectly aligned with, and a perfect metaphor for, American domestic and foreign policy of the time: President Harry S. Truman's disciplinary doctrine of 'containment':

Containment, with its image of an enclosed space surrounded and sealed by American power, was the central metaphor of closed-world discourse ... it differed from its predecessors, however, in its genuinely global character, in the systematic, deliberate restructuring of American civil society that it entailed, and in its focus on the development of technological means to project military force across the globe.[88]

Consistent with Foucault's 'double integration' security technologies, Edwards describes how the Truman Doctrine and McCarthyism served to authorize and reinforce a disciplinary closed-world political and cultural environment in a 'triple sense' during the Cold War. In one respect, the closed-world was deeply linked to a clandestine, secretive, and repressive communist society, which found itself contained within an open world of democracy and capitalism. At the same time, the closed-world could also be positioned to contain the capitalist system, understood as threatened at its margins by Communist invasion. And finally, in the largest sense, the closed-world could be seen as containing the overall globe, as a closed political and economic battlefield,

---

85 Heims, *John von Neumann and Norbert Wiener*, p. 319.
86 Thomas Schelling, *The Strategy of Conflict*, Cambridge: Harvard University Press, 1960.
87 A. Rapoport, *Strategy and Conscience*, New York, NY: Harper and Row, 1964; A. Rapoport,
    Two-Person Game Theory: The Essential Ideas, Ann Arbor: University of Michigan Press, 1969.
88 Edwards, *The Closed World*, p. 8.

...within which the struggle between freedom and slavery, light and darkness, good and evil was being constantly joined in every location – within the American government, its society, and its armed forces as well as abroad. Each side of the struggle had, in effect, a national headquarters, but the struggle as a whole went on everywhere and perpetually.[89]

Post-World War II, the bilateralism that us ll them caesuras in closed-world discourse enabled, served to authorize and reinforce the systematic reduction of the conflicts of the world to one grand battle between the free world and its wicked, insipid communist enemies. And this epic and perpetual tale of real life-or-death struggle between good and evil is the primary metaphor of closed-world discourse. Closed-world discourse also sets up a global stage, on which the world is always divided against itself, wherein actions consist of attempts to invade and parries at containment. Closed-world discourse supports a taken-for-granted view of the globe as a closed stage of action, where the mise-en-scene consists entirely of the struggles between the free world and its foes. Indeed, post-World War II, the grand tale of closed-world discourse allowed the United States to increasingly be viewed as '...the manager, either directly or by proxy, of the entire global political, economic, and military scene'.[90]

Moreover, early massive computer systems developed by the US Defense Department to act as nuclear warning and control devices (i.e. SAGE), can be seen as epitomizing closed-world discourse, fully embodying, supporting, and self-elaborating through their technological structure and practices the globe as the stage of this epic and undeniable struggle between good and evil. 'SAGE was far more than a weapons system. It was a dream, a myth, a metaphor for total defense, a technology of closed-world discourse.'[91] And such disciplinary notions of global technological enclosure quickly spread as the computer's extension of mathematical formalizations to military planning and global politics were equally applicable in social and economic fields and domains, bringing forth a new sense of progress and order through the automated technological delimitation and policing of abnormal or 'risky' elements in uncertain global entropic milieus.

Both Edwards[92] and Heims[93] analyze in detail how such 'systems discourses' of the Cold War, along with their attendant techniques and tools, authorized and reinforced a language and ideology of technical control across a large swath of research fields, domains, and objects of knowledge, including social structures, institutions, and government bodies, and their specific programs, policies, procedures, and activities. From their work we can conclude that systems, or closed-world discourse, can also be understood as unequivocally linking technology to social, military, and global strategy through the methods associated with mathematical and computer modeling. The more computers enabled the modeling and simulation of complex social, economic, and military problems, the more they created an ever-greater need for themselves in such milieus – the double integration effects that are the hallmark of the apparatuses of security.

---

89 Edwards, *The Closed World*, p. 10.
90 Edwards, *The Closed World*, pp. 13-14
91 Edwards, *The Closed World*, p. 11.
92 Edwards, *The Closed World*.
93 Heims, *John von Neumann and Norbert Wiener*; Heims, *Constructing a Social Science for Post-war America*.

Culled From the Vast Seas of Entropy: Enter the Cyborg Class

In her discussion of plutonium and genetically engineered and modified organisms Donna Haraway in *Modest Witness@Second_Millenium: Femaleman©_Meets_Oncomouse™* speaks to the question of classification through technoscientific practices emerging in the Cold War era and beyond:

> What interests me about the proportion that links plutonium with genetically engineered organisms and situates them in their historical chronotopes, World War II through the Cold War of the 1940s through the 1980s, and the New World Order of the early 1980s to the present, is the question of taxonomy, category, and the natural status of artificial entities – kinship in short. Kinship is a technology for producing the material and semiotic effect of natural relationship, shared kind.[94]

In the same way that Haraway argues that kinship is a technology for producing the effect of a shared kind, this chapter and work overall argue that lists are similarly a technology for producing the teleological effects of establishing 'natural' relationships or shared kinds between living beings, things, and knowledge, a primary characteristic of life subsumed in entropic milieus of circulation. A discerning reader might wonder: where has the list gone in all of this? Is it now subsumed, as a disciplinary mechanism of computer technologies, merely serving the administration, organization, and development of knowledge, like computer code and its reams of listed operations? The answer is no, the list has not disappeared, nor is it merely redeployed in the mechanisms of statistics and computer technologies in such mundane capacities; its role has just, to this point in the event of the emergence of the modern computer, remained rather limited, for the early computer's use immediately following WWII hinges almost exclusively on the administration, management, and organization of only two listed players: the free world and communist forces.

> Of all the technologies built to fight the Cold War, digital computers have become its most ubiquitous, and perhaps its most important, legacy. Yet few have realized the degree to which computers created the technological possibility of Cold War and shaped its political atmosphere, and virtually no one has recognized how profoundly the Cold War shaped computer technology. Its politics became embedded in the machines – even, at times, in their technical design – while the machines helped make possible its politics, we can make sense of the history of computers as tools only when we simultaneously grasp their history as metaphors in Cold War science, politics, and culture.[95]

In a world where classifications of 'us' and 'them' were heightened, cybernetic, game, and systems theory provided, then and today, a means to delimit and police the movement of threats of all kinds; the automated classification of living beings and things into factors of net-worth and risk, inputted as registered data and outputted as lists of threats. In other words, from Nazi governmentality through to the Cold War era and beyond, the more computers

---

94 Haraway, *Modest Witness@Second_Millenium*, p. 53.
95 Edwards, *The Closed World*, p. ix.

have been engaged to comb ever-expanding sets of social data, the more they have produced the teleological effect of establishing seemingly 'natural' relationships between people, things, and knowledge or what Haraway calls kinships. And the more computers and statistics have been engaged to establish kinships and define lists, the more they have self-elaborated their own taken-for-granted role in producing these powerful closed-world regimes of truth. In this way, conjunctions of computers, statistics, and lists during the Cold War installed milieus of circulation where the 'risks' of communist elements were always being weighed, and at the same time, they served to authorize, reinforce, and further embed these underlying values, myths, and divisive practices, these politics, right back into the design and development of the next generation of machines.

Turning to Haraway's earlier work, in *Simians, Cyborgs and Women* she says:

> Communication technologies and biotechnologies are the crucial tools recrafting our bodies. These tools embody and enforce new social relations for women world-wide. Technologies and scientific discourses can be partially understood as formalizations, i.e., as frozen moments, of the fluid social interactions constituting them, but they should also be viewed as instruments for enforcing meanings. The boundary is permeable between tool and myth, instrument and concept, historical systems of social relations and historical anatomies of possible bodies, including objects of knowledge. Indeed, myth and tool mutually constitute each other.[96]

Following on Haraway's argumentation, there is no separating the computer or contemporary installations of apparatuses of security from their historical links to myths surrounding the techniques and technologies they help authorize, reinforce, and install; and particularly, in the case of the computer, from the discourse of game theory and the 'us vs. them' myths it specifically helped reinforce in the delimitation and policing of the movement of the Communist threat. From McCarthy's blacklists to today's no-fly lists (explored in the next chapter), post-World War II the world has been and continues to be increasingly translated into what Haraway calls a 'problem in coding',[97] where everything reduces to quantities, rates, directions, distribution, probabilities, and flows of elements in and between populations; and where information makes no distinction and asserts no boundaries between people, objects, and knowledge. With the emergence and widespread application of 'systems theory' to a litany of fields and domains of knowledge, the human species is further 'naturally' subdivided, classified, and listed as cyborg.

> The term cyborg was coined by Manfred Clynes and Nathan Kline[98] to refer to the enhanced man who could survive in extraterrestrial environments. They imagined the cyborgian man-machine hybrid would be needed in the next great technohumanist challenge – space flight ... One of their first cyborgs was a standard white laboratory rat

---

96 Haraway, *Simians, Cyborgs, and Women*, p. 164.
97 Haraway, *Simians, Cyborgs, and Women*, p. 164.
98 Manfred E. Clynes and Nathan S. Kline, 'Cyborgs and Space', *Astronautics* (September, 1960): 75-76.

implemented with an osmotic pump designed to inject chemicals continuously. Conse-
quently, my people are akin to field mice who have entered the anomaly in evolutionary
space – a wormhole – called the laboratory. Like the science-fictional wormhole in an
episode of the television show *Deep Space Nine*, the laboratory continues to suck us
into uncharted regions of technical, cultural, and political space. Passing through the
wormhole of technoscience, the field mice emerge as the finely tailored laboratory ro-
dents – model systems, animate tools, research material, self-acting organic-technical
hybrids – through whose eyes I write this essay. Those mutated murine eyes give me
my ethnographic point of view. Cyborg anthropology attempts to refigure provocative-
ly the border relations among specific humans, other organisms and machines. The
interface between specifically located people, other organisms, and machines turns
out to be an excellent field site for ethnographic inquiry into what counts as self-acting
and as collective empowerment. I call that field site the culture and practice of technoscience.[99]

By constituting the intermingling of living beings and technological devices as information
machines and systems susceptible to technoscientific probing for regularities and patterns,
the kind of governmentality that emerged post-World War II also significantly helped to inte-
grate and acclimatize people into thinking of themselves and society as complex techno-social
automated systems, subject to pervasive and ubiquitous segmenting, research, and testing.
Haraway's argument for cyborgs leaves little doubt that in today's technoscientific order our
lives have been increasingly consumed and contained by the isolated techno-social systems
Wiener cautioned against.

The term cyborg has come to be understood as the intermingling of living beings and
machines, '...a fusion of the organic and the technical forged in particular, historical, cultural
practices'.[100] The emergence of cyborg discourse provided the incunabula for new identities,
subjectivities, and mythic imaginings fitting of the coming information age. Throughout the
Cold War and into today, cyborgs can be understood as yielding new possibilities for identity
and political action, but always from the vantage point of containment within closed isolated
systems, whether in the individual human body or up to the internet, globe, and universe.
Cyborg discourse would inevitably encourage much more than a new set of subject positions for people; ultimately it would enter them into profound reciprocal relationships with
computers themselves. As Sherry Turkle[101] has shown us, 'life on the screen' would come
to encompass 'second selves' for people; and as she has demonstrated, when computers
and minds are equated, notions of the self are significantly altered in processes involving
decentering, fragmenting, and ultimately, reunifying the self as an information-processing
device, constituted by the transmission of information between modular, windows-like, mental
programs. Indeed, for Edwards:

---

99 Haraway, *Modest Witness@Second_Millenium*, pp. 51-52.
100 Haraway, *Modest Witness@Second_Millenium*, p. 51.
101 Turkle, *The Second Self*; Turkle, *Life on the Screen*.

The experience of the computer as a second self *is the experience of the closed-world of a rule based game*. The second self computer users find within the machine is, in general, a 'hard', quasi-scientific, male self, an experience of reality in the terms of closed-world discourse.[102]

In this way, the second self of the cyborg, despite existing in a vast and complex world, never escapes the disciplinary enclosure of conjunctions of security technologies; as individuals increasingly are reduced to numerical values of worth and risk, they are also subjected to increasing research and experimentation. And like all populations, cyborgs are delimited, policed, and listed, seen as digital elements that are subject to 'disassembly, engineering, and reconstruction'.[103] In this way, where closed-world discourse serves to systematically reduce social and political issues to disciplinary 'problems in coding', they also self-elaborate, imagining one's life and society as closed systems, susceptible to endless probing for regularities and patterns and infinite possibilities for delimitation, re-assembly, and policing. Furthermore, where closed-world discourse and the apparatuses of security authorize and reinforce a disciplinary technoscientific politics and practice pivoting on global control systems, modern and contemporary governmentality installs global milieus of circulation, which further 'naturalize' imagining oneself as automaton—as an isolated cybernetic organism circulating in a closed mechanical system, contained in a global milieu where the boundaries between living beings, things, and knowledge, and between humans and machines, have been totally eviscerated.

In order to understand how Bowker and Star's[104] 'global classification infrastructures' are deployed as milieus of circulation installed by the apparatuses of security under governmentality, one development in communication research, despite pre-dating World War II and the widespread automation of life through computer technologies, needs to be examined here: Walter Lippmann and Harold Lasswell's notions of 'persuasive communication' which emerged in the 1920s and evolved onwards.[105]

---

102 Edwards, *The Closed World*, p. 172.
103 Edwards, *The Closed World*, p. 2.
104 Bowker and Star, *Sorting Things Out*.
105 Walter Lippmann, *Public Opinion*, New York: Macmillan, 1922; Walter Lippmann, *An Inquiry into the Principles of the Good Society*, Boston: Little Brown and Company, 1937; Walter Lippmann, *The Good Society*, New York: Grosset & Dunlap, 1943; Walter Lippmann, *The Cold War: A Study in U.S. Foreign Policy*, New York: Harper, 1947; Walter Lippmann, *Essays in the Public Philosophy*, Boston: Little Brown, 1955; Walter Lippmann, *Drift and Mastery: An Attempt to Diagnose the Current Unrest*, Englewood Cliffs: Prentice-Hall, 1961; Walter Lippmann, *Public Opinion*, New York: Macmillan, 1965; Walter Lippmann, *Early Writings*, New York: Liveright, 1970; Walter Lippmann and Godkin Lectures at Harvard University, *The Method of Freedom*, New York: Macmillan, 1934; Harold Dwight Lasswell, 'The Structure and Function of Communication in Society', in L. Bryson (ed.), *The Communication of Ideas: A Series of Addresses*, Religion and civilization series, New York: Jewish Theological Seminary of America and the Institute for Religious and Social Studies, 1948, pp. 37-51; Harold Dwight Lasswell, *Politics: Who Gets What, When, How*, New York: Peter Smith, 1950; Harold Dwight Lasswell, *Psychopathology and Politics*, New York: Viking Press, 1960; Harold Dwight Lasswell, *Propaganda Technique in the World War*, New York: Garland Pub, 1972; Harold Dwight Lasswell, Daniel Lerner, and Hans Speier, *Propaganda and Communication in World History*, Honolulu: published for the East-West Center by The University Press of Hawaii, 1979; Harold Dwight Lasswell and Arnold A. Rogow, *Politics, Personality,*

These early pioneers in the field of communications research, whose work taken together ultimately spawned the domain of 'public relations' research,[106] took as their maxim 'persuasive communication', wherein mass communication technologies, conceived of as necessary tools for managing elites to craft and shape 'public opinion' were understood as instruments for the administration, organization, and management of populations through the manipulation of the distribution of elements that could be deciphered through the constitution of public opinions. Beginning in an era, the 1920s, when the delimitation and management of 'risks' was critically ensured through physical assemblages of policing (men, guns, batons), the idea of 'persuasive communication' seemed far more humane and enlightened than the violence of physical policing. Critical to this functionalist view aimed at policing populations through mass communication means is technology, which is seen as an '…instrument for imposing one's will on others, and preferably on masses of others'.[107] The communications legacy of Lippmann and Lasswell would profoundly weigh on how the apparatuses of security (computers, statistics, and lists) would install contemporary global classification infrastructures as a worldwide milieu of circulation.

The List Serves: Who, Says what, in Which Channel, to whom, with what Effect?

Who?
Says What?
In Which Channel?
To Whom?
With What Effect?[108]

So begins Lasswell's *The Structure and Function of Communication in Society*, a short address, in an obscure edited anthology published by the Institute for Religious and Social Studies, that takes as its point of departure this list of questions. As we have already seen, each answer to a question on a list will surely and inevitably generate infinitely more lists of questions. And so, we must investigate further. This seemingly glib list of 'dictum' summarizing his earlier works with Bruce L. Smith and Ralph D. Casey in *Propaganda, Communication, and Public Opinion*, was intended to be anything but superficial. For Lasswell this list of questions not only works as succinctly enclosing communications research as a scientific field and domain of knowledge, but it also formed the building blocks for his techniques for the materialization of elements circulating in milieus of public opinion that could be acted upon. In fact, this list of questions, an early form of metadata, would come to constitute a 'natural' and 'truthful' way of seeing and doing communications as an empirical discipline. This basic list is a 'dictum that is practically inscribed in stone

and Social Science in the Twentieth Century: Essays in Honor of Harold D. Lasswell, Chicago: University of Chicago Press, 1969; Bruce Lannes Smith, Harold Dwight Lasswell, and Ralph Droz Casey, *Propaganda, Communication, and Public Opinion: A Comprehensive Reference Guide*, Princeton: Princeton Univ. Press, 1946.
106 Simpson, *Science of Coercion*.
107 Simpson, *Science of Coercion*, p. 18.
108 Lasswell, 'The Structure and Function of Communication in Society', p. 37.

over portals of those US colleges offering communication as a field of study'.[109] For when Lasswell's *who says what in which channel to whom with what effect* dictum is correlated with Lippmann's techniques for delimiting public opinion, 'persuasive communication' begins to take on the form and characteristics of a technology of security in its own right:

> The pictures inside the heads of these human beings, the pictures of themselves, of others, of their needs, purposes, and relationship, are their public opinions. Those pictures which are acted upon by groups of people, or by individuals acting in the name of groups, are Public Opinion with capital letters.[110]

It is argued here that the dominant legacy that 'persuasive communications' left behind for communication studies was precisely the correlation of the techniques of Lippmann and Lasswell, and how they together exhibit the hallmark 'double integration' of security technologies. The joint functions of statistically delimiting populations through techniques like Lippmann's early Public Opinion surveys, coupled with the operations of materializing lists of elements from Lasswell's techniques dissecting *who says what in which channel to whom with what effect* are characteristic of the 'double integration' effect, which serves both the delimitation and reconstitution of elements in a self-elaborating process of knowledge development. In this way the conjunction of Lippmann's Public Opinion and Lasswell's 'dissection techniques', like all security technologies act on the very populations and elements they delimit.

For Lasswell,[111] applying a disciplinary scientific method, like in the study of biology, to the study of communication, involved taking complex unmeasurable phenomena, analyzing and breaking them down into discrete parts, and then building up a purportedly objective understanding of the phenomena as a whole from the reconstitution of these parts and their subsequent steering into harmonious action. It is interesting to also note here that the concept of 'persuasive communications' that came to be associated with Lippmann and Lasswell was not lost on the Nazis, who in fact were great innovators in the instrumental use of public opinion surveys and computerized technologies to establish *who says what in which channel to whom with what effect* inside Hitler's Germany.[112]

> We gain perspective on human societies when we note the degree to which communication is a feature of life at every level. A vital entity, whether relatively isolated or in association, has specialized ways of receiving stimuli from the environment. The single-celled organism or the many-membered group tends to maintain an internal equilibrium and to respond to changes in the environment in a way that maintains this equilibrium. The responding process calls for specialized ways of bringing the parts of the whole into harmonious action.[113]

---

109 Simpson, *Science of Coercion*, p. 18.
110 Lippmann, *Public Opinion*, p. 29.
111 Lasswell, 'The Structure and Function of Communication in Society'.
112 Simpson, *Science of Coercion*.
113 Lasswell, 'The Structure and Function of Communication in Society', p. 38.

We can see Lasswell arguing for a form of biopolitics inherent in persuasive communication, wherein the entropic milieu of circulation of messages and information are tamed by the same mechanical means as those that tame nature itself, in organisms, and in the populations and societies in which they move about freely. With the proliferation of positivist practices and techniques of delimiting, classifying, and dividing communication into the discrete individual parts of *who says what in which channel to whom with what effect*, elements circulating in populations factored as public opinions could be acted upon and reconstituted or re-distributed through the installation of new technological conjunctions, the very same techniques that mark the biological, economic, and physical sciences, and their fields, domains, and objects of knowledge. This positivist or disciplinary scientific communications legacy that seeks to analyze, break down, calculate, predict, and build up 'natural' and 'truthful' connections between 'information' elements circulating in public opinions would come to install a massive, modern, and contemporary milieu of circulation that would pivotally serve contemporary governmentality: a global classification infrastructure of epic proportions that would ultimately evolve into the internet and other massive assemblages of living beings, things, and objects of knowledge. So says Foucault:

> The public which is a crucial notion in the eighteenth century, is the population seen under the aspects of its opinions, ways of doing things, forms of behavior, customs, fears, prejudices, and requirements; it is what one gets a hold on through education, campaigns, and convictions. The population is therefore everything that extends from biological rootedness through the species up to the surface that gives one a hold provided by the public. From the species, to the public; we have here a whole field of new realities in the sense that they are pertinent elements for mechanisms of power, the pertinent space within which and regarding which one must act.[114]

The legacy of *who says what in which channel to whom with what effect* listed by Lasswell in his 1948 address is profoundly like Lippmann's Public Opinions, which continue to have significant effects on the delimitation and policing of populations and provide a critical way of seeing and doing 'security'. A presentation at the New Network Theory 2007 conference in Amsterdam epitomized this legacy. Speaking on 'Open Source Network Analysis', Valdis Krebs, a US-based management consultant described how his company explicitly engages Lasswell's *who said what to* whom-model in the material mapping of terrorist networks. Engaging a simple strategy of probing reams of print-based news data, asking *who* said *what* to *whom,* descending two levels, and materializing the results as network images that display kinships and connections between people, Krebs described how the form of pictures of networks carried with them great power, establishing strong ties between people visually.

> "People like pictures," he declared, "and even if we don't understand exactly what these connections between people mean, they clearly indicate that they know each other."[115]

---

114 Foucault, '25 January 1978', p. 75.
115 Valdis Krebs, 'OSNA – Open Source Network Analysis', talk presented at New Network Theory conference, 28-30 June 2007, Institute of Network Cultures, Amsterdam, http://networkcultures.

Describing how his network mapping method and tool were engaged to establish the terrorist network behind the 9/11 attacks, Krebs said that the CIA turns to his company's network visualizations when publicly articulating Al-Qaeda networks, as the CIA's own maps and visualizations are classified matters of national security. Despite a series of acknowledged 'misidentifications' contained in his visualizations of the 9/11 terrorist networks, he described how his network map of the 9/11 terrorists has spread itself far and wide across the internet; making life very difficult for some innocent, yet unwittingly listed people.

Given the power of pictures he described with respect to establishing *who says what in which channel to whom with what effect*, it would appear that the use of such visualizations to identify 'them' would be approached with great caution and trepidation. However, in a world where the probing of entropic milieus of circulation for factors of 'worth' and 'risk' is firmly installed, techniques and technologies surrounding the visualization of networks of *who said what to whom and with what effect* are merely taken for granted, as well as the presence of such network maps in the public domain of the internet. As we shall see in the next chapter on no-fly lists, 'misidentification' is the cost of the installation of such contemporary apparatuses of security. Such network mapping practices and contemporary forms of lists will continue to pervasively and ubiquitously serve the interests of power, further self-elaborating closed-world apparatuses of security, so long as the inherent power to correlate, which such monumental classification conjunctions afford, remains subsumed in our techno-social woodwork, unloosened and unchallenged.

> In the past 100 years, people in all lines of work have jointly constructed an incredible, interlocking set of categories, standards, and means for interoperating infrastructural technologies. We hardly know what we have built. No one is in control of the infrastructure; no one has the power to centrally change it. To the extent that we live in, on and around this new infrastructure, it helps form the shape of our moral, scientific, and esthetic choices. Infrastructure is now the great inner space.[116]

In *Sorting Things Out: Classification and its Consequences*, Bowker and Star argue that it is possible to understand 'the networks that shape much of daily life in cyborg fashion',[117] by examining and interrogating the 'ubiquitous classification systems and standards' that increasingly come to make up distinctions and kinships between living beings, objects, and knowledge. Drawing directly on the work of Haraway,[118] Bowker and Star argue that cyborgs, understood as the intermingling of information technologies, representations, politics, and people, are characterized by the utter evisceration of the boundaries between living beings, objects, and knowledge. For Bowker and Star, the creeping pervasiveness and ubiquity of a 'global classification society' involves the ongoing and pervasive transformation of local classification schemes into international standardized schemes, which are in turn streamed up and aligned with standardized global-scale information systems.

---

org/networktheory/1-network-theory/program/.
116 Bowker and Star, *Sorting Things Out*, p. 319.
117 Bowker and Star, *Sorting Things Out*, p. 301.
118 Haraway, *Simians, Cyborgs, and Women*.

In this process, it is becoming easier for the individual to act and perceive him or her self as a completely naturalized part of the 'classification society' since the thicket of classification is both operative (defining the possibilities for action) and descriptive. As we are socialized to become that which can be measured by our increasingly sophisticated measurement tools, the classifications increasingly naturalize across wider scope.[119]

Here I want to pick up on Bowker and Star's warnings for critical engagement with and fundamental rethinking of information systems.

We need recognize that all information systems are necessarily suffused with ethical and political values, modulated by local administrative procedures. These systems are active creators of categories in the world as well as simulators of existing categories. Remembering this, we keep open and can explore spaces for change and flexibility that are otherwise lost forever.[120]

It is indeed politically and ethically crucial to recognize the pervasive, ubiquitous, taken-for-granted and vital role of our classification infrastructures in our increasingly 'built moral environment'.[121] What might appear to be banal and purely technical issues involving the naming of things and categories, or the articulation of lists, in fact constitutes much of our everyday interactions. In this respect, it is crucial to raise awareness of the organizational and political dimensions of engaging classifications and lists of people, culled from the vast entropy of our global information milieu of circulation, and at the same time to ensure that such classifications and lists retain traces of their builders and construction.

The List Serves: An Example of Entropy and Contemporary Governmentality

It is with great concern that I begin to temporally shift my study of how lists serve from modern governmentality to a contemporary example. I recently received a postcard in the mail from the Right Honorable Stephen Harper, Canada's Prime Minister, wishing a former roommate and his family 'good wishes' for a Jewish New Year '...filled with happiness, health, prosperity and peace'. After all that has been analyzed here, it seems both ironic and fitting to ask this question: how exactly did the Right Honorable Prime Minister of Canada Stephen Harper, get a list of Jews to write to? What computerized and mathematical operations were involved in probing our entropic global classification infrastructures – these milieus of circulation – for regularities and patterns that would see my former (and very Liberal) roommates' name factor on a list of Jews, a population delimited for 'good' wishes and seasons tidings from the Conservative Party? Did my old roommate register himself and his family as Jews with the Conservative Party of Canada, or anyone for that matter, including Statistics Canada, whose data we are told is sacrosanct to the Canadian nation? Given that my former roommate never

---

119 Bowker and Star, *Sorting Things Out*, p. 326.
120 Bowker and Star, *Sorting Things Out*, p. 321.
121 Bowker and Star, *Sorting Things Out*, p. 326.

registered himself at my address with the Conservative Party, nor anywhere as such, how did he and his family come to be classified as Jews, listed at my address, and solicited through the post by the Right Honorable Stephen Harper?

Given the historical trajectory and unloosening of 'governmental reason' presented here, the answers to such questions might prove to be very disturbing and shocking to ordinary Canadians, should we ever care enough to interrogate them in the public domain. The apparatuses of security that correlate computers, statistics, and lists in the delimitation, administration, organization, and development of populations and their elements are so deeply subsumed in our social woodwork, that when the fundamental biopolitical caesuras that characterize them materialize in an expression of 'good wishes' for a 'prosperous' new year from a prime minister to a Jewish family, it might go completely unnoticed, taken merely as a natural phenomenon, part and parcel of entropy and contemporary governmentality.

> In the best of all possible worlds, at any given moment, the past could be reordered to better reflect multiple constituencies now and then. Only then we will be able to fully learn the lessons of the past. In this same optimal world, we could tune our classifications to reflect new institutional arrangements or personal trajectories – reconfigure the world on the fly. The only good classification is a living classification.[122]

In this same spirit, and drawing on Bowker and Star's argumentation for critical engagement with classifications, I argue that the only good list of people is a living list of people, one which explicitly states the criteria by which it was formed, next to the builders and building processes – the techno-human couplings – responsible for its creation. Just as Bowker and Star suggest that 'classifications should be reclassified', I want to state that *lists should be re-listed*, as pivotal and contested sites of contemporary governmentality.

Conclusion

A constant interplay between techniques of power and their object gradually carves out in reality, population and its specific phenomena. A whole series of objects were made visible for possible forms of knowledge on the basis of the constitution of the population as a correlate of techniques of power. In turn, because these forms of knowledge constantly carve out new objects, the population could be formed, continue, and remain as the privileged correlate of modern mechanisms of power.[123]

Being a child of the 1970s, I can remember a time when people like my grandparents were extremely wary of, and approached any form of involvement in scientific research and testing, whether medical or social, with a highly skeptical eye, mostly avoiding being the subject of experimentation their whole lives. Moreover, my grandparents were not only skeptical of scientific research and experimentation, but also, having felt the chilling effects of their families being registered, listed, experimented upon, and exterminated as Jews by the Nazis, were

---

122 Bowker and Star, *Sorting Things Out.*
123 Foucault, '25 January 1978', p. 79.

also highly skeptical of government operations involving registering individuals and populations through disciplinary census mechanisms. How quickly times change. For today, it would be near impossible to imagine how one might heed my grandparents repeated warnings against involvement in scientific research, let alone how to avoid registering oneself through census and other contemporary identification and tracking operations, when the basis of all everyday software and technology end-user license agreements take as their foundation the immediate release of the rights of the 'cyborg' to the data they generate, in the interest of 'future' research and development of products, 'security' technologies, and correlations of capitalism and governmental power.

In the same way that Haraway[124] argues that kinship is a technology for producing the effect of a shared kind, this work argues that computers, statistics, and lists are similarly technologies of security which produce the teleological effects of establishing 'natural' relationships between people, or shared kinds of things and populations. In this way, post-World War II and throughout the Cold War into the 1980s and beyond, increasingly pervasive closed-world game theory discourses, operating through policing assemblages of computers, statistics, and lists, can be understood as reinforcing divisive 'us vs. them' classification practices, particularly concerning the risks posed by possible communist threats in the 1940s, 50s, and 60s, and eventually coming to exert great force in how we delimit and police 'terrorist' movements today.

In a world where questions of 'us vs. them' are heightened, and epic battles between black and white classifications of opposing forces are seen as ongoing and never-ending, the powerful operations of practices involving delimiting and policing 'threats' through lists are subsuming further and further into our techno-social woodwork. Securing 'freedom' through the automated, divisive, and dehumanizing classification of living beings as measures of worth/risk in global information infrastructures and policed through list technologies is clearly on the rise. The more computers and algorithms are engaged to comb ever-expanding sets of social data for regularities and patterns of 'threatening' people and things, the more these self-elaborating processes produce the teleological effect of establishing 'natural' good versus bad global relationships, the more lists are used to delimit and police the movement of threats. And the more we take this self-elaborating form of governmentality for granted.

In this chapter we have seen how open-human and closed-world discourses operated in conjunction with computer, statistical, and list technologies as an economy of discourses, correlated by the apparatuses of security which installed a global milieu of circulation in which we would come to see ourselves and our societies as technoscientific cultural constructions of cyborg elements and populations, circulating in entropic information environments where the boundaries between people, objects, and knowledge are eviscerated. In this way, the emergence of modern computers while ushering in awe-inspiring developments in massive assemblages of living beings and machines, also served to increasingly isolate cyborgs in global classification infrastructures, subjecting them to evermore pervasive and ubiquitous delimitation, policing and nullification. Building on Bowker and Star's[125] assertions, it is argued that

---

124 Haraway, *Modest Witness@Second_Millenium.*
125 Bowker and Star, *Sorting Things Out.*

like classifications, lists are powerful ubiquitous technologies that are so deeply embedded in our working infrastructures that they have become relatively invisible, despite never losing any of their power in the self-elaborating processes of sublimation. Just as categories and classifications are culled into working infrastructures and become ways of seeing and doing everyday life that are increasingly taken for granted, lists too coalesce into working infrastructures that are integrated into and aligned with local, national, and global information systems.

The next chapter, 'Fear and No-fly Listing in Canada', demonstrates how in the entropic global milieus of circulation that were installed with the birth of modern computers, the assemblage of policing (computers, statistic, and lists) deployed to patrol and regulate these uncertain and ever-expanding power/knowledge environments continues to play a pivotal role in contemporary governmentality. This chapter explores what in chapter 4 I call contemporary no-fill-in-the-blank list culture, which increasingly factors elements circulating as risks, and delimits and polices their movement in more and more everyday environments. No-fly lists and broader no-blank list culture, which has emerged in Canada, the United States, and worldwide post-9/11, both culls and calls the modern 'terrorist' into reality. Out of the vast disorder of uncertain entropy into increasingly streamlined global classification infrastructures, contemporary 'us' nations like Canada continue to attempt to identify, predict, and police 'them' terrorists, through the installation of assemblages of policing, underpinned by the critical 'security'

CHAPTER 3. FEAR AND NO-FLY LISTING IN CANADA (MARCH 2006 - NOVEMBER 2007)

Introduction

> A no-fly list is collective punishment for a population that has done no wrong, it violates the rule of law and it will not stop terrorists from murdering innocent people. The no-fly list should be grounded.[1]

On June 18th 2007, amidst much controversy and contestation[2], massive failure with the same endeavor in the United States, and warnings from Canada's Privacy Commissioner Jennifer Stoddart about the 'chilling position' of being mistakenly identified on the list and the 'nightmare' of subsequent redress to the 'so-called' Office of Reconsideration[3], Transport Canada Minister Lawrence Cannon put into effect a no-fly list, promised to consist of the names of no more than 1,000 Canadian citizens deemed to be threats to domestic and international aviation security. Known formally as *The Specified Persons List*, Canada's no-fly list was introduced as a part of Canada's *Passenger Protect Program*, first announced on October 27th, 2006[4] which required in January 2007 that all outgoing Canadian air travelers provide a government issued identification in order to board commercial flights; and then as of June 18th, 2007 required that all airline carriers departing from within Canadian soil screen all passengers, whether domestic or international, through Transport Canada's *Specified Persons List*, with the intention of securing Canada's skies and aviation industry from the threats of domestic and global terrorism. When the plan was publicly unveiled on Friday October 27th, 2006, the Canadian Broadcasting Corporation reported Public Safety Minister Stockwell Day saying the following:

1   The Vancouver Sun Editorial Staff, 'No-fly List Won't Thwart any Terrorist', 17 January 2007, *The Vancouver Sun*, http://www.canada.com/vancouversun/news/editorial/story.html?id=633061d1-cc09-42dc-a797-578c055aa704.

2   CBC News Services, 'Critics Alarmed by Canada's No-fly List', 18 June 2007, http://www.cbc.ca/canada/ottawa/story/2007/06/18/no-fly-list.html; see also Gloria Galloway, 'No-fly List Grounds up to 2,000 People', *The Globe and Mail*, 19 June 2007, http://www.theglobeandmail.com/servlet/story/LAC.20070619.NOFLY19/PPVStory?URL_Article_ID=LAC.20070619.NOFLY19&DENIED=1; and CTV.ca News Staff, 'As Many as 2,000 Names on No-fly List', 19 June 2007, CTV.ca, http://www.ctv.ca/servlet/ArticleNews/story/CTVNews/20070619/cdn_no_fly_list_070619/20070619?hub=Canada; and New Democratic Party of Canada Press Release, 'NDP Rejects Harper's No-fly List', 19 June 2007, Ottawa, ON, http://www.ndp.ca/page/5460.

3   Andrew Mayeda, 'Gov't May Use Biometric Data to Back up No-fly List', *CanWest News Service*, 18 June 2007, http://www.canada.com/reginaleaderpost/news/story.html?id=b9e9a4ec-ebd7-469a-9f16-0d28f6a91152.

4   Transport Canada, 'Canada's New Government Announces Details of Passenger Protect Program', 27 October 2007, http://www.tc.gc.ca/mediaroom/releases/nat/2006/06-gc014e.htm.

Recent events such as the alleged terror plot in the United Kingdom highlight the importance of a program like Passenger Protect. We must remember that Canada is not immune to the threat of terrorism and we must remain vigilant.[5]

As of June 18th, 2007 remaining vigilant 'to the threat of terrorism' – to alleged terror plots – means that individuals 'calculated' to be 'terrorist' or 'predicted' to commit a 'life-threatening crime' involving airline security in Canada will be placed on the *Specified Persons List*, as decided on a case by case basis by an Advisory Group headed up by Transport Canada, and including members of The Royal Canadian Mounted Police (RCMP) and The Canadian Security Intelligence Service (CSIS). On October 27th, 2006 Transport Canada announced the criteria for the inclusion of individuals on the *Specified Persons List*:[6]

- An individual who is or has been involved in a terrorist group, and who, it can reasonably be suspected, will endanger the security of any aircraft or aerodrome or the safety of the public, passengers or crew members;
- An individual who has been convicted of one or more serious and life-threatening crimes against aviation security;
- An individual who has been convicted of one or more serious and life-threatening offences and who may attack or harm an air carrier, passengers or crew members.

Inspired by its American counterpart which had been re-invigorated in the wake of the 9/11 attacks through the enacting of the US Aviation and Transportation Security Act on November 19th 2001, which formally established the Transportation Security Administration (TSA) as the administer of the US no-fly list and was subsequently moved and housed in the US Department of Homeland Security in March of 2003, Canada's no-fly list program resulted from the *Public Safety Act of 2002*, which bequeaths the federal Transport Minister with the legal right to take measures to identify individuals who pose risks to aviation security, as well as the legal right to administer and maintain a list of such individuals[7]. Unlike the US government, who will not divulge the criteria by which people's names are included on the list, the Canadian government has provided the vague criteria outlined above for the inclusion of cases on the list.

Where in the US the number of people on the list fluctuates, is kept secret, and is acknowledged by the US Department of Homeland Security to contain the names of tens of thousands of people[8] (where more independent estimates actually place the number in the hundreds of

---

5   CBC News, 'Ottawa Plans No-fly List by 2007', 27 October 2006, http://www.cbc.ca/
    canada/story/2006/10/27/flying-rules.html.
6   Transport Canada, 'Passenger Protect: Questions and Answers', accessed 15 September 2007,
    http://www.tc.gc.ca/vigilance/sep/passenger_protect/Q&A.htm#4.
7   Caroline Alphonso, 'First Day of "No-fly" List Trouble Free', *The Globe and Mail*, 19 June 2007,
    http://www.theglobeandmail.com/servlet/story/LAC.20070619.DAYONE19/PPVStory/?DENIED=1;
    see also Canada's *BILL C-17: THE PUBLIC SAFETY ACT*, 2002, Amended March 2003, http://
    www.parl.gc.ca/common/bills_ls.asp?Parl=37&Ses=2&ls=c17.
8   Alphonso, 'First Day of "No-fly" List Trouble Free'.

thousands[9]), in Canada the number of names on the list also fluctuates, but was promised to contain the names of no more than 1,000 people when the program was first announced.[10] Ironically, on the first day of its formal incorporation into Canadian aviation culture on June 18th, 2007, this promise was already broken. Transport Minister Lawrence Cannon acknowledged that the list had already mushroomed to some 2,000 names, doubling in size in under a day.[11]

Regarding appeal processes for getting names removed from the no-fly lists, the US Congress legislated in 2004 that the TSA create a system that allows people to correct inaccurate information that misidentifies them on their no-fly list, while also directing the Department of Homeland Security to create an oversight board to ensure that anti-terrorism measures do not infringe upon individual privacy, human rights, and civil liberties.[12] In Canada any person who has been misidentified on the list has the right to appeal to Transport Canada's 'Office of Reconsideration'. Canadian citizens also have the right to take the case of misidentifications on the *Specified Persons List* to Federal Court.[13]

The emergence of Canada's *Specified Person List* will be examined in this chapter as a case for list technologies understood as operating in apparatuses of security and assemblages of police, which correlate the techniques of computers and statistics and operate in a global milieu of circulation and classification. In this correlation of power or governmentality, practices surrounding the delimitation and policing of the movement of risky elements through statistical worth/risk assessment techniques, technologies, and uses, are yet again redeployed, now serving and enforcing divisive fractures through a security assemblage critically supported by the list. Building on the theoretical analysis and discursive threads constructed in the previous chapters, this chapter interrogates global news and popular culture media sources, spanning a time period that begins just over one year (March 2006) before the implementation of Canada's *Specified Persons List* on June 18th, 2007, up until November of 2007, probing for discursive regularities and patterns surrounding the no-fly list apparatuses of security. As such, this work aims to understand no-fly lists as a part of and partially constituted in and through national and global popular culture news sources and information channels.

The emergence of Canada's no-fly list epitomizes how the correlations of power that lists pivot, as unloosened in the preceding chapters, can be exhumed from the woodwork of history and propelled into an analysis of contemporary operations of power that pivot on computers, risk assessment techniques, and global classification infrastructures, underpinned by the critical practice of delimiting and policing lists of human beings as a means and ends to seeing and doing local, national and global security. The practices associated with probing our ever-expanding and ever-disordered entropic global classification infrastructures for regularities and patterns that constitute threatening cases – people reduced to worth/risk

9   BBC News Services, 'US "to Halve" No-fly Watch List', 18 January 2007, http://news.bbc. co.uk/2/hi/americas/6274221.stm.
10   Transport Canada, 'Canada's New Government Announces Details of Passenger Protect Program'.
11   CTV.ca News Staff, 'As Many as 2,000 Names on No-fly List'.
12   Alphonso, 'First Day of "No-fly" List Trouble Free'.
13   Transport Canada, 'Passenger Protect: Questions and Answers'.

assessment scores – comes to the fore of this interrogation of contemporary popular news surrounding Canadian and international no-fly list security technologies, particularly around cases of misidentification.

Anyone who has flown into or out of America, or any large Western society's airport in the post-9/11 era, and has been pulled over by an over-zealous customs agent, has certainly felt the chilling effects of the apparatuses of security, particularly when the 'freedom of movement' that Foucault's *Governmentality*[14] ensures is suspended. Agamben's[15] biopolitical perspective would argue that the suspension of rights that detention in such enclosures imply is further evidence of 'bare life' as the fundamental essence and unit of contemporary political life; sovereign spaces where the layers of the onion that both shield and constitute our political identities are at once revealed and at the same time stripped away. For the moment, despite which biopolitical analysis is engaged, suffice it to say, 'what happens when you book an airline ticket'[16] is increasingly what happens when you make a phone call, send an email, engage in a debit/credit card-based commercial transaction, or drive a GPS (Global Positioning System) enabled vehicle – your actions and your person are registered and classified, transformed into delimited, tracked, and policed objects; bits of information in global classification infrastructures, which efface the boundaries between people, objects, and knowledge.

Legal, Technoscientific, and Popular Conceptions of No-fly Lists

What pre-existing ideas underpin no-fly lists and what real-world entities do they represent? An everyday common-sense answer to such a line of questioning would suggest that no-fly lists are underpinned by national and international laws and security agendas, and contain and represent the names of known and alleged terrorists who would seek to board airplanes and wreak havoc in the sky. But such an answer would be facile, for as the work of Paula Treichler[17] in 'AIDS, Homophobia and Biomedical Discourse' has clearly demonstrated, our common-sense view of language may be that it transmits pre-existing ideas and represents real-world entities, when put to the test, it does neither. Treichler demonstrated through her interrogation of popular news sources that AIDS is less a clear-cut disease entity and more an invented label, classification, and technoscientific cultural construction given birth to in scientific naming practices and discourses in popular news sources, which carry with them stigmatizations of imagined threatening bodies. This chapter is intended to demonstrate that threats listed on no-fly lists are equally an invention; in this case not for a clear-cut disease entity, but nonetheless a threatening disease in metaphor – the contemporary epidemic spread and need for policing of viral 'terrorist' bodies.

---

14 Foucault, '1 February 1978 *Governmentality*'.
15 Agamben, *Homo Sacer*.
16 Colin J. Bennett, 'What Happens when You Book an Airline Ticket? The Collecting and Processing of Passenger Data Post-9/11', in Elia Zureik and Mark B. Salter (eds), *Global Surveillance and Policing: Borders, Security, Identity*, Cullompton; Portland: Willan, 2005, pp. 113-138.
17 Paula A. Treichler, 'AIDS, Homophobia, and Biomedical Discourse: An Epidemic of Signification', in D. Crimp and L. Bersani (eds), *AIDS: Cultural Analysis, Cultural Activism*, Cambridge: MIT Press, 1988, pp. 31-86.

Just as Treichler argued that the nature of AIDS is constructed through the language and discourses of medicine and science, I argue that no-fly lists, and also the 'nature' of terrorists, are constructed through the technoscientific language of computers, statistics, risk assessment, and global classification infrastructures, which retain the legacy of closed-world security discourses and their underpinning 'us' versus 'them', 'good' versus 'evil' dichotomies. The construction of no-fly lists and their constituent 'terrorists' are only 'true' or 'real' insofar as they help to successfully guide local, national, and international security agendas, intended to further separate (or shield) 'us' from 'them' through the streamlining and converging of global classification infrastructures, in a series of self-elaborating processes.

In this way, I argue that the term 'no-fly list' constructs the 'terrorist' anew, shifting the epistemological locus from physical, corporeal bodies and the potential risks they pose, to identity-based representations of people, cases, and elements circulating in global classification infrastructures which efface the boundaries between living beings, things, and knowledge, and at the same time make intelligible the greatest pervasive and ubiquitous 'epidemic' of our time – the terrorist threat. The more 'terrorists' are reified on lists, the more we see how lists serve the construction of imagined 'threatening' bodies in a self-elaborating discursive process that clearly exhibits the hallmark of the technologies of security, namely double integration. The delimitation of populations of worth/risk assessed objects further authorizes, reinforces, and validates the ongoing and pervasive reduction of people to worth/risk assessment scores and to listed elements for policing. This self-referential and self-elaborating 'double integration effect' of the technologies of security[18] serves to efface the boundaries between living beings, objects, and knowledge, and at the same time to redeploy the technologies themselves, further correlating and streamlining the global security policies, practices, and classification infrastructures they themselves constitute.

There is no doubt that terrorists do represent real dangers, threatening and killing real human beings. Because of this it is tempting – and in some instances imperative – to view risk assessment techniques and global classification infrastructures as providing a technoscientific discourse about terrorist threats closer to the 'truth' or 'reality' of what constitutes a 'terrorist' than what we are capable of making intelligible ourselves in our everyday lives. After all, most of us have never knowingly come into contact with a 'terrorist' and therefore have little but popular conceptions to build our ideas upon. The use of computers to probe entropic global classification infrastructures, using statistical techniques to calculate and predict patterns of terrorist movements, and in turn delimiting threatening cases listed on no-fly rosters for policing, is a cultural construction that would seemingly offer reassurance in a highly insecure, but increasingly connected global milieu of circulation, where we are told invisible threats lurk everywhere.

The question of what constitutes a 'terrorist', who poses threats, as well as the policies, practices, and discourses surrounding how names are delimited on no-fly lists – an increasingly pervasive how-to strategy for containing the overall 'epidemic' spread of threats post-9/11 – is

---

18 Foucault, '29 March 1978'.

at once a question of local, national, and global law and governance, of disciplinary techno-scientific systems, and what Treichler has called an 'epidemic of meanings or significations'. Following Treichler, the use of the term epidemic here 'refers to the exponential compounding of meanings as opposed to the simpler spread of a term through a population'.[19] Indeed, epidemics of meanings and significations surrounding 'the war on terror' are crucial to explore, for try as we might to understand and treat 'terrorist' threats as what Haraway[20] has called 'problems in code' that can be delimited and policed through conjunctions of juridical-disciplinary mechanisms of security like no-fly lists, no such contemporary listing apparatus has ever succeeded in stopping a known terror threat. Yet despite such ironies, meanings of what constitutes 'terrorists' and the installation of security conjunctures like no-fly lists to both call 'them' into reality and at the same time police them, continue to multiply and spread wildly at an extraordinary rate, broadening into what I call no-fill-in-the-blank list culture in the next chapter.

Also like Treichler, who derives 'signification' from the linguistic work of Ferdinand de Saussure the term is used here to call attention to the way in which 'no-fly list' operations are increasingly organizing our conceptions of and language surrounding 'terrorists', and discussions on how to control threats to other social contexts and institutions – how we are increasingly doing and seeing security through watch lists. As such, no-fly lists can be understood as key signifiers of contemporary terrorist realities. In this way, we can also begin to see how despite a no-fly list policy and program that has been highly contested in the US since its increased use and exponential growth post-9/11, the operations and language of 'watch lists' are proliferating like wildfire in the US and worldwide in many areas of everyday life.[21]

This 'epidemic of meanings' is readily apparent in the complex, contradictory, and chaotic assemblage of understandings of 'no-fly lists', 'terrorists', and further, 'watch lists', which have emerged in the time frame studied here. The enumeration of some of the ways no-fly lists have been characterized in the global press suggest their enormous power to generate meanings pertaining to terrorist threats and local, national, and global security realities, namely:

1. As crucial key tools in the war on terror.[22]
2. As utterly useless in the war on terror.[23]
3. As protecting innocent citizens in their rights to mobility and free movement, 'only bad guys are on these lists'.[24]

---

19 Treichler, 'AIDS, Homophobia, and Biomedical Discourse', p. 32.
20 Haraway, *Modest Witness@Second_Millenium*.
21 Ryan Singel, 'A Watch List is Born', *Wired News*, 4 April 2007, http://www.wired.com/politics/onlinerights/news/2007/04/watchlist3.
22 Epitomized by US Department of Homeland Security Secretary Michael Chertoff's assertions of a global surveillance society in Michael Geist, 'Privacy Threats no Longer "Terra Incognita"', *The Ottawa Citizen*, 2 October 2007, p. D.1.
23 United Press International (UPI), 'No-fly List Said Growing into Uselessness', 11 June 2006, *The Washington Times*, http://washingtontimes.com/upi/20060611-023518-2050r.htm; also in Faisal Kutty, 'Too Guilty to Fly, Too Innocent to Charge', 18 March 2007, *Media Monitors Network*, http://usa.mediamonitors.net/content/view/full/41774.
24 Mimi Hall, 'Fliers Headed to USA Face Scrutiny', 12 July 2006, *USA TODAY*, http://www.usatoday.com/travel/news/2006-07-11-flier-checks_x.html.

4. As abetting terrorism in their own right, providing a vetting system for would-be terrorist candidates. Those who make it through the lines being the best candidates.[25]
5. As rendering privacy law irrelevant.[26]
6. As presenting a real danger for people misidentified on them.[27] As misidentifying and mislabeling innocents, removing their fundamental rights and liberties, subjecting them to mistreatment.[28]
7. As perfectible technological solutions in iterative development.[29]
8. As highly fallible techno-social systems that limit civil rights and liberties.[30]
9. As tools for individual, local, national, and global security.[31]
10. As tools that can be misused for carrying out political agendas[32] and revenge (most notably the case of Senator Edward Kennedy of the US appearing on the no-fly list).[33]
11. As a political tool that could wind up in the wrong hands.[34]
12. As broadening beyond securing terrorist threats, to a plethora of elements that pose risks to all populations, including health threats, gang threats, etc.[35]

---

25 Bruce Schneier, 'They're Watching', *Forbes Magazine*, 8 January 2007, http://www.forbes.com/free_forbes/2007/0108/032.html.
26 Don Butler, 'Privacy Commissioner Wary of No-fly List', 16 May 2006, http://www.canada.com/ottawacitizen/news/story.html?id=eecd8149-295c-43b0-b095-5e7963e6b182.
27 CBC News, 'US No-fly Lists still Grounding Canadians, Says Civil Rights Group', 9 July 2006, http://www.cbc.ca/story/canada/national/2006/07/07/no-fly.html.
28 Canadian Press, 'Back off on Arar: Ambassador Tells Stockwell Day to Lay off Trying to Get Canadian off U.S. Security List', 24 January 2007, *The Toronto Star*, http://www.thestar.com/defaultNews/article/174407.
29 Carolyn Canville, 'Flying Blind? No-fly List Way off the Mark', aired 27 February 2007, *FoxNews*, http://www.myfoxhouston.com/myfox/pages/Home/Detail;jsessionid=43EEBB1857CA566904B-7CC3642E17CD9?contentId=2512844&version=6&locale=EN-US&layoutCode=VSTY&page-Id=1.1.1&sflg=1.
30 Guy Gugliotta, 'Data Mining still Needs a Clue to Be Effective', *The Washington Post*, 19 June 2006, http://www.washingtonpost.com/wp-dyn/content/article/2006/06/18/AR2006061800524.html
31 Associated Press, 'US No-fly List Reroutes Plane', 8 August 2006, *The Edmonton Sun*, http://www.edmontonsun.com/News/World/2006/08/08/1724189-sun.html.
32 Murray Dobbin, 'Deep Integration: The Plan to Disappear Canada', 11 June 2007, *Rabble.ca: News for the Rest of Us*, http://www.rabble.ca/columnists_full.shtml?x=59973.
33 Steve Kroft, 'Unlikely Terrorists on No-fly List: List Includes President of Bolivia, Dead 9/11 Hijackers', originally aired on CBS Broadcasting Corporation's *60 Minutes*, 8 October 2006, producer Ira Rosen, transcript: http://www.cbsnews.com/stories/2006/10/05/60minutes/print-able2066624.shtml.
34 Globe and Mail News Staff, 'Government Admits that No-fly List Could be Misused', 6 June 2007, *Globe and Mail*, http://www.theglobeandmail.com/servlet/story/LAC.20070606.NATS06-4/TPStory/National; also in Richard Brennan, 'Inquiry Told of No-fly List Danger', 5 June 2007, *The Toronto Star*, http://www.thestar.com/News/article/221760; Canadian Press Services, 'No-fly List Will End up in Foreign Hands', 6 June 2007, *The Edmonton Sun*, http://www.edmontonsun.com/News/Canada/2007/06/06/4238186-sun.html; Jim Bronskill, 'Ottawa's No-fly List Won't End Use of US Roster in Canada', 22 May 2007, *The Globe and Mail*, http://www.theglobeandmail.com/servlet/story/RTGAM.20070522.wnoflylist0522/BNStory/National/home.
35 Singel, 'A Watch List is Born'.

Such contradictory conceptualizations of no-fly lists are also coupled with fragmentary inter-
pretations of the specific elements of the legal policies and procedures surrounding them and
how classifications of 'terrorists' and their 'organizations' are derived and correlated in the first
place. Confusion over whom and what constitutes a terrorist threat and terrorist organization
respectively, have made the misidentification and mislabeling of innocents on terrorist watch
lists, like no-fly lists, a common and routine news story.[36] While many still believe that only
'bad guys' are on 'watch lists', Canadians are increasingly learning that no-fly list culture
means that the misidentification and mislabeling of innocents as threats is becoming a more
common experience of everyday life[37]. Indeed, according to global news sources, the misidentification of innocents on no-fly lists is quite clearly a much bigger story than their role in
protecting innocents from terrorist threats, as no 'no-fly list' has ever succeeded in 'nabbing'
a single terrorist threat:[38]

> In the United States, more than 100,000 people have been "accidentally" harassed by
> the no-fly list, and it has caught a grand total of zero terrorists or criminals. Although it
> has caught dozens of police, military officers, small children and practically everyone
> with the name Mohammed, I've yet to see anyone claim that it's doing a good job.[39]

In this way, no-fly lists can be read as instilling more of a fear for one's own self being misidentified, or in Agamben's terms, for the exposure of one's own 'bare life', over and above
any reassurance they would seemingly offer in an uncertain and dangerous world inhabited
by circulating terrorists. After all, as the Americans have seen, if Senator Edward Kennedy can
be on the US no-fly list, why wouldn't the names of other innocent Americans be there too?[40]

We cannot effectively understand the implications of the emergence of Canada's *Specified
Persons List* if we approach it exclusively from the lens of legal and constitutional rights and
liberties or technoscientific practices. Popular conceptions and myths surrounding no-fly lists
and what constitutes a 'terrorist' in general need to be understood as well. The emergence of
Canada's *Specified Persons List* represents not only a new legal imperative and conception for
airlines and air travel, but also an emerging way of seeing and doing broader governmentality;
pivoting on the delimitation and policing of the movement of people and things that pose risks,
and taking for granted that they be on *watch lists*.

No matter how much we may desire thinking about Canada's *Specified Persons List* as an
exclusively juridical-legal disciplinary mechanism designed to protect citizens and try to ana-

---

36 Louise Dickson, 'No-fly List Snags 78-Year-Old Saanich "Mr. Nice Guy"', *Victoria Times-Col-
    onist*, 19 June 2007, http://www.canada.com/victoriatimescolonist/news/story.html?id=-
    fa518d78-1fb7-426e-9429-beef51de2f8a&k=99491.
37 CanWest News Services, 'No-fly for You, Woman Told', *The Province*, 6 March 2006, http://www.
    canada.com/theprovince/news/story.html?id=e6ca1d58-2bfe-4b30-a300-916c774aa25f.
38 Canville, 'Flying Blind?'.
39 Nicholas Cotton, 'No-fly in the Ointment', 30 October 2006, *The Globe and Mail*, http://www.
    theglobeandmail.com/servlet/story/LAC.20061030.LETTERS30-10/PPVStory/?DENIED=1.
40 A case mentioned ad infinitum in news reports, but most notably as a focus in CBS News Televi-
    sion's *60 Minutes* piece. See also: Kroft, 'Unlikely Terrorists on No-fly List'.

lyze it as such, it is also a global social metaphor, representing the semantic and linguistic work of Canadians and populations of the world making sense of a 'war on terror', conducted on a global stage, in an era of pervasive and ubiquitous worth/risk assessment scores, classification infrastructures, and milieus of circulation. I am arguing, not that the legal dimensions of Canada's *Specified Persons List* are to be ignored, but rather that the technoscientific, social, and metaphorical dimensions are far more central than we might think and therefore merit privileging and intensive scrutiny in their own right. In order to effectively analyze Canada's *Specified Persons List* and develop future policies and procedures surrounding its existence, we must not only take its legal dimensions into account, but also how it operates as a discourse, what it means for how Canadians see themselves, and how we do 'security' in the world in which we live.

Moreover, our cultural construction of no-fly lists as tools in a war on terrorism are based not on a legal, objective, or technoscientifically determined reality of terrorist threats to aviation and other areas of global society, but rather upon what we are told about this reality – this ongoing war on terror – and how we choose to talk about it. Therefore, there are no distinctions but rather a continuum between popular, technoscientific, and legal discourses surrounding no-fly lists, which are in many ways the same as 'a continuum between controversies in daily life and those occurring in the laboratory'.[41] These controversies play out and are revealed in language and metaphor in an indeterminate space where everyday life is increasingly circumscribed by digital technologies and experimented upon through data mining and risk assessment techniques. Consider the thoughts of security 'expert' Bruce Schneier on this state of affairs, specifically pertaining to 'risk assessment' and 'no-fly lists' in an article in *Forbes Magazine*, January 8th, 2007, entitled 'They're Watching':

> [The Automated Targeting System] assigns a "risk assessment" score to people entering or leaving the country, or engaging in import or export activity. This score, and the information used to derive it, can be shared with federal, state, local and even foreign governments. It can be used if you apply for a government job, grant, license, contract or other benefit. It can be shared with nongovernmental organizations and individuals in the course of an investigation. In some circumstances private contractors can get it, even those outside the country. And it will be saved for 40 years. Little is known about this program. Its bare outlines were disclosed in the Federal Register in October. We do know that the score is partially based on details of your flight record – where you're from, how you bought your ticket, where you're sitting, any special meal requests – or on motor vehicle records, as well as on information from crime, watch list and other databases ... any system like this will generate so many false alarms as to be completely unusable. In 2005 Customs & Border Protection processed 431 million people. Assuming an unrealistic model that identifies terrorists (and innocents) with 99.9% accuracy, that's still 431,000 false alarms annually. The number of false alarms will be much higher than that. The no-fly list is filled with inaccuracies; we've all read about innocent people named David Nelson who can't fly without hours-long harassment.

---

41   Bruno Latour and Steve Woolgar, *Laboratory Life: The Construction of Scientific Facts*, Princeton: Princeton University Press, 1986, p. 281.

Airline data, too, are riddled with errors. The odds of this program's being implemented securely, with adequate privacy protections, are not good. Last year I participated in a government working group to assess the security and privacy of a similar program developed by the Transportation Security Administration, called Secure Flight. After five years and $100 million spent, the program still can't achieve the simple task of matching airline passengers against terrorist watch lists.[42]

Based on such an assessment from a highly regarded security expert, should we be comfortable with legal policies being enacted that take as their basis technoscientific procedures involving the automated probing of data environments and reductive risk assessment scores to identify and list human beings? Moreover, hearkening to Cold War players and the origins of the no-fly list apparatus' closed-world discursive legacy, Schneier concludes with sharp criticism:

There is something un-American about a government program that uses secret criteria to collect dossiers on innocent people and shares that information with various agencies, all without any oversight. It's the sort of thing you'd expect from the former Soviet Union or East Germany or China. And it doesn't make us any safer from terrorism.[43]

But the point here is not whether this security expert is right or wrong, but rather that ambiguity and uncertainty are features of technoscientific practices surrounding the risk assessment of terrorists, and as such are uncertainties – like those unearthed in the laboratory – that must be socially and linguistically managed. Almost a year to the day before Canada implemented its no-fly list, 19 June 2006, Guy Gugliotta in an article entitled 'Data Mining Still Needs a Clue to Be Effective' in *The Washington Post* writes:

Computers can jump to conclusions just like humans ... To make the correct inference requires deep, intellectual thinking; these systems are significantly less reliable than lie detector tests. Still, even the best technicians are going to find themselves searching multiple blind allies in navigating a mega-database such as telephone logs, the experts said, so much so that the time needed to clear false positives may outweigh the odds of finding a terrorist.[44]

What we are told is at stake here are innocent peoples' lives, threatened at every turn by terrorists who lurk in every corner of an increasingly globalized, yet highly connected and (in this contradictory way) shrinking world. What we tend to take for granted in this conception is that the delimitation and policing of terrorist movements takes as its basis legal and technoscientific amalgamations of network technologies, automated statistical risk assessment techniques, and global information infrastructures, whose outputs for policing are watch lists.

---

42 Schneier, 'They're Watching'.
43 Schneier, 'They're Watching'.
44 Gugliotta, 'Data Mining Still Needs a Clue to Be Effective'.

It is important to note that no-fly lists in addition to listing threatening human elements, also contain everyday household objects. Headlines like 'Feds Add Juice, Sprays to No-fly List'[45] from *The Ottawa Sun* in August of 2006 have become commonplace. It's now taken for granted that both living beings and things have unique 'security identities' and associated scores, and that all populations as such, animate and inanimate, must be screened before flight, whether by government officials or by the subjects of such disciplinary mechanisms themselves.

> The disciplinary mechanism also constantly codifies in terms of the permitted and forbidden, or rather the obligatory and the forbidden, which means that the point on which the disciplinary mechanism focuses is not so much the things one must not do, as the things that must be done.[46]

In this way, contemporary governmentality of the milieu of global aero-circulation can be characterized as redeploying a disciplinary space, that through the positing of prohibitive norms (such as the increasingly complex no-fly list of carry-on items), offers prescriptive remedies for 'secure' circulation by placing the responsibility for 'the things that must be done' onto the passengers themselves, who are increasingly trained to 'screen' their own bags and selves, ensuring they do not contain prohibited no-fly list items. The taken-for-granted nature of the effacing of boundaries between people and inanimate objects, as well as technoscience's pivotal role in such processes, is exemplified in a September 2006 *Forbes Magazine* article entitled 'Will it Fly?':

> "Since the initial total ban [on liquids] experts from around the government and our national labs have conducted extensive explosives testing to get a better understanding of this specific threat," said Hawley [Kip Hawley, assistant secretary of Homeland Security for the TSA], speaking yesterday at the Ronald Reagan National Airport in Washington, D.C. "While this novel type of liquid explosive is now an ongoing part of the terrorist playbook and must be dealt with, we now know enough to say that a total ban is no longer needed from a security point of view." So what's now off the no-fly list? Vindicated toiletries include lip gloss, saline solution, shampoo, toothpaste, shaving cream, gel deodorant and liquid antibacterial soap – all of which were banned last week but are now allowed in 3-ounce packages. Lipstick and solid deodorant were never subject to the ban and are therefore still allowed on commercial flights. And, there are some oddities in what's permitted and not in the cabin – yes on knitting needles, no on pool cues, for example.[47]

Herein we see no-fly list security discourses figuring the laboratory as central to the fabrication of factual, or truthful, knowledge about risky elements and populations. Contemporary

---

45 CP (Canadian Press Services), 'Feds Add Juice, Sprays to No-fly List', 13 August 2006, *The Ottawa Sun,* http://ottsun.canoe.ca/News/National/2006/08/13/1752098-sun.html.
46 Foucault, '18 January 1978', p. 46.
47 Sophia Banay, 'Will It Fly?', *Forbes Magazine*, 26 September 2006, http://www.forbes.com/travel/2006/09/26/travel-ban-changes_life_travel_cx_sb_0926airban.html.

apparatuses of security make no distinction whatsoever between the detection of human and inanimate threats to aviation, and all the while self-elaborate 'the laboratory' as the pervasive and ubiquitous site of security solutions. Indeed, the laboratory is also the ultimate 'vindicator' for establishing whether 'toiletries' or innocent people are risks or threats and for placing them on lists. Building on Foucault,[48] it is argued that the challenge for governmentality in the global milieus of circulation installed by the apparatuses of security is to 'train' people and things alike to be self-screeners so as not to be misidentified as 'threats', and in the event that they are, how to cope and manage these 'inconveniences' until such time as the technoscientific laboratory susses out the situation and makes prescriptions for what can and cannot circulate.

In the face of such colossal uncertainty surrounding who and what constitute a 'threat', it seems only reasonable that our conceptions of 'terrorist' would differ wildly and often derive from stereotypical notions and racial profiles, since the majority of 'us' have never engaged with 'them' – known terrorists. As Treichler argues, 'what is distasteful in peoples conceptions'[49] must nonetheless be considered, and in this way there are few differences between the AIDS and 'terrorist' epidemics in terms of the oft-discriminatory operations of significations, meanings, and misconceptions:

> To label them misconceptions implies what? Wrongful birth? That only facts can give birth to proper conceptions and only science can give birth to facts?[50]

Despite our best efforts, there appears to be no exact science on the horizon to wage war on this terrorist epidemic, one that could accurately and precisely define, predict, and give unequivocal fact to a naturalized 'terrorist' class. And so we are left on the one hand with vague, if not 'black-box' government criteria, policies, and procedures by which terrorists and their organizations are constituted, and on the other, and more pervasively, with our widespread popular conceptions of what a terrorist is, which post-9/11 sadly tends to center on racial profiles built on Muslim stereotypes. In this way, the argument here is that there is no clear boundary between the facticity of legal, technoscientific, and popular conceptions of no-fly lists wherein 'us' versus 'them', stereotyped, ambiguous, cloudy, and confusing definitions of 'terrorists' circulate in osmotic discursive fashion. This is but the operations of an economy of discourses and more profoundly, this represents the ethical and moral implications of reducing human lives to scores, fracturing 'threatening' elements and labeling 'dangerous' cases in an uncertain, but increasingly automated and classified world; and as such these issues must be deeply and critically considered in future policy.

Writing about 'The International Data Protection and Privacy Commissioner's Conference' in September of 2007, Michael Geist in *The Ottawa Citizen* articulates the moral and ethical conundrum inherent in blurred techno-legal boundaries, describing how the conference emphasized,

---

48 Foucault, '1 February 1978 *Governmentality*'.
49 Treichler, 'AIDS, Homophobia, and Biomedical Discourse', p. 36.
50 Treichler, 'AIDS, Homophobia, and Biomedical Discourse', p. 36.

...the growing 'toolkit' of responses, including privacy audits of public and private sector organizations, privacy impact assessments that are used to gauge the effect of new regulations and corporate initiatives, trust seals that include corporate compliance programs, and emphasis on global co-operation in a world where personal data slips effortlessly across borders. While the effectiveness of these measures has improved in recent years, there remained a pervasive sense that these responses are inadequate. Part of the unease arises from the growing realization that the legal foundation of privacy law is being rendered increasingly irrelevant.[51]

Canadian privacy law at its core relies on two fundamental principles – those of 'notice' and 'consent' – and these 'twin pillars' are designed to ensure that Canadian consumers are notified of and should consent to the collection, use, and disclosure of their personal 'identifiable' information. As Geist notes, 'Critics argue that both notice and consent today are little more than legal fictions, as consumers ignore overly complex notices and shrinking technology makes it virtually impossible to obtain informed consumer consent'.[52] Furthermore, Canadian privacy law also makes distinctions between 'personally identifiable' (legally protected) and 'non-identifiable' (not legally protected) information, which global classification technologies, practices, and infrastructures are also rendering irrelevant. Geist writes:

Technology threatens the ability to easily distinguish between the two as powerful computers and ever-expanding databases make it easier to identify individuals from what was once thought to be non- identifiable information. In a room full of privacy advocates, [Michael] Chertoff [US Secretary of Homeland Security] came not with a peace offering, but rather a confrontational challenge. He unapologetically made the case for greater surveillance, in which governments collect an ever-increasing amount of data about their citizens in the name of security. In the process, his vision of a broad surveillance society – supported by massive databases of biometric data collected from hundreds of millions of people – presented a chilling future.[53]

Chertoff's assertion of a broad security and surveillance society epitomizes not only the legal and technoscientific transformations of how we now materially identify and constitute 'terrorists', but also a new inscribed meaning for their bodies, namely as listed objects. What changed for Canadians with the implementation of the *Specified Persons List* were not so much the terrorist and threatening bodies as material entities in their own right, but the way we would now construct them linguistically and understand them metaphorically, as objects on lists – the fundamental pivot of Chertoff's 'broad surveillance society'. With each such announcement and articulation of the fundamental use of risk assessment techniques and global classification infrastructures in the war on terror, not only do these apparatuses of security further sublimate themselves into Canadian social woodwork, but also a new dominant meaning for 'terrorists' is invoked, reinforced, and validated: that 'threatening' people

---

51 Geist, 'Privacy Threats no Longer "Terra Incognita"'.
52 Geist, 'Privacy Threats no Longer "Terra Incognita"'.
53 Geist, 'Privacy Threats no Longer "Terra Incognita"'.

and things are listed; that such lists are subject to sharing and manipulation between and by corporations, governments, and nations; and that such lists are rife with misidentified, innocent people.

In this way, no-fly lists are to be understood not only as 'double integration' technologies of security, but also as a linguistic and material reality; 'a duality inherent in all linguistic entities',[54] wherein the 'terrorist' label associated with 'no-fly list' discourse can carry with it highly dehumanizing and possibly life-threatening consequences for those listed as such. Without such an understanding and vision, we cannot begin to read the story of no-fly lists accurately, nor formulate intelligent interventions surrounding them in the future. No case better exemplifies this than that of Canadian Maher Arar, who, as a result of having his name appear on the US no-fly list, was extradited to Syria where he endured over one year of imprisonment and torture, and subsequently, despite having been declared innocent of any terrorist actions or affiliations by the Canadian Government, has yet to receive an apology from the US Government, and have his name removed from their no-fly list.[55]

Intelligent Interventions into No-fly Listing

All of the above is not to say that intelligent interventions have not helped shape the discourse surrounding the *Specified Persons List*; quite the contrary. Although over the timeline studied here the Canadian Government remained 'tightlipped' about its 'terrorist criteria' and whether, how, and when it would share its no-fly list data with the United States and other foreign governments,[56] Canada's Privacy Commissioner Jennifer Stoddart certainly did not, warning repeatedly about the infringement on individual Canadians' rights to privacy and the destructions of the 'twin pillars' of privacy law – notice and consent – that the sharing of the *Specified Persons List* with the United States would imply.[57]

On June 8th, 2007 CanWest News Service's Don Butler wrote in *The Ottawa Citizen* that 'Stoddart said the list represents a "serious incursion" into the privacy and mobility rights of Canadians'.[58] Under the program, which took effect for all domestic and international flights in Canada on June 18th, 2007, anyone deemed a threat would now be prevented from boarding. Further on, he noted even more critical warnings from Stoddart, who on June 17th warned Canadian citizens that,

---

54 Treichler, 'AIDS, Homophobia, and Biomedical Discourse', p. 40.
55 Canadian Press, 'Back Off on Arar'.
56 Don Butler, Canada Tight-Lipped over No-fly List Plans: No Doubt Information Will Be Shared With Allies, Experts Say', CanWest News Service, *The Vancouver Province*, 15 January 2007, http://www.canada.com/vancouversun/news/story.html?id=2340027b-945c-4a6e-8039-5db923f9d036.
57 Don Butler, 'No-fly List Could be a Nightmare: Will Passengers Expect to Be Challenged?', 8 June 2007, CanWest News Service *The Vancouver Province*, http://www.canada.com/theprovince/news/story.html?id=4e7e91cd-4701-4b47-b18f-948e86800c07.
58 Also reported in Ronda MacCharles, 'Canada to Launch No-fly List in June', *The Toronto Star*, 12 May 2007, http://www.thestar.com/News/article/213185.

...the increasingly intrusive use of your identity in order to make decisions about you as an individual are pretty drastic. This could turn into quite a nightmare for some ordinary citizens. Every time we go to the airport, do we expect to be challenged? That may be the new world. Increasingly one wonders how effective is this going to be. Is this simply going to widen into another net through which to filter civil categories of people?[59]

Yet despite Stoddart's warnings and verbal interventions into this divisive caesuric social practice that was initiated by the Canadian Government, for the most part Canadians stood back idly and watched as the no-fly list began to sublimate itself further into our woodwork, with no substantial arguments raised against it in the 75-day period of public rebuke that came into effect as of its announcement on October 27th, 2006. The lack of interest in the topic by Canadians over the course of this research and the lack of serious public debate around the *Passenger Protect Program* and its *Specified Persons List*, were epitomized by the headline from the Canadian Press Service on January 27th, 2007: 'Canada Quietly Working on own No-fly List'.[60]

While at times the Canadian press did approach the question of the implementation of the *Passenger Protect Program* with a critical eye during this period, mostly when Jennifer Stoddart spoke, or Michael Geist, Don Butler, and major Canadian news department editorial staffs wrote on the topic, for the most part the majority of the mainstream press stood by and watched as 'Canada's No-fly List Sped Towards Lift-off'.[61] Indeed, despite Stoddart's highly publicized statements on October 27th, 2006, the day of the announcement, Meagan Fitzpatrick of *The National Post* opted to omit Stoddart's criticism in her article the next day, merely waving a hand at questions of privacy and civil liberties by suggesting that 'Alexi Wood of the *Canadian Civil Liberties Association* is not sure if the no-fly list is necessary'.[62]

Throughout the research period, not only were the 'Feds Mum on the No-fly List'[63] and how it would work (but for Transport Canada's initial public announcement of the vague criteria for inclusion on the *Specified Persons List*, and how the advisory board would be constituted), but the Canadian government also adamantly refused to divulge whether or not they planned to share the list with the US and other allies. Nick Butler writes that,

---

59 Butler, 'No-fly List Could Be a Nightmare'.
60 Canadian Press, 'Canada Quietly Working on own No-fly List', 27 January 2007, http://www.ctv.ca/servlet/ArticleNews/story/CTVNews/20070127/no_fly_070127/20070127?hub=Canada.
61 Meagan Fitzpatrick, 'Canada's No-fly List Speeding Towards Lift-off', CanWest News Service, in *The National Post*, 28 October 2006, http://www.canada.com/topics/news/story.html?id=223f0998-daae-4c3e-8289-c6687576427c&k=97291.
62 Fitzpatrick, 'Canada's No-fly List Speeding Towards Lift off'.
63 Don Butler, 'Feds Mum on No-fly List', CanWest News Service, in *The Ottawa Citizen*, 15 January 2007, http://www.canada.com/topics/news/national/story.html?id=a836c50c-54ff-48d1-96b4-f48ecd66643a&k=36497.

...security experts say there's little doubt Canada will share no-fly information with its allies, including the U.S., when the list is activated ... One thing is beyond dispute: every airline that flies into and out of Canada will have access to the no-fly list.[64]

With such 'corporate' sharing already an assumption of the *Passenger Protect Program*, there is little doubt that as of this writing the United States and other foreign nations are in full possession of Canada's no-fly list. There is also clearly something unsettling about a Canadian air travel culture that prior to the initiation of the *Passenger Protect Program* and its *Specified Persons List*, had already been turning a blind eye to the constitutionally questionable practice engaged by Air Canada of screening its passenger names through the US no-fly list prior to departure:

> Transport Canada is putting the finishing touches on its no-fly list, called Passenger Protect, that all airlines will be required to use to screen passengers. The goal is to identify individuals who pose an "immediate threat to security". But Air Canada already applies a no-fly list using intelligence data from Canadian and U.S. authorities. "As part of our security measures, we do screen for names", said a spokesman. He wouldn't elaborate. "I don't think you'd expect a bank to talk about the steps it takes to keep its money safe," he said.[65]

Moreover, no provisions have ever been stipulated in Transport Canada's *Passenger Protect Program* that bar such practices, before or after the implementation of the *Specified Persons List*; practices which then and today expose Canadian air travelers, at least on Air Canada flights, to the massive American no-fly list. The dangers of practices that frame individuals in legally contradictory guilty-before-proven-innocent contexts are epitomized by the case of Canadian Maher Arar.[66] Just how are the rights and liberties of Canadians protected when they travel by air and have their names screened through lists derived from what amount to anonymous builders working with unspecified construction materials – data-bases and data-pools – culled from the entropy of global classification milieus?

Not surprisingly, racial profiling and stereotyping play into the discursive mix as well, as on the day of the initiation of the *Specified Persons List* the Canadian Council on American-Islamic Relations were already calling for its 'scrapping', voicing concerns with how '...the measure could lead to racial and religious profiling and the blacklisting of innocent people', a CTV.ca story noted.[67] It is ironic that just as Canada was considering how to adopt its own no-fly list in June of 2006, a *Baltimore Sun* headline stated that 'No-fly list said growing into uselessness' in the United States, citing the TSA's admission that the no-fly list was getting so large and cumbersome that it was increasingly becoming obsolete.[68] 'The federal government [of

---

64 Nick Butler, 'The Management of Populations', *Ephemera: Theory and Politics in Organization* 7 (3, 2007): 475-480.
65 CanWest News Services, 'No-fly for You, Woman Told'.
66 Canadian Press, 'Back Off on Arar'.
67 CTV.ca News Staff, 'As Many as 2,000 Names on No-fly List'.
68 United Press International (UPI), 'No-fly List Said Growing into Uselessness'.

the United States] has inflated the 'No Fly List' to 200,000 names. But the list has nabbed more members of Congress than it has terrorists,' wrote James Bovard in *The Boston Globe* on July 24th, 2006.[69]

With the number of people on Canada's *Specified Persons List* doubling in a mere day,[70] how long will it be before it approaches the six digit figures associated with its American counterpart? And how many people on the list will be listed merely because of their race? In a culture that has already become comfortable with profiling and listing in powerful contexts that reduce people to delimited and policed digital worth/risk elements, increasingly subdivided in populations housed in massive global information infrastructures, what impact do the Canadian Privacy Commissioner and The Canadian Council of American-Islamic Relations interventions really have? Can the 'stringent' criteria for inclusion on the *Specified Persons List* set forth by Transport Canada have any real impact on securing innocent people like Maher Arar from the 'misidentifications' that rule the day when computers, statistics, and lists are correlated in assemblages of police that patrol the global milieus of circulation installed by the apparatuses of security?

As the year progressed there was surprisingly no interrogation in the Canadian Press of the definition of the term 'terrorist' itself, which indicates its deep sublimation as a taken-for-granted but highly vague, provisional, and ambiguous classification in Canadian society. But despite a murky definition of 'terrorist', questions pertaining to the clearing of false 'terrorist positives' began to bubble to the surface of concerns voiced in the Canadian press,[71] while paying little mind to the term itself. The criteria associated with a person being placed on the no-fly list in Canada are so vague, and the practices engaged by the Canadian Specified Persons List Advisory Board for delimitation on the list so closed off, that despite the fact that individuals can petition to be removed from the no-fly list to the so-called Office of Reconsideration,[72] the reasons for which they were placed on the list in the first place and who was responsible for the decision will never be disclosed to the listed.[73] In this respect, and following on Bowker and Star's[74] conclusions regarding classification systems as living entities that explicitly contain traces of their builders and construction, it is a troubling trend that the construction and builders of *The Specified Persons List* in Canada remain obscured behind black-box policies, practices, and criteria by which they are probing entropic milieus of circulation for regularities and patterns that constitute terrorists and their organizations – classified matters of the highest national security.

---

69 James Bovard, 'The "Terrorist" Batting Average', *The Boston Globe*, 21 July 2006, http://www. boston.com/news/globe/editorial_opinion/oped/articles/2006/07/21/the_terrorist_batting_average?mode=PF.

70 Bovard, 'The "Terrorist" Batting Average'.

71 Montreal Gazette Editorial Staff, 'Ground Canada's No-fly List Now', 16 January 2007, *The Montreal Gazette,* http://www.canada.com/montrealgazette/news/editorial/story.html?id=77c6dc-da-a949-475c-a9d1-d2d8c25ab0f2.

72 A review and advisory board consisting of independent, unnamed advisors and former judges.

73 Mayeda, 'Gov't May Use Biometric Data to Back up No-fly List'.

74 Bowker and Star, *Sorting Things Out.*

Canadian Privacy Commissioner Jennifer Stoddart's four main concerns regarding the no-fly list also reflect this questionable state of affairs. As Don Butler in *The Ottawa Citizen* chronicled on May 16, 2007 in an article entitled 'Privacy Commissioner Wary of No-fly List',[75] Stoddart's first concern centers on whether or not and if so, how, the no-fly list will be shared with foreign governments. 'Though most security experts say there's little doubt they will be shared, the government has refused to say, citing security considerations.' Her second concern is the risk of misidentification of innocent Canadian citizens through the establishment of 'false positives' on the list. Stoddart's spokesperson Florence Nguyen '...noted the no-fly list in the United States has been plagued by false positives. Children have been listed as suspected terrorists, she said, and Senator Ted Kennedy was once denied boarding because his name was on the list.' Her third concern is how Canadian airline travelers will be informed of the presence of their name on the no-fly list. '"Will that information be communicated privately?" Ms Nguyen said. "In front of everyone, it could be embarrassing."' And perhaps most poignant to the research presented here, Stoddart's fourth concern is more broadly reflective of an ongoing trend towards

> ...identity-based versus physical-based screening systems ... What makes a person an immediate threat is more about what they are physically doing than who they are or who they have associated with.[76]

Butler concludes by noting, 'Ms. Stoddart has asked Transport Canada for studies or other evidence that no-fly lists improve airline security ... Ms. Nguyen said no such studies or evidence had ever been provided.' So where reports of Stoddart's and other critical interventions emerged throughout the year in the assembled news corpus, the only thing they have seemed to make clear for Canadians is that challenging increasingly streamlined and converged classification infrastructures, risk assessment scores, and apparatuses of security in general – whose meanings are deeply entrenched in the social and historical codes outlined in earlier chapters – requires considerable tenacity, and as some stories that emerged in the corpus reveal, extreme courage.

The Case of Christopher Soghoian

Challenging no-fly lists and associated security agendas means engaging the cultural and material resources available to those intervening, and in the case of no-fly lists, such interventions begin with a key technological support of the apparatuses of security; networked computer infrastructures. While computer technologies and global classification infrastructures are subsumed deeply in our social woodwork, rendering them near-invisible in how no-fly list conjunctures are represented, it was precisely when the computer's status as a taken-for-granted, underlying technology of US airline security was compromised in the timeframe studied here, that its crucial operations in the apparatuses of security were revealed.

---

75 Butler, 'Privacy Commissioner Wary of No-fly List'.
76 Butler, 'Privacy Commissioner Wary of No-fly List'.

On October 28th, 2006, a headline in *The Chicago Sun-Times* read 'Student Shoots down No-fly List',[77] which went on to chronicle how Christopher Soghoian, a Ph.D. student in the School of Informatics at Indiana University, was distracted and bored during a lecture on cryptography, and quickly designed and developed a website that would generate Northwest Airlines boarding passes. Any visitor to the site could type in any name and any flight number, and Soghoian's application would then prepare a facsimile for printing of a Northwest Airlines boarding pass containing the desired information.

Despite not being usable to actually board a plane, the boarding pass facsimile allowed anyone to pass through airport security checkpoints, completely subverting the no-fly list screening procedures engaged by Northwest Airlines prior to clearance into secure pre-boarding facilities. Indeed, this case was used to justify the need to remove pre-boarding security screening responsibilities from airlines themselves, placing no-fly list measures in the hands of the US Transport Safety Administration directly, streamlining them into their broader classification infrastructures and the watch lists of the Department of Homeland Security.[78]

Randall Stross in *The New York Times* on December 17th, 2006, described how Soghoian had stated on his (quickly dismantled) website that the project was simply intended 'to demonstrate that the TSA. Boarding Pass/ID check is useless',[79] but from a political perspective it clearly represented far more than that. Without compromising any computer airline system, without cracking any code, and without visiting any airport, Soghoian used simple computer and web-based techniques and technologies to completely compromise the United States' no-fly list program, and in turn, aviation security procedures across that nation, at the very least as they were intended to secure boarding facilities at airports that accommodated Northwest Airlines flights. And although Soghoian had presented Homeland Security with an opportunity to make strong arguments to further streamline and unify security watch lists and procedures across the nation and internationally, and even evidence to support them,

> [t]o thank Mr. Soghoian for helping the government identify security weaknesses, the T.S.A. sent him a letter warning of possible felony criminal charges and fines, and ordered him to cease operations, which he promptly did. It was too late, however, to spare his apartment from an F.B.I. raid.[80]

While Soghoian was subsequently cleared of any charges,[81] one has to wonder what kinds of watch lists his name can now be found on. 'The message it sends to the community

---

77 *Chicago Sun-Times*, 'Student Shoots Down No-fly List', 28 October 2006, http://www.suntimes. com/news/nation/115306,CST-NWS-fake29.article.

78 Randall Stross, 'Theater of the Absurd at the T.S.A', *The New York Times*, 17 December 2006, http://www.nytimes.com/2006/12/17/business/yourmoney/17digi.html?adxnnl=1&ref=yourmoney&adxnnlx=1192028686-OR6Bceht1ETM4RfmVF82pA.

79 Stross, 'Theater of the Absurd at the T.S.A'.

80 Stross, 'Theater of the Absurd at the T.S.A'.

81 Ryan Singel, 'Boarding Pass Hacker not Prosecuted', *Wired News*, 28 November 2006, http:// blog.wired.com/27bstroke6/2006/11/boarding_pass_h.html.

is that if you do security research, someday the FBI will come knock on your door,' said Soghoian.[82] Surely, Soghoian's manipulations of technoscientific infrastructures, and his intervention into the practices that partially constitute no-fly list apparatuses of security in the United States through the development of a simple computer or web-based application that anyone with a home computer and digital photo manipulation software could have easily accomplished, had the effect of labeling him a 'bad guy'. And not surprisingly, 'expert' analysis of the case inevitably framed questions of conducting security research as involving ethical and moral dilemmas revolving around the categorization of 'good guys' and 'bad guys'; conundrums that place researchers working in security contexts in difficult and compromising situations.

Matthew Blaze, an associate professor of computer science at the University of Pennsylvania, investigating domestic and international computerized security systems, framed the dilemma for security researchers working in a 'black' and 'white' world of global security, wherein their research can be interpreted as abetting the 'bad guys' agendas, as such:

> "Why should we help the bad guys?" The answer, he said, is that the bad guys aren't helped – because they almost certainly already know a system's weak points – and that disclosing the weaknesses brings pressure on government agencies and their suppliers to improve security for the good guys... "If a grad student can figure it out," he said, "we can assume agents of Al Qaeda can do the same."[83]

Blaze and his graduate students had discovered a series of techniques for subverting and thwarting government wiretapping systems the previous year, but they hesitated when it came time to publish their findings.[84] Blaze described how they adhered to the assumption that if they had discovered the techniques, 'terrorists' and 'criminals' had undoubtedly discovered them too, and therefore, in the interest of scientific advancement and in order to push the research, corporate, and military-industrial complex to address the security weaknesses their work revealed, they needed to publish their findings. But despite these rational principles, Blaze and his students still contacted the FBI before publishing their results, explaining their assumptions, elaborating on their findings, and providing the Department with a schedule for pending publications. The contradictions of their rational assumptions coupled with their cooperation with the FBI leads one to wonder if their 'openness' came from a patriotic impulse, or whether it was rather emblematic of their fear for their own identities being constituted as risks? Possibly delimited as security threats in their own right – possibly classified as 'bad guys' for tampering with security systems – with little to no redress for re-listing.

> "To their credit," Professor Blaze said, "they [the FBI] understood and did nothing to try to stop it."[85]

---

82 Singel, 'Boarding Pass Hacker not Prosecuted'.
83 Stross, 'Theater of the Absurd at the T.S.A'.
84 Stross, 'Theater of the Absurd at the T.S.A'.
85 Stross, 'Theater of the Absurd at the T.S.A'.

What Soghoian's intervention and Blaze and his students' conundrum reveal, is that despite the computer being deeply sublimated in the apparatuses of security and the operations of global classification infrastructures and further governmentality, when it is used or revealed as a tool of resistance, either for 'good' or for 'bad', the risk factor for those involved in exhuming this power from our social woodwork can be elevated and listed for policing; a historical legacy traceable to both Nazi governmentality and the embodiment of Cold War politics in computer, statistics, and list conjunctions outlined in the previous chapters. It is far from a stretch to suggest that the raids on Soghoian's house, his identity factored as a risk, his name on security watch lists, is precisely what Blaze and his students feared, and exactly what Soghoian experienced.

> Soghoian, who flies often and fears being put on the no-fly list, said he will probably cease working on airport security research, despite having had other ideas he wanted to test. "I travel and I see the risks and I want them to be fixed, but I'm not going to get to try them, and if Al Qaeda is the first one to test it then we failed. Al Qaeda should never be the first one to test the system," Soghoian said. As for the lessons he's learned? "You don't do anything two weeks before an election," Soghoian said. Also he suggests that his experience fits with those of security researchers pursued by the feds for their exposure of faults with Cisco and Adobe products. "The message it sends to the community is that if you do security research, someday the FBI will come knock on your door."[86]

The case of Christopher Soghoian's challenge of, or more precisely, intervention into US aviation security and its no-fly list program, not only demonstrates the extent of tenacity and courage required to challenge no-fly lists, global classification infrastructures, and their associations in the apparatuses of security, but at the same time requires us to acknowledge and examine the multiple ways in which our social constructions pivot on discursive dichotomies – how 'no-fly lists' guide our vision of the material reality of 'terrorists' in extraordinarily black and white terms.

Reconstructing No-fly Lists

> As Christine Brooke-Rose demonstrates, one must pay close attention to the way in which these apparently fundamental and natural semantic oppositions are put to work. What is self and what is not-self? Who wears the white and who wears the black hat? (Or in her discussion, perhaps, who wears the pants and who the skirt?)[87]

There is now not only broad consensus amongst privacy policy analysts and activists that no-fly lists represent significant incursions into and outright violations of privacy law, civil right, and liberties,[88] but there is also contradictory consensus among worldwide governments, particularly those of the US and Canada, that security assemblages such as no-fly

---

86 Singel, 'Boarding Pass Hacker not Prosecuted'.

87 Treichler, 'AIDS, Homophobia, and Biomedical Discourse', paraphrasing Christine Brooke-Rose, 'Woman as a Semiotic Object', in *The Female Body in Western Culture: Contemporary Perspectives*, ed. Susan Rubin Suleiman, Cambridge, Mass.: Harvard University Press, 1986, pp. 305-316.

88 MacCharles, 'Canada to Launch No-fly List in June'; and Don Butler, 'No-fly List Puts Rights at Risk: Critics', 14 January 2007, *The Ottawa Citizen*.

lists are the way to go in a never-ending and ever-expanding war on terrorism. The latter is highly emblematic of an emerging and pervasive tendency towards engaging technoscientific closed-world conjunctions involving the probing of global classification infrastructures through risk assessment techniques and technologies, wherein outputted watch lists pivot the delimitation and policing of 'terrorist' elements as a means and an end of practicing a global surveillance society.

Clearly, the multiplicity of meanings, significations, and stories which no-fly lists represent are neither simple nor under any specific discursive control. No-fly lists exist at a point where many entrenched narratives intersect, each with its own problematic context in which the 'terrorists' they represent acquire meaning. Therefore it is no wonder that most of us cannot resist the temptations and reassurance of pervasive and ubiquitous good/bad and black/white discourses surrounding no-fly lists and terrorists. Herein we inherit what Treichler calls '...a series of discursive dichotomies; the discourse [of e.g. no-fly lists] attaches itself to other systems of difference and plays itself out there':[89]

- us and them
- good guys and bad guys
- Islam and the 'free world'
- religion and secularity
- capitalism and communism
- certainty and uncertainty
- humans and machines
- physical bodies and identities
- freedom and repression
- innocents and perpetrators
- self and other

There is little doubt that for many people the emergence of no-fly lists lends force to their fear of terrorists – to their fear of others – and at the same time provides reassurance in an increasingly uncertain world. And there is little doubt that for some, in a post-9/11 era, no-fly lists would seem to provide a legitimate forum and mechanism for enabling racial profiling, which in this era means seeing Muslims as those primarily listed.[90] The complications associated with racial profiling and listing and policing 'terrorist' elements are exemplified by a story that emerged in late summer of 2006. On August 30th a *Reuters* worldwide headline declared: 'Pakistani-American Teen, Father Barred from US',[91] a story that subsequently generated over thirty news articles in subsequent weeks, all chronicling how two relatives (Mohammed and Jaber Ismail) of a father and son who were recently

---

89 Treichler, 'AIDS, Homophobia, and Biomedical Discourse', p. 63.
90 CTV.ca News Staff, 'As many as 2,000 Names on No-fly List'.
91 Reuters News Service, 'Pakistani-American Teen, Father Barred from US', 30 August 2006, http://today.reuters.com/news/newsArticle.aspx?type=domesticNews&story-ID=2006-08-31T002935Z_01_N30222713_RTRUKOC_0_US-SECURITY-TEENAGER.xml&archived=False.

convicted of terrorism charges in the US (Umer and Hamid Hayat), had been placed on the no-fly list while in Pakistan and thus had been barred from American soil, unless they agreed to be interviewed by the FBI in Islamabad. Despite there being no direct evidence of 45 years old Mohammed Ismail and his 18 years old son Jaber Ismail's involvement in a terrorist network, their bloodlines to those recently convicted (and intensely interviewed) terrorists made them 'guilty enough' to be placed on the US no-fly list. *The New York Times* reported on August 29th, 2006 that Hamid Hayat mentioned Jaber Ismail in a marathon F.B.I. interrogation before he was charged, according to transcripts. He said his cousin had attended a camp in the past couple of years, but he was not sure if it was the same one he had attended.[92]

What the Ismail's were doing in Pakistan at the time of being placed on the US no-fly list – the son participating in a vaguely defined 'religious' camp coupled with the father's refusal to cooperate with the FBI interviewers – was unclear and could be deemed suspicious. But as one of the Ismail's lawyers was quick to note, suspicion is not law, and 'If the government had evidence instead of innuendo ... then they would be charged with a crime instead of being held hostage in a foreign land.'[93]

What the Ismail's case demonstrates is that to talk of racial profiling as though it were a simple or easily detectable and recognizable phenomenon in popular global news culture is impossible. When we review the various conceptions of 'terrorist' which are produced by the term 'no-fly list' and how we construct meaning surrounding lists of risky circulating elements, we find very limited and narrow discourses of 'black' and 'white' dichotomies – of good guys and bad guys; us vs. them; good vs. evil; terrorist vs. the free world; self vs. other, etcetera.

At first, many Americans and Canadians undoubtedly believed that the names of innocent citizens would never be contained on no-fly lists – that they themselves would never be mislabeled 'bad guys' – but such myths were quickly shattered as the misidentification of innocent citizens on no-fly lists continued to be the focus of mainstream news on no-fly lists,[94] most notably epitomized by CBS Television's newsmagazine *60 Minutes* segment on no-fly lists entitled 'Unlikely Terrorists on No-fly Lists'.[95] The original airing of the episode of *60 Minutes* on October 8th, 2006 became news in its own right, yielding Associated Press international headlines including one in *The Jerusalem Post* on October 6th, 2006: 'Report: US No-fly List Includes Foreign Officials'. The short *Associated Press* news brief read:

> A no-fly list meant to keep terrorists off airplanes contains the names of Bolivia's President Evo Morales and Nabih Berri, Lebanon's parliamentary speaker, according to a report by a television news show. The story by CBS' "60 Minutes" builds on previous reports that detailed how young children and well-known Americans like Sen. Edward

---

92 Randal C. Archibold, 'U.S. Blocks Men's Return to California from Pakistan', 29 August 2006, *The New York Times,* http://www.nytimes.com/2006/08/29/us/29hayat.html?ref=washington&pagewanted=print.
93 Archibold, 'U.S. Blocks Men's Return to California from Pakistan'.
94 Dickson, 'No-fly List Snags 78-Year-Old Saanich "Mr. Nice Guy"'.
95 Kroft, 'Unlikely Terrorists on No-fly List'.

M. Kennedy have been stopped at airports because their names match those on lists. Critics say the government does not provide enough information about the people on the lists, so innocent passengers can be caught up in the security sweep. The number of names on watch lists increased into the tens of thousands since the September 11, 2001, terror attacks on the United States.[96]

The news of *60 Minutes*' revelations about the 'misidentification' of world leaders on the US no-fly list were quickly rebuked by the Associated Press on October 10th, 2006 saying that 'Richard Kopel, acting director for the Terrorist Screening Center of the Justice Department, said Bolivia's Evo Morales and Nabih Berri, the Lebanese parliamentarian, are not on the list, but he did not say whether they ever have been', in a report entitled 'U.S. Breaks Silence on No-fly List' published in *The International Herald Tribune*.[97] Whether they were or weren't on the list, what this *60 Minutes* segment revealed is a taken-for-granted 'truth' of no-fly list apparatuses of security: anyone and everyone is equally susceptible to this powerful web – as Senator Edward Kennedy, who has also been on the US no-fly list, would know.[98]

One of the other key revelations in the *60 Minutes* segment pointed to just how contradictory and ambiguous the practices associated with risk assessment and the automated probing of global classification infrastructures can be: 14 of the 19 names of the 9/11 hijackers are still identified on the no-fly list. When asked about the presence of the names of the dead hijackers on the no-fly list, Donna Bucella, who spearheads the FBI's Terrorist Screening Center which has been responsible for evaluating information and intelligence from various agencies post-9/11 and ultimately for compiling the US no-fly list, replied: 'Well, just because a person has died doesn't necessarily mean that their identity has died. People sometime carry the identities of people who have died.'[99]

Repeated warnings that terrorists are everywhere among us, even in death, suggest that technoscientific, legal, and popular discourses surrounding no-fly lists all take as their underlying assumption that fears borne of everything and everyone are legitimate in an unending array of social contexts in the age of global terrorism, wherein 'terrorists' are seen to lurk in every corner of an ever-threatening global milieu of circulation of good guys and bad guys, and that are served, validated, reinforced, and self-elaborated by no-fly lists. In this way, the 'terrorist' constructed around the term 'no-fly list' in Canadian and global news sources, the multiplicity of meanings it invokes, is driven in large part by a historical need and tendency to create evermore oppositions between people, to constantly distinguish

96 Associated Press, 'Report: US No-fly List Includes Foreign Officials', *The Jerusalem Post*, 6 October 2006, http://www.jpost.com/servlet/Satellite?cid=1159193380734&pagename=-JPost%2FJPArticle%2FShowFul.
97 Associated Press, 'U.S. Breaks Silence on No-fly List: Bolivian, Lebanese Politicians Are not on It', 7 October 2006, *The International Herald Tribune*, http://www.iht.com/articles/ap/2006/10/07/america/NA_GEN_US_Airline_Screening.php.
98 Lisa Wiehl, 'Privacy: A Thing of the Past?', 12 July 2007, *FOX Fan Central*, http://www.foxnews.com/printer_friendly_story/0,3566,203195,00.html.
99 Kroft, 'Unlikely Terrorists on No-fly List'.

between 'us' and 'them'. Indeed, the dichotomous meanings enabled through no-fly lists continue to be layered into existing discourses, evidenced in the slippery slope between listing cases that pose 'terrorist risks' and those that pose 'health risks'.[100] In other words, as the next chapter on no-blank list culture demonstrates, no-fly lists and their constituent 'terrorists' are signifiers that in many ways have been and can be embraced forever, in an unending array of social contexts.

How to disrupt, intervene, and renegotiate the powerful cultural narratives and discourses surrounding no-fly lists as they operate in the apparatuses of security is a complex question that requires significant tenacity and courage to approach, as Canada's Privacy Commissioner Jennifer Stoddart's efforts attest and the case of Christopher Soghoian clearly demonstrates. Fear of the 'other' is inscribed within no-fly list discourse at such a deep level that it is very difficult to dislodge. When our Public Security Minister tells us that 'Canada is not immune to terrorism' and that 'we must remain vigilant to the threat' he is merely validating, reinforcing, and redeploying a message that has been conveyed time immemorial, and one that has been used historically to justify increasingly invasive security and surveillance measures and divisive caesuric practices: 'they' lurk out there in every corner, posing mortal threat to 'us'. The only 'truth' that no-fly lists reveal is that any separation of 'others' (terrorists) from 'us' (general global population) is now quite literally impossible, yet such hegemonic discursive dichotomies and attempts at governmentality continue to rule the day.

Conclusion

The discursive mechanisms that no-fly lists pivot as described here are systems of difference – of significations and meanings of 'us' and 'them' – that lists have reinforced at least since the dawn of Nazi governmentality. But what we have also seen is that no-fly lists further shift the focus from the physical, corporeal assessment of risks to identity-based screening, involving deploying assemblages of policing in entropic global classification infrastructures and milieus of circulation. While there continues to be debate about how no-fly lists render the twin pillars of Canadian privacy law – notice and consent – irrelevant, as the government increasingly leverages indistinguishable 'identifiable' and 'non-identifiable' information to assess terrorist movements, the Canadian and American governments have quite clearly opted to disregard these conundrums – the perils of precarious guilty-before-proven-innocent legal positions – privileging a technoscientific vision and unproven approach to the management of terrorist threats locally, nationally, and globally. In a never-ending war on terror, the misidentification of 'innocents' is seen merely as a 'problem in code', perfectible through the engagement of increasingly sophisticated computer, statistical, and list techniques and technologies deployed to probe massive classification infrastructures in global milieus of circulation.

Moreover, underpinning this technoscientific correlation of power is a discourse of 'national security' wherein the criteria by which risks are calculated and contained on no-fly lists

---

100 CNN News Services, 'Border Security Scrutinized After TB Patient Slips in', 1 June 2007, http://www.cnn.com/2007/HEALTH/conditions/05/31/tb.flight/index.html.

are considered sacrosanct strategic intelligence, the highest 'classified' matters of national and global security. For even those who have been misidentified cannot know why, how, or when their identities came to be listed amongst terrorist populations, as surely this would impact the 'freedom of movement' that juridical-disciplinary mechanisms like no-flight lists deployed by the apparatuses of security are expressly supposed to ensure. We have also seen how the terrorist as a listed object is not merely viewed a threat to local and Canadian national security, but presents a global danger that makes the criteria by which this critical object of contemporary knowledge is constituted and called into reality even more precious and protected, and all the more important to unloosen as a key site of struggle.

My own view is unequivocal: technoscientific discourse cannot be privileged in this way. It represents a slap in the face to both legal rights and any form of *open-human discourse*. Historically, we have seen how privileging technoscientific conjunctions to articulate differences between people are dangerous practices and represent a very slippery slope for organizing society—one that teeters on, if not outright becomes, fascist. It is my view that the 'terrorist' is at once a socially constructed object and a historical subject; a very real source of threat in contemporary life, albeit one that remains for the most part invisible and highly provisional.

Intervening into no-fly list assemblages of policing and security will require us to relinquish some of the most pervasive and ubiquitous myths of the ages; our epic tales of good and evil – of us and them – and the fallacies and dangers of approaching such questions from an exclusively technoscientific lens. We need to use what technoscience has given us in ways that are open, critical, self-conscious, legal, just, and pragmatic. We need to understand that 'no-fly lists' and their 'terrorist' constituents are historical, provisional, and deeply problematic signifiers. Above all, we need to resist thinking pervasively and ubiquitously about risks and threats all around us – how we can shield 'us' from 'them' through no-fill-in-the-blank list apparatuses of security – and get in touch with real people, in real time, placing the weight of our beliefs in each other, in Norbert Wiener's islands, existing in a vast but isolating sea of entropic expansion and uncertainty.[101]

---

101 Wiener, *Cybernetics*; Wiener, *The Human Use of Human Beings*, 1950.

CHAPTER 4. NO-BLANK LIST CULTURE, OR HOW TECHNOSCIENCE 'TRUTHFULLY' CONSTRUCTS THE 'TERRORIST'

Introduction

Culture is one of the two or three most complicated words in the English language.[1]

As the 'war on terror' becomes a reality that is more and more taken for granted in a post-9/11 world, the no-fill-in-the-blank list's significance as a legal, technoscientific, and popularly conceived solution to our local, national, and global security 'crises' is increasingly becoming clear. What the emergence of the *Specified Persons List* and the overall *Passenger Protect Program* has shown is that as the Canadian government has tried to 'get ahead of the game' with new 'border' technologies and 'changing practices of government',[2] the probing or 'data-mining' of entropic global classification milieus of circulation for regularities and patterns that constitute risks continues to expand in an ever-expanding array of new watch lists. In this context, *no-blank list* is short for *no-fill-in-the-blank list*, a term meant to connote the unending expansion of the use of security watch lists, whether they be no-fly lists, no-buy lists, no-stay lists or no-work lists, or future watch lists that have yet to be imagined. True to their 'double integration' form,[3] no-blank list technologies of security serve as justification for the redeployment of their own praxis in the self-elaborating processes involving the constitution of fields, domains, and objects of knowledge. The legal, popular, and technoscientific conception that threats and risks lurk everywhere amongst us in a highly uncertain yet ubiquitously connected world, and the seemingly incumbent need to list and police the movements of elements circulating in populations and global milieus as such, was epitomized in Canadian Privacy Commissioner Jennifer Stoddart's 'welcome message' to 'The International Data Protection and Privacy Commissioner's Conference' held in Montreal in September 2007, called '*Terra Incognita*'.

> Our theme, *Privacy Horizons: Terra Incognita* points to the challenge for us as privacy guardians entering into uncharted territory, to anticipate and plan our readiness to tackle the "unknowns" in our field. Technology and terrorism are transforming the world. Information outsourcing and the exponential growth of transborder data flows as well as illicit data trafficking have become commonplace. *Terra Incognita* is our chance to assess this shifting privacy landscape and to map out our responsiveness and capacity to address emerging issues that trouble us as privacy professionals.
>
> By bringing together some of the world's foremost data protection experts to boldly chart the challenges ahead, we can explore ways of protecting and enhancing the pri-

---

1   Raymond Williams, *Keywords: A Vocabulary of Culture and Society*, London: Fontana/Croom Helm, 1976.
2   Katja Franko Aas, '"Getting Ahead of the Game": Border Technologies and the Changing Space of Governance', in Zureik and Salter (eds), *Global Surveillance and Policing*, pp. 194-214.
3   Foucault, '29 March 1978'.

vacy rights of all people. Thought-provoking workshops and interactive roundtables will plumb the depths of difficult issues such as data mining, authentication and identity management in our volatile, globalized and interconnected world. The emphasis will be on offering practical advice so you can develop your own solutions. Experts will bring forward the latest on new and alarming technologies such as brain scans and smart dust.[4]

The field of *Terra Incognita* and the domain of 'data protection experts', can be classified as a 'closed-world' disciplinary technoscientific way of seeing and doing 'terrorism' through the listing and policing of the movement of circulating risks or threats. Through this disciplinary conjunction, which takes shape in research and experimentation conducted in the techno-scientific laboratory, the terrorist is made real; at once fabricated and at the same time materialized as fact, through correlations of computers, statistical data mining, risk assessment techniques, and no-blank lists. All of these technoscientific forces are clearly in evidence in Jennifer Stoddart's 'welcome message'; n her emphasis on 'new and alarming technologies' and the critical role of 'identity management' in a 'shifting privacy landscape', deployed to 'anticipate and plan our readiness to tackle unknowns in our field'. Indeed, in *Terra Incognita,* the calculation, prediction, classification, and listing of 'threats' are practices that are pervasively expanding in the vast and ubiquitously connected, but highly insecure, milieu of circulation installed by the apparatuses of security that serve contemporary governmentality.

Here I argue that 'technologies of security' (like computers, statistics, and lists) and 'terrorism' are not merely 'transforming the world' in which we live, as Stoddart said, but are also transforming how we conceive of, talk about, symbolically represent, and materialize 'terrorists' in their own right: as naturalized, truthful, and classified listed objects. In a post-9/11 world, no-blank lists have seemingly become a taken-for-granted way of both seeing and doing local and global security; through the visualization, materialization, and policing of 'terrorist' or 'threatening' elements delimited on lists. Increasingly pervasive technoscientific practices surrounding the collection, analysis, and disclosure of 'personal' information in global classification milieus of circulation are permeating the way we think, and talk about terrorism and terrorists in general; as a 'listed' reality in a highly insecure and irruptive world, where dubious elements are understood as mined, listed, and policed for the safety of the 'general population', ensuring their 'free' and 'secure' circulation.

This year's conference theme was 'Terra Incognita', a reference to the unknown lands that typify the fear of the unknown in a world of rapidly changing technologies that challenge the core principals of privacy protection. Yet despite a dizzying array of panels on new technologies such as ubiquitous computing, radio-frequency identification (RFID) and nanotechnology, it was a reference by U.S. Secretary of Homeland Security Michael Chertoff to a simple fingerprint that struck the strongest chord ... In support of his security agenda, he noted that U.S. forces in Iraq once gathered a single fingerprint from a steering wheel of a vehicle that was used in a bombing attack and matched it to

---

4   Jennifer Stoddart, 'Privacy Horizons: Terra Incognita – 29th International Conference of Data Protection and Privacy Commissioners Welcome Message', September 2007, http://www.privacy-conference2007.gc.ca/Terra_Incognita_home_E.html.

one obtained years earlier at a U.S. border crossing. He added that there was a similar instance in England, where one fingerprint in a London home linked to a bombing was matched to a fingerprint gathered at a U.S. airport (the identified person was actually innocent of any wrongdoing) ... Rather than terra incognita Chertoff seemed to be saying that there is a known reality about our future course and there is little that the privacy community can do about it.[5]

With the Montreal conference placing the spotlight on the 'growing toolkit of responses' available to security specialists to address the uncertainties of *Terra Incognita*, where personal data slips effortlessly across borders, a future course did seem to be taking hold in Montreal: one in which individuals are increasingly understood as listed objects, mathematically and statistically derived worth/risk assessment scores, delimited and listed as risks circulating in global classification milieus that further efface the boundaries between people, things, and knowledge; all legally validated, reinforced, and naturalized as truth, in government programs like no-fly lists.

No-blank List Culture Emerges

In addition to constituting our contemporary 'surveillance society' as a conjunction of computer technologies, surveillance techniques, and privacy discourses, which hinge on cyborg reductions of humans and machines to information, David Lyon has also argued that 'the border is everywhere'.[6] Identities are increasingly being managed through biometric and surveillance techniques and technologies[7] like 'new' micro data-mining devices; while at the same time local security classifications are increasingly being streamlined and unified into 'global surveillance and policing' standards, technologies, infrastructures, and discourses.[8] The work presented here argues that this movement towards a global surveillance society revolves around the articulation and deployment of watchlists with questions surrounding who builds them and how risks are calculated being paramount. The interrogation of the emergence of the *Specified Persons List* in Canada in the preceding chapter demonstrates how no-fly lists are powerful discursive entities that are becoming deeply embedded in our working infrastructures and in this way risk losing visibility, despite never losing any of their power in their self-elaboration and further sublimation. No-fly lists are but the tip of the iceberg of *no-blank list culture*.

Throughout this period of research, numerous worldwide news sources reported the emergence of a variety of other watchlists that are also increasingly being used to manage 'threats' to other areas of local, national, and global security. On April 16th, 2006 Ryan Singel writing for *Wired News* described how over and above the US no-fly and selectee lists (people who

---

5 Geist, 'Privacy Threats no Longer "Terra Incognita"'.
6 David Lyon, *The Electronic Eye*, Minneapolis: Univ. of Minnesota Press, 1994; David Lyon, *Surveillance Society: Monitoring Everyday Life*, Buckingham, Philadelphia: Open University Press, 2002; David Lyon, 'The Border is Everywhere: ID Cards, Surveillance and the Other', in Zureik and Salter (eds), *Global Surveillance and Policing*, pp. 66-82.
7 Benjamin J. Muller, 'Borders, Bodies and Biometrics: Towards Identity Management', in Zureik and Salter (eds), *Global Surveillance and Policing*, pp. 83-96.
8 See, Zureik and Salter (eds), *Global Surveillance and Policing*.

can fly but are designated for extensive screening and interrogation before boarding), new watch lists are being born every day in the United States. Singel provided a 'field guide' to US watch lists post-9/11, including:

1. *The Unified Watch List* – a master watch US list said to contain more than 200,000 names of suspected foreign or domestic terrorists ranging from Al-Qaeda operatives to radical environmental activists.
2. *The Violent Gang and Terrorist Organizations File* – a list including citizens and residents suspected of being associated with gangs or terrorists.
3. *The Terrorist Identities Datamart Environment* – a massive global database and repository of intelligence data from US and global intelligence services that (hearkening back to Lasswell's 'who said what to whom' mantra) Singel describes as 'likely to have the name of anyone who ever called anyone who ever called Al Qaeda'.
4. *The Interagency Border Inspection System* which can be seen as completely effacing the boundaries between people, things, institutions, organizations, and knowledge, containing over a billion records on individuals, businesses, cars, trucks and planes; all 'tagged' with worth/risk scores by the,
5. *Automated Targeting System* that rates the suspicion level of every single person and vehicle and their cargo traveling in and out of the United States.
6. *The Consular Lookout and Support System* – a global database that leverages American and other governments' terrorist watch lists to assess visa requests and allocations.
7. *The Interpol Terrorism Watch List* – a unified list shared between intelligence, border and law enforcement agencies worldwide.
8. *The Warrant Information Network* – a list maintained by the US Marshals Service that keeps a watch on everyone in the United States with an existing federal warrant.[9]

As the emergence of this avalanche of watch lists attests, no-blank list culture begins with the reduction of people and things to digital elements with associated worth/risk scores through the techniques of correlating computers and statistical technologies, like in the operations of *The Automated Targeting System.* Indeed, no-blank list culture continues with the streamlining of these worth/risk assessed objects into entropic global classification infrastructures, like *The Terrorist Identities Datamart Environment, The Interagency Border Inspection System,* and *The Consular Lookout and Support System,* in which objects are further data-mined and probed for factors that constitute risks. Finally, no-blank list culture fulfills itself with the fracturing practices of listing and policing 'terrorists', like through the operations of *The Unified Watch List* and *The Interpol Terrorism Watch List,* which attempt to nullify the movement of risks or threats through their patrol by even finer-grain list technologies of security, such as no-fly lists, no-buy lists, no-work lists, etcetera. It is argued here that these provisional and self-elaborating techniques and correlations continue to serve, reinforce, and validate the form of governmentality that the apparatuses of security install: milieus where 'freedom of movement' is of preeminent concern and where risky elements are calculated, predicted, and outputted on watch lists for policing. In the struggle over

9   Singel, 'A Watch List is Born'.

this most critical production of knowledge – of who and what is classified a threat – power very much rests in the associations and representations of no-blank lists, with who builds them, and how they define and constitute risks.

> This calculation of risk shows straightaway that risks are not the same for all individuals, all ages, or in every condition, place, or milieu. There are therefore differential risks that reveal, as it were, zones of higher risk and, on the other hand, zones of less or lower risk. This means that one can thus identify what is dangerous.[10]

Post-9/11, the identification of risks through no-blank lists emerged in milieus or circulation that we have long seen as 'zones of higher risk', like airports, but they are now also being installed in milieus we assume to be 'zones of lower risk', like hotels. On February 16th, 2007, Misty Harris writing in *The Ottawa Citizen* reported that a no-stay database and list have been increasingly employed in Australia to track hotel guests who might pose a threat to the security of registered hotels and chains in that country.[11] No-stay lists in the hotel industry did not end in Australia, as they were also being debated in the United States in this research time frame, including in an article by Kitty Bean Yancey in *USA Today* on September, 15th, 2006, which explored questions of whether or not US hotels should have a 'blacklist' for guests.[12]

No-blank Lists as Technoscientific Cultural Constructions

To call no-blank lists 'cultural' may mean simply acknowledging that legal, technoscientific, and popularly conceived discursive amalgamations like no-fly lists and their constituent risky elements have significantly affected social life, symbolic expression, talk, and material reality. But as we have seen through the research of Paula Treichler[13] into AIDS and bio-medical discourse in the preceding chapter, no-fly lists are less clear cut entities and more invented labels, cultural constructions given birth to in the closed-world laboratory through its scientific naming practices. In this way, the research presented here argues that to call no-blank lists 'cultural constructions' means acknowledging how they serve the conceptual, and material establishment of truth, invoking debate about the nature of knowledge and the nature of living beings and things, as they exist and are classified in the everyday world. As Foucault argues, these are the critical sites of power that must be unloosened: struggles over the production of 'truthful' knowledge related to living beings.[14]

---

10 Foucault, '29 March 1978'.
11 Misty Harris, 'Australian 'No-stay' Database Tracks Hotel Guests Behaving Badly', *The Ottawa Citizen*, 16 February 2007, http://www.canada.com/ottawacitizen/news/story.html?id=8635fd6d-025d-4b18-a81b-d3859836fe61.
12 Kitty Bean Yancey, 'When Irate Guests Pounce: Should Hotels Have a Blacklist?' *USA Today*, 15 September 2006, http://www.usatoday.com/travel/news/2006-09-14-bad-guests_x.htm.
13 Treichler, 'AIDS, Homophobia, and Biomedical Discourse'.
14 Foucault, *The Order of Things*; Foucault, Burchell, Gordon, and Miller, *The Foucault Effect*; Foucault, Senellart, and Davidson, *Security, Territory, Population*.

What we have seen thus far is that no-blank list culture pivots on the reduction of people and things to worth/risk assessment scores, classified in global technological infrastructures that at once efface the boundaries between living beings, objects, and knowledge, and at the same time invoke new meanings for the term 'terrorist'; understood as a listed object. Given the complex correlations of the apparatuses of security installing global milieus of circulation and the delimiting and policing of the movement of risks or threats that lists serve, I would like to now assert that no-blank lists are, in all these ways, thoroughly 'cultural constructions'.

In a later work entitled *AIDS, HIV, and the Cultural Construction of Reality*, Treichler traces the legacy of the term 'cultural construction' from Karl Manheim's groundbreaking *Ideology and Utopia*,[15] which concerns itself with how knowledge is bound up with being, how '...any object of knowledge becomes clearer with the systematic and cumulative analysis of different ways of seeing it'[16], to Kuhn's *The Structure of Scientific Revolutions*,[17] which argues that radical 'scientific' ideas coalesce and produce moments of rupture in knowledge development; to Peter Berger and Thomas Luckman's influential work *The Social Construction of Reality*,[18] which explores how we experience the world in the form of multiple realities continuously in our everyday lives; and onto the work of Karin D. Knorr-Cetina who explores how science is a discourse like all others, where 'fact' is understood as a 'fabrication' of the laboratory, which serves the central purpose of 'making things real' and 'making things work'.[19] What Treichler concludes from this analysis is that, as per Foucault, culture is about the discursive construction of knowledge, hinging on the etymological connection between 'fact' and 'fabrication'. In this way, culture, like that of technoscience, is a 'made phenomenon' of the laboratory.[20]

A constant regularity in no-blank list culture is that when things go awry in its operations, questions are put right back on the disciplinary technoscientific mechanisms themselves to prescribe solutions. The laboratory of technoscience calls on itself to resolve problems when things do not work with no-blank lists, and as such, the laboratory is a double integration technology of security in its own right.

> Written communication crystallizes the laboratory's entire argument and stakes its claim. Science, as a discursive field of interaction, is directed at and sustained by the arguments of others; writing is, therefore, at the heart of its social and symbolic foundation.[21]

15 Karl Mannheim, Louis Wirth, and Edward Shils, *Ideology and Utopia: An Introduction to the Sociology of Knowledge*, London, New York: Harcourt Brace and company, 1936, 1985.
16 Treichler, 'AIDS, Homophobia, and Biomedical Discourse', p. 70.
17 Thomas S. Kuhn, *The Structure of Scientific Revolutions*, Chicago: University of Chicago Press, 1962; Thomas S. Kuhn, *The Structure of Scientific Revolutions*, Chicago: University of Chicago Press, 1996.
18 Peter L. Berger and Thomas Luckmann, *The Social Construction of Reality: A Treatise in the Sociology of Knowledge*, New York: Doubleday, 1967.
19 K. Knorr-Cetina, *Epistemic Cultures: How the Sciences Make Knowledge*, Cambridge: Harvard University Press, 1999; K. Knorr-Cetina and Aaron Victor Cicourel, *Advances in Social Theory and Methodology: Toward an Integration of Micro- and Macro-Sociologies*, Boston: Routledge & Kegan Paul, 1981.
20 Treichler, 'AIDS, Homophobia, and Biomedical Discourse', p. 73.
21 Treichler, 'AIDS, Homophobia, and Biomedical Discourse', p. 73.

Bruno Latour and Steve Woolgar's *Laboratory Life* is similarly inspired, arguing that fact simultaneously constructs what is fabricated, as well as what is not fabricated. In a similar way to how lists operate as 'intellectual technologies', Latour and Woolgar argue that scientific accounts are inherently uncertain and provisional, that facts are constructed through 'slow, practical craftwork by which inscriptions are superimposed and accounts are backed up or dismissed. It is through practical operations, that a statement can be transformed into an object or a fact into an artifact.'[22] Latour and Woolgar argue that there is no inherent dichotomy between the material (the lab's technological apparatuses) and the nonmaterial dimensions of its cultural constructions (scientific ideology). Technoscientific accounts of phenomena are understood as transforming into reified objects, ultimately emerging as a reality that self-elaborates its own praxis. In turn, Latour and Woolgar characterize the social or cultural study of scientific phenomena as 'the construction of fictions about fiction construction'.[23]

What does this mean in terms of this research into no-blank list culture? It means that a risk or a threat and the no-blank lists that delimit and call them into reality, are both cultural constructions, fictional representations whose legitimacy is established, validated, and reinforced through a series of interacting and self-elaborating technologies, scientific practices, and ideologies that take shape in the laboratory. How the terrorist is produced – the classification of this most critical of contemporary knowledge – must be taken seriously and unpacked, rather than passively accepted as hegemonic reality. This is the challenge that this research into no-blank list culture brings to the table: *that the issue is not the cultural construction of the terrorist, but rather, the technoscientific construction of terrorism, or terrorist culture.*

No-blank list culture must be understood as a legal, scientific, and popular imagining that most often privileges disciplinary 'closed-world' technoscientific constructions, whose classifications are increasingly experienced by people as natural, as what *is*. The more data about individual identities is collected, sniffed, worth/risk assessed, and classified in global information infrastructures – the more people are reduced to scores on no-blank lists – the more the technoscientific laboratory's account and construction of terrorist realities, classifications, and the 'truth' about the ongoing war on terror becomes a taken-for-granted reality self-elaborated through no-blank list culture. And in this highly uncertain, but pervasively connected global culture, it is precisely these underlying technoscientific discourses and their embodied technologies that appear to become precisely what need not be examined. In this way, the stage on which the realities of terrorist dramas unfold, the milieus of circulation installed, are validated and reinforced almost invisibly by the apparatuses of security that serve contemporary governmentality.

If there is another constant in the history of no-blank list culture presented here, besides that of the technoscientific construction of 'terrorists', it is the further sublimation of the computer's crucial and unquestioned role in combating 'good' and 'evil' in this global struggle over the production of 'terrorist' knowledge – its role as a pivotal 'closed-world' technology of security governing operations that probe entropic milieus for patterns and regularities that constitute

---

22 Latour and Woolgar, *Laboratory Life*, p. 236.
23 Latour and Woolgar, *Laboratory Life*, p. 284.

risks. Couplings of humans and machines, cyborgs, data-mined at every moment, worth/risk assessed, and distributed in populations circulating in increasingly ubiquitous and pervasive classification milieus that completely efface the boundaries between people, things, and knowledge, have in many ways become a hegemonic reality of contemporary governmentality. The unfolding global popular news items on 'watch lists' reads like a case-study on this point, documenting on the one hand the utter instability and uncertainty involved in practices of identifying terrorists through risk assessment techniques and global classification infrastructures, and on the other, the efficient and effective ways in which technoscience can repair this instability and uncertainty – that it is a just a matter of time until the perfect mathematical algorithms and technoscientific system is developed to combat this contemporary plague of terrorism.

The contestation surrounding the sharing of Canada's no-fly list with other nations, specifically the US, explored in the previous chapter, is not merely a question of privacy law, civil rights, and liberties but also clearly demonstrates how we are coming to increasingly understand, see, and accept our selves as technoscientific objects of knowledge; distributed in populations that are continuously experimented upon through data-mining, risk assessed, coded, classified, and streamlined into international information standards and systems. Global adherence to such standardized systems, beginning with the underlying technological infrastructures enabling the internet, global telephony, and cellphone networks in general, are standards which for the most part have been developed by the United States,[24] and that not only form the infrastructure of global telecommunication, but are also the de-facto pivot in post-9/11 cooperative efforts to manage terrorist threats worldwide. In these ever-creeping ways too, no-blank list culture expands, going hand in hand with staunch technoscientific governmental efforts, which in the case of the emergence of the Canada's no-fly list, saw increased pressure being placed on the Canadian government to share their lists and databases and adhere to increasingly stringent US standards, policies, and procedures that seek to delimit and police the movement of risks and threats in more and more milieus of circulation.

The idea of terrorists as listed objects is quite clearly the remnant of Cold War 'closed-world' discourse, validated and reinforced through mainstream global news sources, with each and every utterance of good guys and bad guys, us and them, etcetera. At the same time we have seen oppositional discourse appear in mainstream news, centered generally on privacy law and the protection of basic civil rights and liberties associated with 'free movement'. Such discourse, characterized by open-human conceptions, has certainly also helped shape no-blank list culture. We have seen that resistance and opposition to no-blank list culture is not futile, specifically in the case of no-fly lists, but does become evermore difficult with the powerful technoscientific 'security' agendas that enable global surveillance milieus sublimating themselves deeper into our social woodwork. At times, it is even difficult to distinguish between dominant and oppositional views of no-blank lists, as 'friends and foes' often agree that there is 'no better solution' to security than this technoscientific one – the installation of no-blank lists.[25]

---

24 Bowker and Star, *Sorting Things Out*.
25 Tyche Hendricks, 'The Immigration Debate: Identifying Legal Workers – Ways to Verify Eligibility

On May 24th, 2007, Kathy Kiely reported in *USA Today* that an immigration bill had been proposed and was being debated in the US Senate that would make provisions requiring that every person who applies for a job in the United States need to demonstrate that they are legally eligible to work.[26] Like the no-fly list, a no-work list was being developed by the United States' Department of Homeland Security, which would ultimately allow all US employers to verify the legal-status of their employees through comparative screening processes like those of the no-fly list program. Indeed, such technoscientific practices involving 'verifying the eligibility' of identities by screening them against no-work lists are increasingly being 'seen [by the US government] as key to immigration control'.[27] But such a technoscientific vision for immigration control, despite the powerful governmental forces behind it, is far from taken-for-granted, as competing and contradictory meanings surrounding no-work lists also abound in mainstream reporting.

> Civil liberties advocates worry that an extensive database linking Social Security data with immigration information would invade Americans' privacy and could lead to warrantless government data mining, be a ripe target for identity thieves and foster a "no work" list akin to the federal government's "no fly" list. Other experts fear that a multi-billion-dollar, mandatory system – which would be almost 1,500 times the size of a pilot program that already has encountered logistical problems – would be rife with errors and delays. But friends and foes of immigration alike say there's no better solution.[28]

According to this report, the competing legal discourses of a civil liberties vision of no-work lists, set against the efficiency and effectiveness of technoscientific approaches to controlling immigration, both take as their basis an agreed upon, yet highly provisional foundation: that there is 'no better solution' than that derived from the laboratory and its no-blank list technoscientific policing conjunctions. In a world where 'threats' lurk everywhere and need be managed and controlled through watch lists, the obliteration of privacy law becomes a taken-for-granted reality too: a passive agreement that human existence in a world plagued by pervasive and ubiquitous threats to local, national, and global security – from terrorist threats, to threats to immigration, and employment – can be secured trough technoscientific data-mining and screening practices.

> "Everybody who wants there to be meaningful (immigration) enforcement recognizes that the centerpiece has got to be workplace enforcement, and employment verification is a central component of that," said Steve Camarota, research director at the Center for Immigration Studies in Washington, D.C., a think tank that favors reducing both legal and illegal immigration. The American Civil Liberties Union has long opposed such a plan, which it considers a step toward a national identity card that the government could use to track the movements of Americans without their consent.

Seen as Key to Immigration Control', 23 May 2006, *The San Francisco Chronicle*, http://www.sfgate.com/cgi-bin/article.cgi?file=/c/a/2006/05/23/MNGIOJO95U1.DTL&type=printable.

26 Kathy Kiely, 'Employer-verification Proposal Draws Fire', *USA TODAY*, 24 May 2007, http://www.usatoday.com/news/washington/2007-05-24-employer-verification_N.htm.

27 Hendricks, 'The Immigration Debate: Identifying Legal Workers'.

28 Hendricks, 'The Immigration Debate: Identifying Legal Workers'.

"This will create privacy consequences that are profound," said Tim Sparapani, the ACLU legislative counsel for privacy rights. "We'll be gathering enormous amounts of sensitive information in an unsecured format ... These databases will inevitably be used by the government for purposes other than employment verification. The government has an insatiable appetite, post 9/11, for information. And it will take and aggregate and sift and data mine any source of information about the populace that it can get its hands on."[29]

As fabricators of fact, no-blank lists have become technoscientific industries in their own right, ways of doing and seeing that are extremely costly, both economically and in terms of their degradations of human beings to data bits, highly susceptible to misidentification and the 'inconveniences' of being placed in guilty-before-proven-innocent contexts. Furthermore, despite having thus far provided no 'return-on-investment', no-blank lists are increasingly being seen as so critical to ensuring 'freedom of movement' and 'security' in a highly uncertain world, that it appears they will not be given up on lightly. We have clearly seen that their use is expanding evermore pervasively across an 'unknown' but ubiquitously connected milieu of circulation – *Terra Incognita* – both fabricating and giving 'truthful' fact to terrorist realities.

Double Integration, or Good Guys 0, Bad Guys 1

What is involved in this analysis of mechanisms of power is the politics of truth, and not sociology, history or economics.[30]

The case of the emergence of the *Specified Persons List* in Canada, explored in the previous chapter, epitomizes the creeping pervasiveness and ubiquity of a global classification society[31] wherein local classification schemes (i.e. Canada's no-fly list) are transformed into international standardized schemes (i.e. US no-fly list practices and policies), which are in turn aligned with standardized global-scale information systems (i.e. unification and alignment of many governments no-fly lists in global surveillance and policing networks). Furthermore, with the case of no-fly lists, we have seen how international forces, particularly those exerted by the United States, are acting to cement a common global classification infrastructure that at its core completely effaces the boundaries between people, things, and knowledge. Indeed, both the Canadian and American no-fly list programs derive from the same technoscientific assumption: that a terrorist is functionally equivalent to an information bit, identifiable and controllable as it bounces between states, countries, security checkpoints, and computer nodes.

No-blank lists derived from the tabulation, sorting, analysis, and coding of human beings are becoming evermore pervasive and ubiquitous in our global classification society, receding further and further into the fabric of an everyday culture that is increasingly turning

---

29 Hendricks, 'The Immigration Debate: Identifying Legal Workers'.
30 Foucault, '11 January 1978', p. 3.
31 Bowker and Star, *Sorting Things Out*.

to lists to manage threats to local, national, and global security. The historical legacy of Nazi governmentality's practices of reducing individuals to statistical objects with associated values cannot be denied in contemporary no-blank list culture. The more the Nazis devised quantitative means and mechanisms for differentiating between 'biopolitical' lives in the Greater Reich, the more social policies and programs revolving around empirically reductive and caesuric differentiation flourished and became an increasingly taken-for-granted way of seeing and doing security and surveillance. Beyond the biopolitics the historical imperative is clear, particularly when propelled into a contemporary analysis: the more comfortable people become with the liberty, rights, and mobility of their selves being reduced and tracked as worth/risk assessed digital elements, ultimately regulated and policed through lists, the more social policies and procedures are accepted and implemented that rely on such reductions of people to digital elements. These are the self-elaborating discursive processes, the double integration effects of technoscientifically constructed no-blank list culture.

But while we can see similar patterns and regularities in today's no-blank list culture as in Nazi governmentality, there are differences, which involve the kinds and the scope of information gathered and warehoused in global classifications infrastructures – the direct effects of which are the rendering irrelevant of distinctions between what Canadian privacy law calls 'identifiable' and 'non-identifiable' personal data, and also the twin pillars of 'notice' and 'consent' – and also, how automated statistical techniques involving work/risk assessment have come to take center stage. With increased emphasis on encoding life as worth/risk objects and approaching it as a 'problem in coding', come self-elaborating policies, procedures, and practices of mathematically reducing people to scores, and assessing and classifying them as risks. According to James Gilden's headline in *The Los Angeles Times* on November 19, 2006, such 'Math Could Help Protect Against Terrorism'[32]. Chronicling how 'operations research' follows the numbers in assessing the efficiency and effectiveness of current no-fly list screening systems, Gilden writes that '...there is the problem that there is no clear picture of what a terrorist looks like'.[33]

> "Whenever you divide people into two categories – more suspicious and less suspicious – you invite the bad guys to figure out how to get into the 'search-me-less line' ... There's this myth that somehow there is a profile of the bad guys, and it's not true," Schneier said. "There's an enormous danger and enormous insecurity in relying on a profile," Schneier said. "Pre-identification doesn't really help much, so why are we bothering?"[34]

Despite the assumed reassurance of such screening practices, the terrorist continues to remain invisible in technoscientifically constructed no-blank list culture, and thus, is faithfully and eternally profiled, stereotyped, and constructed as a 'bad guy' in need of

---

32 James Gilden, 'Pi in the Sky: Math Could Help Protect Against Terrorism', *The Los Angeles Times*, Travel Insider Section, 19 November 2006, http://travel.latimes.com/articles/la-tr-insider19nov19.
33 Gilden, 'Pi in the Sky'.
34 Gilden, 'Pi in the Sky'.

further policing. Moreover, while such practices have proven to be inefficient, no-blank lists can also be thought of as instruments at the disposal of would-be threats, in terms of how they can be used oppositionally, as vetting systems for 'terrorist candidates'.

> Critics of Secure Flight note that it would be simple for terrorists to probe the system, sending their members on flights just to see who would be selected for secondary screening. Those who were not selected by the government would become the lead candidates for any planned terrorist act.[35]

However, despite such problematic conceptions of no-fly lists and further no-blank lists as 'dangerous' technoscientific cultural constructions, in the over 500 news articles that appeared in the corpus, only three articles (and a *Fox News* television report) actually probed deeper into the specific mathematical algorithms and risk assessment techniques of watch lists. Quite shockingly, these three reports revealed that the

> U.S. federal government is using the Soundex concept to match traveler names against the No Fly List. Soundex, developed in 1918 for census analysis, removes vowels from names and assigns a numerical value to remaining consonants. The result is hundreds of "false positive" matches and unnecessary inconvenience for tens of thousands of airline passengers.[36]

Over and above the disturbing revelation that the US no-fly list program at its core engages an inefficient mathematical risk assessment algorithm first developed in 1918, which has never succeeded in 'nabbing a single terrorist',[37] is the source of this information: a *Public Relations Newswire* for S3 Matching Technologies of Houston.[38] It is even more distressing that the second source of this technoscientific revelation was a report filed by Carolyn Canville for *FOX News*'s Houston outlet on February 27th, 2007 where she, too, revealed the underlying 1918 mathematical algorithm on which America's *Secure Flight No-fly List* was based.[39] Not surprisingly, Canville's segment concludes with what is little more than a commercial plug for local Houston-based S3 Technologies.

The final report which addressed this story came from the United Kingdom's *The Register*, which ran the following headline on March 14th 2007: 'George Bush fingered as terrorist by US feds.' This short article ends with a conclusion epitomizing the situation:

---

35 Gilden, 'Pi in the Sky'.
36 PR Newswire, 'S3 Matching Technologies: Outdated TSA Software Matches Clinton, Obama, and McCain with Potential Terrorist Names on No Fly List. Concept Used by TSA was Created in 1918', 1 January 2007, http://sev.prnewswire.com/computer-electronics/20070131/DAW03631012007-1.html.
37 Canville, 'Flying Blind?'.
38 PR Newswire, 'S3 Matching Technologies'.
39 Canville, 'Flying Blind?'.

Either the terrorist conspiracy has gone deeper than anyone could have thought, or the American feds have gone loco, or perhaps the S3 guys are over-egging the pudding just a tad. Maybe all of the above. [40]

But where such 'news' reports focus on the misidentifications inherent in the use of no-blank lists to patrol threats, at no point do they define what a terrorist is, call such 'truthful' classifications into question, nor raise any criticism of the policies and procedures that strip people of fundamental rights and liberties to 'movement' and 'circulation' on little more than a computationally-derived risk assessment score. Of course, the laboratory is taken-for-granted as providing the solution here, and yet again the invisible body of the terrorist is reduced to the eternal catchall-phrase 'bad guy'.

False matches on a list of 20 names included: Bugs Bunny, Daffy Duck, and Mickey Mouse – he matches up with a suspected terrorist named Max Massou. And while they're [TSA] busy targeting these false matches, the bad guy could be getting away ... We could all wind up on the no-fly list! Along with thousands of other innocent travelers.[41]

But as Canville is quick to reassure us, fortunately 'there is a solution on the horizon' and it comes from none other than the laboratory of 'Houston's own S3 Technologies'. The reduction of the identities of individuals to digital bits, their subsequent algorithmic worth/risk assessment, and reconstitution on security watch lists – the ethical and moral dimensions of people divested of basic liberties and rights in precarious guilty-before-proven-innocent contexts on nothing more than a score – have little to do with the failings of the US no-fly list program, which according to these reports are merely attributable to approaching security and surveillance as a mathematical problem in coding. In these self-elaborating discursive processes, the solution to the problem is of course to be found in the exclusive domain of the laboratory. One such lab may have already solved the no-fly list misidentification conundrum: S3, and their TeraMatch® software technology that leverages innovative and patented mathematical algorithms:

"It's no wonder the No Fly List has never nabbed a terrorist," said Andrea Gillentine, S3's Healthcare Solutions Leader. "Soundex had 97 false positives compared to only 3 turned up by our TeraMatch® technology. It should be pretty obvious to everyone why so many people are upset about the No Fly List."[42]

Quite clearly people are upset with the underlying technologies and mathematical algorithms and the need for their improvement and refinement in this technoscientific construction of no-blank lists, paying little to no mind to the divesting of their privacy and civil rights and liberties to 'free movement'. Terrorists are scary and only the technoscientific lab can save us!

---

40 Lewis Page, 'George Bush Fingered as Terrorist by US Feds', 14 March 2007, *The Register*, http://www.theregister.co.uk/2007/03/14/no_fly_website_jollies/.
41 Page, 'George Bush Fingered as Terrorist by US Feds'.
42 PR Newswire, 'S3 Matching Technologies'.

Either that, or the 'American feds have gone loco'.[43] Whatever the case, what is unquestioned is that terrorist threats, and all living beings and things in general, are reducible to worth/risk scores, delimited through statistical mechanisms and policed through the operations of no-blank lists. The extent to which these invisible threats lurk all around us – this technoscientifically constructed reality and fear central to the technoscientific construction of terrorism – comes right to the fore in Bruce Schneier's *Forbes Magazine* article from January 8th, 2007 entitled 'They're Watching'.[44] 'If you read this piece we'll have to kill you,' he begins,

> If you've traveled abroad recently, you've been investigated. You've been assigned a score indicating what kind of terrorist threat you pose. That score is used by the government to determine the treatment you receive when you return to the U.S. and for other purposes as well. Curious about your score? You can't see it. Interested in what information was used? You can't know that. Want to clear your name if you've been wrongly categorized? You can't challenge it.

Here I argue that the contemporary construction and naturalized classification of 'terrorists' – reduced to numbers, assessed as risks, and placed on no-blank lists – this commitment to categories, scores, and listing, is at once an artifact of the ways in which people have been classified on lists as threats since modern Nazi governmentality, and a highly provisional and emerging phenomenon wherein never-before imagined global classification infrastructures, risk assessment techniques and technologies are leveraged in attempts at pervasive and ubiquitous global security and surveillance on a radically re-spatialized globe, where populations, milieus of circulation, algorithmic logic and predictions of movement rule the day. In this way, despite its invisible risk factors and criteria, no-blank list culture requires an ongoing commitment to 'black' and 'white' classifications based on profiled factors of risk. No-blank lists as technoscientific cultural constructions can thus be seen in all their contradiction:

- As providing reassurance in a highly insecure but pervasively and ubiquitously connected world through the 'truthful' and 'natural' materialization of 'terrorists';
- As rendering the terrorist body even more invisible in this milieu of circulation, un-localizable in our global classification woodwork;
- As reinforcing perpetual fears, that threats to 'us' from 'them' are always lurking out there, somewhere, on a radically re-spatialized globe, where the solution to finding such threats will inevitably come from the technoscientific laboratory.

No-blank Lists Serve: The Naturalization of 'Terrorist' Knowledge

> Officials disclosed that they intended to search for unknown terrorists by buying access to commercial repositories of personal data collected about consumers to look for any possible link between a passenger and a known terrorist like a common address or phone number.[45]

---

43 Page, 'George Bush Fingered as Terrorist by US Feds'.
44 Schneier, 'They're Watching'.
45 Eric Lipton, 'U.S. Official Admits to Big Delay in Revamping No-fly Program', 21 February

Under a form of contemporary governmentality that swallows information up in one big gulp into the bowels of global classification infrastructures, the mislabeling of 'terrorists' and threatening elements in populations – this slippage in the production of some of our most critical constructed knowledge – is virtually ensured. Furthermore, 'innocents' who are miscategorized and who suffer at the long arm of such assemblages of police, are meant to appease their suffering through their unwavering belief in technoscience; that it is only a matter of time until the laboratory unearths the 'right' strategy for 'securing' the milieu of circulation.

> "All of us are anxious to get it started as soon as possible," Kip Hawley [US Transport Security Administrator] said of the problems of scope the revamped no-fly list program in the US was intended to address, with the aim of cutting the overwhelming amount of misidentifications on the list down by at least half. "But we are going to get it right before we set an artificial date and try to rush to it." [46]

A timeline for 'getting it right', the imposition of an 'artificial date', would seemingly be anathema to a never-ending war on terror, in which technoscientific discourse further reinforces, validates, and self-elaborates itself and its laboratories as pivotal in perfecting systems that will inevitably and 'truthfully' classify, calculate, and predict 'terrorist threats' and their movements. When it comes to no-blank lists as cultural constructions, technoscientific discourse would seem to not only trump civil rights and liberties, but also economic practices, since despite the massive expenditures associated with them, no-blank list programs like no-fly lists, rarely, if ever, yield a return-on-investment. If we are to understand no-blank lists as cultural constructions of a symbolic model of reality, then it has become apparent through this analysis that approaching them from a strictly technoscientific standpoint raises several important questions:

- What kind of correspondence do we presume to exist between the technoscientific representation of terrorists on no-blank lists, or in global classification infrastructures, and their material corporeal reality?
- Are the realities of terrorist corporeal threats really reducible to risk assessment scores, factored in populations and classified in global information infrastructures, or are they far more provisional in nature, and as such, invisible?
- What other features of culture determine no-blank list reality?
- What is the role of language in articulating and popularizing no-blank list culture?
- Do different representations of no-blank lists and their threatening elements make a difference in no-blank list cultural constructions?

Three general takes on such questions can be observed in mainstream news reporting on watch lists. Firstly, terrorist threats, whether animate or inanimate, are seen as reducible to risk assessment scores and a high degree of correspondence is assumed between terrorist

2007, *The New York Times*, http://www.nytimes.com/2007/02/21/washington/21secure.html?_r=1&ref=us&oref=slogin.

46 Lipton, 'U.S. Official Admits to Big Delay in Revamping No-fly Program'.

realities and technoscientific discourse. Secondly, once they are reduced to risk assessment scores, threatening elements and in turn terrorist corporeal bodies, can be efficiently and effectively controlled (delimited and policed) through their listing in global classification infrastructures. The misidentification of innocents on watch lists in such practice is seen as a taken-for-granted reality of involvement in a local, national, and global 'war on terror'. A problem inevitably mediated through the language of technoscientific discourse, wherein the solution to misidentification – the perfection of the no-blank list screening of terrorists – is self-elaborated as exclusively realizable in technoscience's closed-world lab. Thirdly, our experience and knowledge of terrorists is inevitably mediated through our symbolic construction of them, as listed objects housed in global classification infrastructures and circulating in vast milieus of uncertainty.

There are pressing and critical reasons for clarifying the concept of no-blank lists as cultural constructions. In the face of an ever-broadening and seemingly never-ending war on terror, the ethical, moral, and technical limitations of these facile symbolic constructions of 'black' and 'white' 'terrorists' that no-blank lists reinforce and validate, should by now be emerging as not only obvious, but dangerous. The current terrorist crisis – with its long-term influence over the direction of policy, research, legislation, and everyday life – makes it all the more imperative to take seriously the conceptual clashes between different symbolic conceptions of 'no-blank lists' and 'terrorists' like those presented here, and how these terms can be clearly read as technoscientific cultural constructions.

> Displayed in themselves, emptied of all resemblance, cleansed even of their colours, visual representations will now at last be able to provide natural history with what constitutes its proper object, with precisely what it will convey in the well-made language it intends to construct. This object is the extension of which all natural beings are constituted – an extension that may be affected by four variables. And by four variables only: the form of the elements, the quantity of those elements, the manner in which they are distributed in space in relation to each other, and the relative magnitude of each element.[47]

It is my hope that by highlighting its ancient and historic instrumental role in the 'naturalization' of 'risky' or 'threatening' classes of people and things through its techniques for visualization and materialization, the list is revealed as a key site of struggle in the production of knowledge: giving the contemporary 'terrorist' form, establishing its quantities, serving the distribution of its elements in relation to each other, and helping to delimit, predict, and modify magnitudes of knowledge about it. Who (or what) are 'us', what (or who) are 'them', and where will 'they' strike next? How are the politics that serve to delimit, predict, police, and nullify the movement of terrorists established? Although the answers to such questions remain fluid and elusive with respect to who builds no-blank lists and how risk is factored, one thing we can be sure of is that 'us' and 'them' can be living beings, things, or combinations thereof.

---

47 Foucault, *The Order of Things*, p. 146.

Of all the stories that could be read from it, the emergence of no-blank lists are multiple stories about an object that in many ways does not exist: that of the 'terrorist'. As Raymond Williams has shown us, culture encompasses both material and non-material meanings; both the concrete objects produced by a cultural community (i.e. airports, airplanes, x-ray machines, no-fly lists, terrorists), as well as the complex intersection of practices, attitudes, beliefs, ideas, stories, and myths that make up a culture's way of life (i.e. terrorists are everywhere and we need to exercise extreme vigilance in delimiting and policing the movement of these 'unknown' threats). Williams also notes that the dichotomous nature of culture does not end there, but that it also serves to distinguish the material from the spiritual, and further to distinguish human from material development – people from objects.

In a contradictory era of ubiquitous global connectedness, coupled with high uncertainty and extreme religious and spiritual fundamentalism, the 'truthful' and 'natural' classification of the terrorist is one that we seem to want and need to materialize and differentiate, that we in many ways, and particularly through no-blank lists, have constructed it ourselves. No-blank lists are pivots of contemporary visions of global surveillance and security societies and as such represent a nexus of technologies, practices, meanings, stories, and legal, technoscientific, and popular discourses that reinforce, subvert, intersect, and overlap each other. Yet clearly within this miasma of densely interwoven meanings and significations, one pivot remains constant, that of the ephemeral 'terrorist'; the elusive and oft invisible threat to the Volk – the Jew or the Communist – figuring centrally in the drive towards the streamlining of global classification techniques and infrastructures.

Moreover, the ambiguities inherent in the label 'terrorist' – in how we construct 'it' as an object of knowledge – can be read as retaining clear traces of Nazi governmentality, involving the practice of valuing human life and assessing risks through the probing of data-pools as a means and an end to the identification and control of threatening elements. Such practices are now deeply sublimated in our classification milieus of circulation, but remain clearly palpable in legal security measures such as the Canadian *Public Safety Act of 2002*, which bequeaths the federal Transport Minister with the right to take measures to identify individuals who pose risks to aviation security, as well as the right to administer and maintain a list of such individuals.[48] Such caesuric social practices involving disaggregating risky or threatening elements from general populations are, while highly provisional, also deeply historical, and so it is not surprising that despite ongoing vague definitions of what constitutes a 'terrorist' in the national and global press – of this most critical classification and knowledge – Canadians implemented a *Passenger Protect Program* in June 2007 hinging on this questionable legacy involving delimiting, policing, and nullifying the movement of 'threatening' circulating elements – terrorist and other – through lists.

---

48 See Canada's BILL C-17: THE PUBLIC SAFETY ACT, 2002, amended March 2003, http://www.
parl.gc.ca/common/bills_ls.asp?Parl=37&Ses=2&ls=c17.

No-blank Lists Serve: The Reemergence of Bare Life

Foucault's[49] critical theorizing of governmentality has clearly helped to identify and unloos-en key constrictions, blockages, and correlations of power of list security technologies in this research. But at the same time, in light of the questions of 'human rights violations' which have emerged in this analysis – of the ethical and moral quandaries surrounding assemblages of juridical-disciplinary mechanisms for policing individual bodies in global entropic milieus of circulation like airports – there has also remained a tangible sense of 'bare life' in this state of affairs, which now compels a re-examination the work of Giorgio Agamben.[50] By way of example, one of the most covered no-blank list stories worldwide in the time frame studied here was about a US citizen who unfortunately contracted a drug-resistant form of tuberculosis while honeymooning in Rome and was placed on the US no-fly list while abroad.[51] Unable to return from Europe to the United States and desperate to get home, Andrew Speaker of Atlanta, Georgia, subverted the no-fly list by boarding a plane in the Czech Republic, and flying into Montreal, then crossing the US border via land.[52]

This story first broke at the end of May 2007, and generated over fifty articles in the assem-bled corpus, most of which illuminated Speaker's body – reduced, assessed, and classified as a risk and threat to the 'health' of US society – as an urgent beacon or signifier for the unification and streamlining of US and Canadian security measures and infrastructures (as well as those of other nations), all in the interest of ensuring the 'free' movement of normal populations in secured global milieus of circulation.[53] But in another way, Andrew Speaker's body can be read here per Agamben as pared down to its 'bare life', stripped of its rights to 'freedom of movement' through the fracture of biopolitical caesuras from legal subjects of right, to disciplinary enclosures where bodies are stripped of humanity and unequivocally and brutally policed at all times, like those in the Nazi concentration camps:

> Whoever entered the camp moved in a zone of indistinction between outside and in-side, exception and rule, licit and illicit, in which the very concepts of subjective right and juridical protection no longer made sense. What is more, if the person entering the camp was a Jew, he had already been deprived of his rights as a citizen by the Nuremberg laws and was subsequently completely denationalized at the time of the Final Solution. Insofar as its inhabitants were stripped of every political status and whol-ly reduced to bare life, the camp was also the most absolute biopolitical space ever to have been realized, in which power confronts nothing but pure life, without mediation.[54]

49 Foucault, '1 February 1978 Governmentality'.
50 Agamben, Homo Sacer.
51 Sikander Hashmi, 'Clement Confident Despite TB Carriers No-fly Voyage', 31 May 2007, The National Post, http://www.canada.com/nationalpost/news/story.html?id=b8de6459-15bd-4d44-b4b7-e1f558def726&k=87708.
52 Hashmi, 'Clement Confident Despite TB Carriers No-fly Voyage'.
53 CNN News Services, 'Border Security Scrutinized After TB Patient Slips in'.
54 Agamben, Homo Sacer, pp. 170-171.

For Agamben, the enclosure of the concentration camp as the most absolute biopolitical space ever to have been realized extends itself well beyond Nazi Germany. Just as practices surrounding the identification and control of bare life were at the center of this modern political formation, inscribed on the bodies of all citizens of the Reich at birth, the concentration camp as disciplinary space for the cloistering of bare life can be seen as transcending its historical realm too, jumping the barbed-wire fence, propelled into contemporary global milieus of circulation.

> The camp as dislocating localization is the hidden matrix of the politics in which we are still living, and it is this structure of the camp that we must learn to recognize in all its metamorphoses into the *zones d'attentes* of our airports and certain outskirts of our cities ... The camp, which is now securely lodged within the city's interior, is the new biopolitical *nomos* of the planet.[55]

Andrew Speaker's body, reduced to an element circulating in an entropic global milieu,[56] in this way is not only emblematic of Foucault's governmentality, but also is evidence of Agamben's contemporary biopolitical caesuras. The layers of the onion that shield bare life, are stripped away in contemporary *zones d'attentes* like airports, where fractured threatening bodies are policed, quarantined, and their rights as *homo sapiens* are rescinded, all in the interest of protecting the sanctity of the global Volk's 'free' movement. Indeed, under a contemporary form of governmentality, which envisions the state as an organic membrane with permeable, leaky borders, nested in a global body, what needs to be policed and patrolled at these osmotic outskirts are the bodies of individual citizens, circulating in chaotic fashion, but inscribed with the fundamental political unit of 'bare life' in birth, and thus being critical sites of contemporary policing.

Agamben argues that the emergence of bare life at the center of modern and contemporary biopolitical policing can be traced back to the United States' Declaration of Rights and Freedoms enacted in 1789, which unequivocally affirms 'that 'men are born and remain free and equal in their rights' and that 'every man is born with inalienable and indefeasible rights'. For Agamben, the emergence of 'individual human rights' as such represents a radical shift in the site of sovereignty; *from divinely authorized royal sovereign, to a dispersed national sovereignty*, situated in the individual bodies of everyday citizens. 'The fact that in this process the "subject" is transformed into a citizen means that birth – which is to say natural bare life as such – for the first time becomes the immediate bearer of sovereignty.'[57] For Agamben charters of rights and freedoms go hand-in-hand with the practice of sovereignty, with each right inscribed on the body forming another layer of protection to shield our absolute biopolitical nature; our bare lives, inscribed on us in birth.

---

55 Agamben, *Homo Sacer*, pp. 175-176.
56 Associated Press, 'Andrew Speaker Case Fuels Calls for Tougher Laws on Movement of Patients', 10 June 2007, *Fox News*, http://www.foxnews.com/story/0,2933,279912,00.html.
57 Agamben, *Homo Sacer*, p. 128.

> Biopolitical caesuras are essentially mobile, and in each case they isolate a further zone in the biological continuum, a zone which corresponds to a process of increasing degradation. Thus the non-Aryan passes into the Jew, the Jew into the deportee … the deportee into the prisoner … until biopolitical caesuras reach their final limit in the camp … Here the wavering link between people and population is definitively broken, and we witness the emergence of something like an absolute biopolitical substance that cannot be assigned a particular bearer or subject, or be divided by another caesura.[58]

In this way, 'bare life', or 'the absolute capacity of the subjects' bodies to be killed, forms the new political body of the West.[59] With each biopolitical caesura that further divides, layers of rights are shed from bodies, until all that remains is bare life. Bare life as such is the fundamental political unit of modern and contemporary existence, an absolute biopolitical substance that cannot be further divided, and around which power is fundamentally practiced. Whether life is subsumed in Nazi totalitarianism or existence takes shape in western liberal democracy, each fracture of people from populations, delimited, listed, and policed as threats, further divests bodies of layers of humanity; ultimately carrying the potential to pare them down to this final and absolute indivisible biopolitical substance – bare life – the capacity to be killed without conscience. And so Agamben's bare life propels the corporeal bodies that Foucault subsumed in populations under governmentality back into the spotlight, and into a pivotal role.

> Behind the long, strife-ridden process that leads to the recognition of rights and formal liberties stands once again the body of the sacred man with his double sovereign, his life that cannot be sacrificed yet may, nevertheless, be killed. Today politics knows no value (and, consequently, no non-value) other than life, and until the contradictions that this fact implies are dissolved, Nazism and fascism – which transformed the decision on bare life into the supreme political principal – will remain stubbornly with us. According to the testimony of Robert Antelme, in fact, what the camps taught those who lived there was precisely that "calling into question the quality of man provokes an almost biological assertion of belonging to the human race".[60]

Following on Foucault's governmentality, we could say that Andrew Speaker's entire life was reduced to the contamination probability that he posed to the US Volk and other global biopolitical populations, was materialized on a no-fly list, and in this way, was nothing more than a factor of risk assigned to an element circulating in a global milieu of circulation, which seeks to subdivide the human species into such categories in the interest of ensuring the normal distribution and circulation of populations. But Agamben also forces us to acknowledge that there is something else going on here that needs to be unloosened, relating to the dehumanizing effects of stripping layers of freedom from circulating bodies, classifying, concentrating, and quarantining subdivisions of the human species as risks and threats. Through the analysis of how lists serve power formations, we are able to see

---

58 Agamben, *Homo Sacer*, pp. 84-85.
59 Agamben, *Homo Sacer*, p. 125.
60 Agamben, *Homo Sacer*, p. 10.

how Foucault's populations and milieus of circulation installed through governmentality are in fact reconcilable with Agamben's 'bare life' as the fundamental political unit of contemporary political life.

Since Foucault[61] understands juridical-disciplinary mechanisms (i.e. human rights and freedoms charters) as redeployed in the apparatuses of security, serving the free milieus of circulation installed under governmentality, what Agamben[62] brings to this analysis of how lists serve governmentality is an elaboration and description of the dehumanizing effects implicit in redeployments of such juridical-legal mechanisms. As we have seen with the case of Andrew Speaker and all the cases of misidentification outlined here, but also as applied to those interned in Guantanamo Bay today, it is precisely because these bodies are divested of humanity, stripped of rights customarily attributed to human beings, and yet still remaining biologically alive (and as such being extreme signifiers of risk), that bare life can be understood as a part of correlations of power that constitute this most critical of classifications of the human species: the terrorist, or what Agamben calls *homines sacres (homo sacer)*.

> Those who are sentenced to death and those who dwelt in camps are thus in some way unconsciously assimilated to *homines sacres*, to a life that may be killed without the commission of homicide. Like the fence of a camp, the interval between death sentence and execution delimits an extratemporal and extraterritorial threshold in which the human body is separated from its normal political status and abandoned, in a state of exception, to the most extreme misfortunes. In such a space of exception, subjection to experimentation can, like an expiation rite, either return the human body to life (pardon and the remission of a penalty are, it is worth remembering, manifestations of the sovereign power over life and death) or definitively consign it to death to which it already belongs.[63]

Through the case of Andrew Speaker, we can see how *homo sacer*, or sacred man – one who is lacking the rights bestowed on other human beings – resides in each and every one of us, and the potential for the exposure of this bare life lies at every turn of existence in global milieus of circulation; a double integration, or double sovereignty each and every one of us assumes in birth and possesses in life. On the one hand, our sovereignty is sanctified in our bodies at birth and is the foundation of our nation-state's legitimacy, which cares for and protects the lives of its citizens through its charters of rights and freedoms. On the other hand, our sacred and bare lives can always be exposed – which is illuminated when one violates the sanctity of the biopolitics of the nation or globe – in the case one is divided, classified, and listed as 'dangerous', 'them', 'terrorist', or 'other'.

When individual human rights, freedoms, and liberties of movement are removed through the operations of no-blank lists, and when the layers of the onion covering sacred life are

---

61 Foucault, '1 February 1978 *Governmentality*'.
62 Agamben, *Homo Sacer*, p. 128.
63 Agamben, *Homo Sacer*, p. 159.

stripped away, the pivotal contemporary operations of both Foucault's governmentality and Agamben's bare life are further exposed. Like the double integration effect characteristic of Foucault's technologies of security, bare life is a double sovereignty that is written into our legal constitutions and is the foundation of political life – biopolitical life – inscribed on us at birth: proud subjects of individual human rights and at the same time subject to their rescission.

> Every society sets this limit; every society – even the most modern – decides who its "sacred men" will be. It is even possible that this limit, on which the politicization of the *exceptio* of natural life in the juridical order of the state depends, has done nothing but extend itself in the history of the West and has now – in the new biopolitical horizon of states with national sovereignty – moved inside every human life and every citizen. Bare life is no longer confined to a particular place or a definite category. It now dwells in the biological body of every living being.[64]

What the case of Andrew Speaker shows us is that the installation of 'secure' global milieus of circulation that take as their chief objective ensuring the 'freedom of circulation' for normal populations, through the delimiting, policing, and nullification of the movement of anything that may stand in the way of this objective, is a reality of contemporary governmentality. The redeployment of juridical-disciplinary mechanisms installed by the apparatuses of security also produce the 'double integration' or 'double sovereignty' effect of calling into reality human rights and freedoms, inscribed on the bodies of individuals, and at the same, nullifying these rights and freedoms in the interest of serving the modus operandi of this self-elaborating form of governmentality, 'freedom of movement'.

> "We only have the ability to put people on watch lists coming into our country," [Michael] Chertoff [United States Department of Homeland Security Secretary] told CNN. "It would have been good if we had a system that allowed us and the Canadians to have a common picture ... The Canadians could have picked up this individual (before) getting into Canada, if the two countries had a fully integrated system to share information on passengers who pose a health threat," Chertoff said.[65]

The people on the watch lists US Department of Homeland Security Secretary Michael Chertoff's describes are fundamentally nothing more than worth/risk elements circulating in populations and milieus that can be probed and subjected to automated risk assessment techniques and technologies; and subsequently listed as 'risky' or 'threatening' objects in global classification infrastructures, stripped of some of the layers of the onion that shield bare life. Such digital identities are also stripped of any trace of humanity, reduced to scores, which serve as the basis for Chertoff's 'common picture'.

---

64 Agamben, *Homo Sacer*, p. 140.
65 Sheldon Alberts, 'Canada, U.S. Need Shared No-fly List: U.S. Homeland Security', 7 June 2007, *CanWest News Service*, http://www.canada.com/topics/news/national/story.html?id=d759a89a-2a1c-40ff-b15f-87d3cce4ecc9&k=68609.

Throughout the coverage into the case of Andrew Speaker's subversion of the US no-fly list, Canada's Health Minister Tony Clement refused to comment on whether or not the idea of creating a specific no-fly list for people with contagious diseases and sharing it with other nations such as the US was an option that would be considered to prevent the recurrence of such an incident in the future.[66] The links between a health derived no-blank list and Nazi governmentality's critical practice of nullifying elements that posed a health risk to the Volk is clearly detectable here.

Despite the fact that the risk that Andrew Speaker actually posed to the health of US society was admitted by Julie Gerberding of the US Centre for Disease Control to be low, '...but we can't rule out zero',[67] this case nonetheless received an inordinate amount of worldwide coverage that inevitably took as its focus the increased urgency for the sharing of no-blank lists and their data between nations, further reinforcing the need for delimiting, predicting, and policing the movement of elements distributed in populations and milieus that pose other kinds of security threats and risks over and above terrorism, like health risks. In the self-elaborating processes of no-blank list culture, more meanings of what is dangerous are inscribed and the bare lives of even more innocent citizens are exposed.

Given Transport Canada's criteria for peoples' inclusion on the no-fly list as strictly pertaining to an individual's involvement in terrorist organizations or the commission of serious life-threatening crimes; how will government officials deal with such health-based risks in the future? Will they construct another no-blank list, or will those victimized by contagious diseases be forced into Canadian no-fly list culture's procrustean 'terrorist' bed? Will the boundaries between such circulating risky 'health' elements and 'terrorists' be completely effaced as they are calculated, predicted, classified, and cross-referenced on lists in global classification infrastructures where misidentification seems to always rule the day?

Speaking to the legacy of how lists brought contradiction to questions of who constituted a 'Jew' or an 'undesirable' in Nazi governmentality – and how such knowledge was 'truthfully' classified – today they can be seen as bringing contradiction to questions of who constitutes a 'terrorist' and how criteria are established to factor 'risks' and place such elements on watch lists. Like the Nazis traced back generations in their classifications of 'who' and 'what' constituted the 'Jewish' population, fiercely deliberating how far bloodlines needed to go, today registration data leveraged from telephone, email, web, and commercial databases are our contemporary bloodlines – *who said what to whom and with what effect* – wherein 'terrorist' movements are established by probing for regularities and patterns between individuals in this time-honored fashion. In this epic, necessary, and never-ending battle between 'us' and 'them', the cost of delimiting and policing the movement of risks to security often means that innocent citizens are misidentified and miscategorized.

66 Hashmi, 'Clement Confident Despite TB Carriers No-fly Voyage'.
67 Hashmi, 'Clement Confident Despite TB Carriers No-fly Voyage'.

We must remember that Canada is not immune to the threat of terrorism and we must remain vigilant.[68]

The unfortunate exposure of the bare lives of innocent Canadians on no-blank lists is clearly one of the costs of remaining vigilant to threats of terrorism in the global war on terror. Throughout the time span of this research a series of articles emerged depicting the trials and tribulations of parents whose children had unwittingly been given 'terrorist' names that were contained on no-fly lists.[69] 'No-fly List Names Cause Baby Blues' read a headline in *The Montreal Gazette* in the summer of 2006. 'It sounds like a joke, but it's not funny to parents who miss flights while scrambling to have babies' passports and other documents faxed.'[70] Other headlines like '4-year-old's Name on US No-fly List',[71] which told the story of how 'the parents of a 4-year-old California boy say their son gets treated like a terrorist because his name is on the US government's no-fly list', were peppered throughout the assembled corpus. The names of infants and toddlers being contained on no-blank lists can be read as evidence that the contemporary apparatuses of security make no distinctions whatsoever when it comes to ensuring 'secure' circulation, even between children and terrorists, exposing the bare life of all. The names of infants and toddlers on no-fly lists can also be read as further evidence of Agamben's[72] conclusion that we are born into *bare life* from the get-go; that *homo sacer*, or sacred man – the threatening class of *homo sapiens* who lacks the rights bestowed on other human beings – resides in each and every one of us, and the potential exposure of bare life, of the 'them' in 'us', lays at every turn of existence, even for toddlers.

It is a double sovereignty each and every one of us assumes in birth and possesses in life. On the one hand, the sovereignty of this 4-year old from California was sanctified in his body at birth and is the foundation of his nation-state's legitimacy, which inscribes, cares for, and protects his life through charters of rights and freedoms and the use of security tools like no-fly lists. On the other hand, his bare life can always be exposed – the boundaries between his identity and those of a 'known terrorist' completely effaced. Cases like that of the 4-year old, misidentified and classified on the no-fly list as a terrorist, demonstrate how bare life can be read in the case of no-blank lists as the foundation of political life, biopolitical life, inscribed on us at birth – proud subjects of individual human rights and at the same time how in powerful global milieus of circulation like airports, policed through apparatuses like no-blank lists, such rights can be stripped so easily away.

---

68 CBC News, 'Ottawa Plans No-fly List by 2007'.
69 Canadian Press Services, 'Islamic Group Planning Challenge to No-fly List', *CTV News Services*, 5 October 2005, http://www.ctv.ca/servlet/ArticleNews/story/CTVNews/20051005/no-flylist_canadianmuslimchildren_20051005/20051005?hub=Canada; also in Rocky Mountain News Services, 'No-fly List Becoming Political Liability', *The Rocky Mountain News*, 19 August 2005, http://www.rockymountainnews.com/drmn/opinion/article/0,1299,DRMN_38_4013121,00.html.
70 Associated Press, 'No-fly List Names Cause Baby Blues', *The Montreal Gazette*, 17 August 2006, p. A7.
71 United Press International (UPI), '4-year-old's Name on US No-fly List', *The Washington Times*, 11 October 2006, http://washingtontimes.com/upi/20061010-111722-9098r.htm.
72 Agamben, *Homo Sacer*, p. 128.

No-blank List Culture as a Critical Site of Struggle

An example of a no-blank list that could seemingly be read as a site of struggle is Canada's do-not-call list. Initiated with Bill C-37 introduced in November 2005 by the Canadian Government, the Amended Telecommunications Act gave the Canadian Radio-Television and Tele-communications Commission (CRTC) the legal authority to establish a disciplinary mechanism called a do-not-call list, intended to protect Canadian citizens from intrusive telemarketing campaigns aimed at a large swath of populations. The bill also included provisions to levy penalties for violations on any and all offenders.[73] But despite 'moving forward with a do-not-call list [which] generated a sigh of relief from millions of Canadians fed up with intrusive, unwanted, and inconvenient unsolicited telemarketing calls',[74] competing visions continue to abound as to the nature of this list, its operations, meanings, and ownership, in addition to a variety of other questions that emerge regarding how such a monolithic technology and practice can be efficiently and effectively administered in the name of millions of 'innocent' Canadians.

> In the past few months, the do-not-call list details have begun to emerge, with the CRTC addressing questions surrounding who will run the list, who will pay for it, and who will investigate consumer complaints. While Canadians might expect most of those responsibilities to rest with the CRTC, the commission appears to have a far different vision, one that involves a near-complete outsourcing of responsibilities to Canada's dominant telecommunications companies.[75]

The ironies inherent in placing the control of the do-not-call list in the hands of the problem creating and ever-offending telecommunications giants themselves, speaks to the enormity of industry required around no-blank list culture; how the design, development, and administration of such 'screening' practices working in the interest of 'innocent' people requires massive human effort and tremendous technological and financial administration and resources to maintain, and the CRTC has clearly indicated and acknowledged that they could never meet such demands. Again, we see an example of the double integration effects of list technologies: wherein the corporations and their laboratories, responsible for the 'problem' of deploying *do-call lists* delimited from elements circulating in the 'public' domain in the waging of massive telemarketing campaigns, are the same players who are invoked as responsible for the solution to the problem, which is self-elaborated as engaging the equal and opposite technological effect of *do-not-call lists* to nullify their own opposing force.

> The CRTC was never particularly supportive of the do-not-call list. Indeed, Charles Dalfen, the former CRTC chairman, told the Canadian Press in 2004 that a do-not-call list was a good idea, but that the commission "isn't equipped to administer such a list and doesn't have the power to enforce it properly".[76]

---

73 For a summary see Sam N.K. Banks, 'Bill C-37: An Act to Amend the Telecommunications Act', in the *Canadian Library of Parliament Legislative Summaries*, 2005, http://www.parl.gc.ca/common/bills_ls.asp?Parl=38&Ses=1&ls=c37.
74 Geist, 'Privacy Threats no Longer "Terra Incognita"'.
75 Geist, 'Privacy Threats no Longer "Terra Incognita"'.
76 Geist, 'Privacy Threats no Longer "Terra Incognita"'.

So where no-blank list culture as a means of opposition to contemporary governmentality is clearly out of the hands of ordinary 'innocent' populations of citizens, due to the massive and inefficient monolithic scope of such projects, nonetheless its expansion across society continues to be never-ending. Kelly Hannon reported in *The Fredericksburg Free Lance-Star* on July 26, 2006 that identities in the United States are also now increasingly being checked when people make major purchases, such as cars, boats, houses, and insurance, as businesses have begun to consult a Homeland Security-derived 'no-buy list' to weed out the names of 'people and businesses associated with drug trafficking, money laundering or terrorism'.[77] On March 28, 2007 Richard Gonzales filed a radio report on the no-buy list for National Public Radio's *All Things Considered* radio news magazine in which he chronicled how the 'no-buy list' is increasingly 'snaring regular citizens in its web', making large purchases difficult for those misidentified.[78]

In an article entitled 'Reliance on Watch Lists Can Threaten Americans' Safety' penned by former US Republican Congress Representative Bob Barr (Georgia) with Azizah Al-Hibri, which appeared in *The Chicago Sun-Times* on May 26th, 2007, the story of Tom and Nancy Kubbany, who were denied a mortgage because Tom's middle name matched an alias known to be used at times by one of Saddam Hussein's sons, was detailed.[79] Strongly opposing no-buy list practices, which clearly place people like the Kubbanys in guilty-before-proven-innocent contexts, Barr and Al-Hibri write:

> We must be cautious in our use of watch lists. First and foremost, watch lists should not be used as "blacklists" to deny employment or other contracts. The Kubbanys' mortgage is far from the only example of a company misusing a watch list. Watch lists are appropriate only when a lengthy investigation is not possible and the potential consequences are extremely grave, as in the case of the no-fly list. Even when watch lists are appropriate, reforms are necessary to promote fairness and accuracy. Since most people will not know they are on a watch list until they experience some harm, it is crucial to maintain accurate lists in the first place. The system requires serious front-end reform, including clear written standards detailing what evidence is needed to place someone on a list. Watch lists can be useful, but only insofar as they are maintained fairly and used appropriately. Liberty and security are mutually reinforcing; we can and must demand both from our government.[80]

---

77   Kelly Hannon, 'Identities are checked for major purchases', *The Fredericksburg Free Lance-Star*, 16 July 2006, http://fredericksburg.com/News/FLS/2006/072006/07162006/204270.

78   Richard Gonzales, 'Critics Say U.S. 'No Buy' List Snares Regular Citizens', radio report on National Public Radio's *All Things Considered*, 28 March 2007, http://www.npr.org/templates/story/story.php?storyId=9190024.

79   Bob Barr and Azizah Al-Hibri, 'Reliance on Watch Lists Can Threaten Americans' Safety Reform Is Crucial to Streamline Investigations and Allow the Innocent to Clear Their Names', 26 May 2007, *The Chicago Sun-Times*, http://www.suntimes.com/news/other-views/402470,CST-EDT-REF26B.article#

80   Barr and Al-Hibri, 'Reliance on Watch Lists'.

Despite such intelligent critical written opposition that clearly strikes an open-human standpoint over the closed-world systems approach generally privileged in this technoscientific conjunction, still no-blank list culture expands evermore. Barr and Al-Hibri explicitly argue that watch lists need to retain traces of their construction materials and builders, and adamantly argue for their use only in exceptionally 'grave' contexts in a major US news paper; and yet no-blank lists remain unchecked as such. Indeed, in a global milieu of circulation where 'You are either with us, or you're with the terrorists!', no-blank lists efficiently and effectively serve this discursive dichotomy of our time, and with this further their self-elaboration. George Bush's post-9/11 mantra is as vague as the risk assessment criteria set forth by Transport Canada for inclusion on the *Specified Persons List*. Who is a terrorist? What is a terrorist organization? And who has the authority to deem either so? How are such risks calculated?

While the answers to these questions are unclear, what is clear is that the fabrication of these facts is the field and domain of the technoscientific laboratory and their data-mining and statistical expertise. Where Transport Canada has seemingly provided quite stringent criteria for an individual's inclusion on the *Specified Persons List*, unequivocally stipulating that this means 'known or suspected involvement in a terrorist organization', what remains completely obfuscated are the criteria or statistical strategies by which organizations are deemed to be 'terrorist' in the first place, how individuals and populations are classified as 'threats', and who has the authority to name them as such. The procedures for defining and materializing 'terrorists' are constantly referred to as 'classified in the interest of national security', yet at the same time they continue to constitute our linguistic and material under-standing of the 'terrorist' object through the lens of technoscience, and as such remain critical sites of struggle to unloosen.

No-blank Lists Serve: New Formations of Security, Territory and Population

The emergence of conjunctions of no-blank lists, pervasive global classification infrastruc-ture technologies, statistical risk assessment techniques, and their derived scores and populations point to a radical new form of global re-territorialization: one that began with the economic mechanisms to counter famines and epidemics installed in the eighteenth century which Foucault[81] describes, continued through to targeting military airplanes in the sky; and ultimately expanded to include the space race. In these vast and uncertain milieus, threats are no longer seen as existing in terms of disciplinary geographical enclo-sures but rather are seen to reside in living beings, things, populations, and knowledge circulating everywhere.

This re-territorialization has involved shifting the meaning of 'threats' from disciplinary spaces and their clearly delimited geographical territories, to elements circulating in populations, a way of seeing and doing governmentality which clearly gained further traction in the wake of the terror attacks of 9/11. Prior to 9/11, the US no-fly list was said to contain some eleven

---

81 Foucault, '1 February 1978 *Governmentality*'.

names,[82] but as of the time of this writing has mushroomed to what independent sources estimate to be between 200,000 and 400,000 names (the precise number has never been stated by the US government who considers it a matter of national security).[83] More and more, from WWII to 9/11 and beyond, the globe has been treated as one whole contested territory – one milieu of circulation – wherein threats and risks are understood to be pervasive and ubiquitous realities existing in all dimensions, in need of constant delimiting and policing through technoscientific risk assessment practices and unified global classification infrastructures. With this transformation, our talk, specifically pertaining to the location of terrorists, has shifted from a language of localizable terrorist organizations in national territorial zones to one of threatening elements circulating everywhere.

In an article appearing in *The International Herald Tribune* on October 12th, 2007 entitled 'Canadian Airlines Rebuke U.S. Call for More Passenger Data,' Ian Austen describes how the United States Department of Homeland Security is attempting to require that Canadian airlines turn over all information about passengers flying above the United States, whether or not the carrier is landing on US soil en route to their destination.[84] The no-blank list milieu of circulation is so pervasively understood to be everywhere, that the United States now demands a vertical reconstitution of geography through its no-fly list program's policies and standards: from the two-dimensional realm of maps, into the *n*-dimensional realm of clouds and satellites, wherein threats, as they have been since the Cold War, are seen to lurk everywhere contained in the bodies of individuals and objects on land, in the air, at sea, and in space.

Conclusion

The concept of cultural construction can be understood as follows. It is a way of talking about how knowledge is produced and sustained within specific contexts, discourses, and cultural communities; it takes for granted metaphor and other forms of linguistic representation; it presupposes that ideas are produced out of concrete contexts and have concrete effects; it takes for granted hermeneutic activity; it is a complex of ideas and operations sustained over time within a given community; hence it is institutionalized. Though often confused with idealism or more recently with a view that 'discourse is everywhere', the notion of cultural construction is not a matter of arbitrarily envisioning an unknowable material reality, but of engaging in highly *non*arbitrary ways with the material world. Although meaning is indeed arbitrary and fluid, this does not mean that it is arbitrary and fluid within a given signifying system. The predictability and stability provided by a given history, society, culture, and set of disciplinary conventions are anything but arbitrary.[85]

---

82 Singel, 'A Watch List is Born'.
83 BBC News Services, 'US "to Halve" No-fly Watch List'.
84 Ian Austen, 'Canadian Airlines Rebuke U.S. Call for more Passenger Data', *The International Herald Tribune*, 12 October 2007, http://www.iht.com/articles/2007/10/12/europe/canada.php.
85 Treichler, 'AIDS, Homophobia, and Biomedical Discourse', p. 89.

Within the cultural construction of no-blank lists, terrorists are both materialized and given meaning; they are rendered nonarbitrary, predictable, and stable, fabricated as fact through technoscientific conjunctions. In an age of global uncertainty where the fear of terrorists lurking everywhere feels increasingly more real, it is no wonder that governments expend great efforts and monies on such technoscientifically derived solutions to combat risks or threats that at once provide a sense of reassurance and security, and at the same time, continue to preserve beliefs in the same amalgamations of computer technologies, statistical practices, and no-blank lists that makes the material realities of terrorists appear to be more stable and controllable – more real and true – on a local, national, global, and even universal level. *But recognizing that the realities of no-blank lists and their delimited and policed 'terrorists' are culturally constructed makes such 'truthful' beliefs impossible.*

Like the realities in the cultural construction of AIDS outlined by Treichler,[86] with no-blank list culture we see a 'division of linguistic labor' wherein people are becoming increasingly more comfortable with ceding the articulation of 'terrorist' realities – their 'black box' definition and constitution – to classified technoscientific data and security expertise, ideologies, and systems. We have seen that the problems and contradictions inherent in identifying and naming individual terrorist threats, the misidentifications, and the infringements to privacy, civil rights and liberties – the exposure of bare life – are all obfuscated by the denotative and disciplinary authority of technoscientific discourse. During a period like the current one, where no-blank list authority can be, and still is challenged, it is with these divisions of linguistic and conceptual labor involved in naturalizing and 'truthfully' classifying, naming, and listing 'terrorists', that opposition must begin.

The naming of terrorists and the listing of risky and threatening elements in global milieus of circulation cannot be approached through the exclusive lens of technoscience and the security establishment's black box criteria for constituting risk. In Canadian Privacy Commissioner Jennifer Stoddart's interventions, and writings like Michael Geist's, as well as that of former Congressman Bob Barr and Azizah Al-Hibri, we can see challenges to the technoscientific construction of no-blank lists: people trying to get in touch with people, speaking and writing about a shifting privacy landscape where identity-based screening over physical corporeal assessment of risks has come to rule the day. As the solution to a global security crisis is named, practiced, and interpreted through a 'closed-world' technoscientific security lens, this investigation into no-blanks lists has served to demonstrate that 'the concepts of culture and cultural construction encompass both material and nonmaterial phenomena and that analysis must emphasize the ongoing interaction and mutual influence between the two'.[87]

We have seen specifically how the correlations of no-blank lists and their constituent 'terrorists' are thoroughly cultural constructions, 'made real' through the apparatuses, practices, and worldview of the technoscientific lab, which at once delimits and polices threats, and at the same time writes their fiction. With the number of misidentifications on no-blank lists continuing to escalate, and still no proof as to their efficiency and effectiveness in prevent-

---

86 Treichler, 'AIDS, Homophobia, and Biomedical Discourse'.
87 Treichler, 'AIDS, Homophobia, and Biomedical Discourse', p. 90.

ing terrorist acts, the moral and ethical limitations of these facile 'good' and 'evil' cultural constructions has hopefully become far more evident too. While it has been very useful to characterize no-blank lists and their constituent terrorists as cultural constructions, it is by no means intended to suggest that terrorism is not a serious danger in our time, quite the contrary. In fact, it argued here that no-blank list culture and terrorism are mutually constituted, both a product and problem of the apparatuses of security, their laboratories, and contemporary governmentality.

CONCLUSION. IN LISTS WE TRUST?

The dimension in which the population is immersed amongst the other living beings appears and is sanctioned when, for the first time, men are no longer called 'mankind' (*la genre humaine*) and begin to be called 'the human species' (*l'espèce humaine*). With the emergence of mankind as a species, within a field of the definition of all living species, we can say that man appears in the first form of his integration within biology.[1]

This work has argued that the list is not simply an innocuous tool of everyday life for administering and organizing the minutiae of mundane existence, but rather is an instrument, or more precisely, a security technology of contemporary governmentality – a critical support of juridical-disciplinary mechanisms and assemblages of police – with the dual role, and *double integration* effect, of self-elaborating and securing the classes of 'factual' knowledge it itself calls into 'truthful' reality. As such, this work has unloosened the relations of power that lists associate, which seek to correlate and secure natural divisions, categories, and classifications of the human species. In other words, this work has revealed the list as a key site of struggle in the constitution of a critical field, domain, and object of modern and contemporary knowledge: *homo sacer*, or the 'threatening' class of *homo sapiens*.

What we have seen in modern and contemporary correlations of list technologies and techniques, is that they have functioned and continue to function to constitute the ongoing and necessary production of fundamental but highly provisional caesuric subdivisions of *homo sapiens*, of 'us' and 'them' – which have been with 'us' since the emergence of natural history. We have also seen how a correlate of the kind of governmentality installed through the redeployment of list security technologies is the appearance of a 'natural' form of knowledge, an order of things, that can only be 'truthfully' known by the use of the same techniques and methods as in the production, classification, and listing of all scientific knowledge. With the emergence of no-blank lists, we have further seen how out of our ever-expanding entropic disorder, the fabricated fact of the laboratory serves to both produce a kind of truthful and natural technoscientific knowledge, and self-elaborate a series of practices that are indispensable to contemporary governmentality: the prediction, delimitation, and policing of risky, threatening and terrorist elements. And in this way, we have seen 'a quite particular relationship of power and knowledge, of government and science',[2] a 'double integration' unity that couples power/knowledge and science/decision as an art of governmentality that models its decisions on its own self-elaborating effects.

It will be necessary to arouse, to facilitate, and to *laisser faire*, in other words to manage and no longer to control through rules and regulations. The essential objective of this management will be not so much to prevent things as to ensure that the necessary and natural regulations work, or even to create regulations that enable

---

1   Foucault, '29 March 1978', p. 75.
2   Foucault, '29 March 1978', p. 351.

natural regulations to work. That is to say, it will be necessary to set up mechanisms of security. The fundamental objective of governmentality will be mechanisms of security, or let's say, it will be state intervention with the essential function of ensuring the security of the natural phenomena of economic processes or processes intrinsic to population.[3]

The emergence of contemporary no-fly lists and no-blank lists – these state interventions – are mechanisms of security that have been created to enable 'natural' regulations to work, specifically regarding the freedom of movement of elements and populations circulating in milieus that contemporary governmentality takes as its maxim. In this way, this research into how lists serve formations of power, or how lists are political technologies and techniques of security, challenges 'us' to take responsibility for the contradictory and problematic nature of technoscientific practices of delimiting, predicting, and policing risky or threatening elements; acknowledging that how we classify terrorists today is at once historical and also highly provisional, based on the calculation of probabilities and the constitution of populations. It has been argued that the fabrication of such critical knowledge carries immense power, and as such cannot be ceded exclusively to technoscientific discourses and expertise, 'black box' security criteria, and their derived 'truthful' classifications.

Inspired by Jack Goody's[4] conception of 'ancient lists' as 'intellectual technologies' and his taxonomy of their operations (administration, organization, and knowledge development roles), the work presented here has bifurcated from such 'structural' communications research traditions to analyze listing practices in modern and contemporary formations of power. Propelling the list's critical operations in the delimitation, prediction, and policing of risky elements from out of history and into a contemporary analysis of power, it has been demonstrated how these correlations of the apparatuses of security continue to factor in the construction and constitution of a most critical and necessary contemporary object of knowledge: the 'terrorist'.

In short, and following on Bowker and Starr's[5] pithy summation of classification systems, I have argued that *lists need to be re-listed*; as 'cultural constructions' of security in correlations of power that produce and police natural 'us' and 'them' categories of knowledge in the interest of securing the safe, necessary, and sufficient movement and distribution of 'normal' elements circulating in the 'free' milieus of contemporary governmentality. The list serves to 'let things happen' – *laisser-faire, passer et aller*.

This explains finally, the insertion of freedom within governmentality, not only as the right of individuals legitimately opposed to the power, usurpations, and abuses of the sovereign or the government, but as an element that has become indispensable to governmentality itself. Failing to respect freedom is not only an abuse of rights with

---

3   Michel Foucault, '5 April 1978', in Senellart and Davidson (eds), *Security, Territory, Population*, p. 353.
4   Goody, *The Domestication of the Savage Mind*.
5   Bowker and Star, *Sorting Things Out*.

regard to the law, it is above all ignorance of how to govern properly. The integration of freedom, and the specific limits to this freedom within the field of governmental practice has now become an imperative.[6]

Listing practices are key techniques in the integration of freedom as Foucault articulates it, acting to 'secure' the specific limits of 'freedom of movement', which is the *modus operandi* of the field of contemporary governmentality. With the event of no-fly lists we have seen how despite abusing privacy rights, and despite their failure to respect 'freedom of movement', and notwithstanding the complete ignorance of how to govern properly they seemingly represent, the pervasive and ubiquitous conjunctive web of no-blank list culture continues to spread itself further.

Foucault writes: 'On the one hand will be a whole series of mechanisms that fall within the province of the economy and the management of the population with the function of increasing the forces of the state.'[7] The list is clearly a part of this series of mechanisms that take as their chief objective the necessary and sufficient administration, organization, development, normalization, and distribution of elements circulating in expanding milieus of uncertainty. 'Then, on the other hand, there will be an apparatus or instruments for ensuring the prevention or repression of disorder, irregularity, illegality, and delinquency.'[8] The list has also been revealed as one of these policing instruments, not only for delimiting and policing the movement of risks to 'disorder', but also for establishing the 'truthful' and 'natural' category of terrorist, further self-elaborating its own praxis in the constitution of this most critical of contemporary knowledge. As a contemporary phenomenon, the list fully exhibits the 'double integration' effects that are the hallmark of the apparatuses of security – a unity that couples power/knowledge and science/decision as an art of this self-elaborating form of governmentality. Following on Foucault, this investigation into how lists serve power/knowledge shows how

[w]e can construct the genealogy of the modern state and its different apparatuses on the basis of a history of governmental reason. Society, economy, population, security, and freedom are the elements of the new governmentality whose forms we can still recognize in its contemporary modifications.[9]

As Foucault also argues, not only can we construct the genealogy of the modern state on a history of governmental reason, we can also unloosen the relations of power it correlates by unpacking and unloosening how political technologies have operated in the constitution of fields, domains, and objects of knowledge, and propelling them into an analysis of contemporary formations of power. For we have seen how under the Nazi regime, a conjunction of juridical-disciplinary mechanisms, redeployed in apparatuses of security, coalesced as a form of governmentality that sought to delimit and police the movement of risky or threatening elements circulating in populations and milieus to an extreme. It was in this moment and

---

6   Foucault, '5 April 1978', p. 353.
7   Foucault, '5 April 1978', p. 353.
8   Foucault, '5 April 1978', p. 353.
9   Foucault, '5 April 1978', p. 354.

under these conditions, that Nazi governmentality first deployed the list as a pervasive and ubiquitous security technology which produced the *double integration* effect of both calling threats into reality and policing them in a wide variety of everyday milieus of circulation, further self-elaborating the extreme biopolitical caesura discourses circulating throughout the Third Reich.

But as the interrogation of the work of Giorgio Agamben[10] has also revealed, the list can equally be characterized as a juridical-legal mechanism under Nazi governmentality: one that produced a double sovereignty effect – at once inscribing individual rights and liberties from charters of rights and freedoms on bodies in birth and exposing 'bare life' as the fundamental political unit on which the removal of such rights turn. In other words, under the Nazi regime the list emerged as a pivot of a form of modern governmentality marked at every turn by the policing of biopolitical caesuras of 'us' and 'them' – a way of seeing and calling 'threats' into reality and a practical basis for nullifying their movement. In other words, lists at once strip away the layers of human rights that shield bare life, and at the same time act as key mechanisms in the policing and securing of milieus. In list culture we can see Agamben's bare life operating within Foucault's governmentality.

> Economic reason does not replace *raison d'État,* but it gives it a new content and so gives new forms to state rationality. A new governmentality is born with the *écono-mistes* more than a century after the appearance of that other governmentality in the seventeenth century. The governmentality of the *politiques* gives us police, and the governmentality of the *économistes* introduces us, I think, to some of the fundamental lines of modern and contemporary governmentality.[11]

The operations of delimiting, predicting, managing and securing the distribution of elements circulating in milieus have been revealed here as a practice completely suffused with the politics of policing in both modern and contemporary formations of power/knowledge. The political assemblage of police that enforces delimitations and patrols the movement of 'freely' circulating elements is integrated with a statistical approach rooted in probabilities that takes as its chief objective 'securing' the 'normal' distribution of elements in populations, all with the intent of serving the best interests of a form of governmentality installed and regulated by the apparatuses of security.

With the emergence of the modern computer we have additionally seen how open-human and closed-world discourses operated in conjunction with statistics and lists in the installation of a global milieu of circulation characterized as a space of entropy, in which we would come to see ourselves and our societies as technoscientific cultural constructions of cyborg elements, circulating in disordered and ever-expanding milieus, where the boundaries between people, objects, and knowledge are completely eviscerated. In this way, we can say that the emergence of modern computers, while ushering in awe-inspiring developments in massive assemblages of living beings and machines, also served to increasingly isolate

---

10 Agamben, *Homo Sacer.*
11 Foucault, '5 April 1978', p. 348.

cyborgs in global classification infrastructures, subjecting them to evermore pervasive and ubiquitous delimitation, policing, and nullification. Building on Bowker and Star's[12] research, I have also argued that like classifications, computers, and statistics, lists are also pervasive and ubiquitous technologies that are so deeply embedded in our working infrastructures that they too have become relatively invisible, despite never losing any of their power in the self-elaborating processes of sublimation. Just as categories and classifications are culled into global computer and network infrastructures, becoming increasingly taken-for-granted ways of seeing and doing everyday life, lists too coalesce into working infrastructures that are integrated into and aligned with local, national, and global security systems.

In the era of the Cold War, when myths relating to us vs. them were heightened and ultimately transformed into epic global battles between black and white classifications of opposing forces, wars – like the contemporary one on terror – began to appear as ongoing and never-ending, further necessitating the self-elaborating operations of assemblages of policing involving delimiting, predicting, and nullifying the movements of risks or threats through listing practices. We have seen through our examination of no-fly lists and no-blank lists, that such cultural constructions are receding further and further into our cotemporary techno-social woodwork. Securing 'freedom' through the automated, divisive, and dehu-manizing classification of living beings as measures of worth/risk circulating in entropic global information infrastructures and policed through list technologies are contemporary practices that are clearly on the rise. As computers and statistics have been increasingly deployed to comb ever-expanding sets of social data for regularities and patterns of 'threat-ening' living beings and things since World War II, these self-elaborating processes have produced the teleological effect of establishing 'natural' and 'global' good vs. evil relation-ships, and the further need to redeploy lists to delimit and police the movement of threats.

This research into how lists have served, and continue to serve, formations of modern and contemporary power can be considered as part of a theoretical tradition that concerns itself with manifestations, technologies, and techniques of surveillance, or social control. Much has been written about integrated technologies, techniques, and discourses surrounding the observing, tracking, and monitoring of individuals and their behavior in modern and contemporary surveillance culture: beginning with Jeremy Bentham's visions of the pan-opticon in 1791, as historicized by Foucault in *Discipline and Punish*,[13] continuing with Gilles Deleuze's short but seminal 'Postscript on Societies of Control',[14] onto Hardt and Negri's highly influential *Empire*,[15] and more currently in the work of David Lyon into *The Surveillance Society*[16] and how *The Border is Everywhere*,[17] as well as in a slew of other contemporary works like Zureik and Salter's edited anthology chronicling contemporary

---

12 Bowker and Star, *Sorting Things Out.*
13 Foucault, *Discipline and Punish.*
14 Gilles Deleuze, 'Postscript on the Societies of Control', in *OCTOBER 59,* Cambridge: MIT Press, (Winter, 1992): 3-7.
15 Michael Hardt and Antonio Negri, *Empire*, Cambridge: Harvard University Press, 2000.
16 Lyon, *Surveillance Society.*
17 Lyon, 'The Border is Everywhere'.

Global Surveillance and Policing.[18] Taken together, this kind of research has emerged as a field and domain that concerns itself with technologies of security, surveillance, and social control as a disciplinary form of power.

This investigation into how lists serve formations of power has also unearthed the indispensable role of mathematical and statistical techniques that factor populations, assess worth/risk elements, and generate populations and 'profiles' in the policing of milieus that do not prohibit or prescribe, but rather let things happen. Questions of social control have been examined not from the perspective of disciplinary enclosures, as has been the focus of much theoretical investigation into surveillance culture, but rather from the standpoint of governmentality.

If we have seen in this work how 'in lists we are', future work needs to specifically address how through contemporary assemblages of humans and machines in digital networks, this state of affairs might be more accurately characterized by a self-elaborating discourse where the motto is more aptly described as 'in lists we trust'. From 'top ten lists', to 'best of lists', to our increasing reliance on listed and ranked information to navigate the ever-increasing entropy of the internet and contemporary networked spaces, we are seemingly relying more and more on these critical instruments of knowledge and security to constitute natural, truthful, everyday facts. For now, it is my hope that the powerful operations of list culture revealed here have served to rupture some of the critical self-elaborating processes of contemporary governmentality, particularly those that further naturalize the ongoing and never-ending segmenting and subdividing of *homo sapiens* into populations of *homines sacres*. In other words, it is my hope that this work has served to dislodge our profound and unequivocal trust in lists.

---

18 Zureik and Salter (eds), *Global Surveillance and Policing.*

References

Agamben, Giorgio. *Homo Sacer: Sovereign Power and Bare Life*, Stanford: Stanford University Press, 1998.

– . *Remnants of Auschwitz : The Witness and the Archive*, New York: Zone Books, 2000.

– . *State of Exception*, Chicago: University of Chicago Press, 2005.

Aly, Götz, Karl Heinz Roth, Edwin Black, and Assenka Oksiloff. *The Nazi Census: Identification and Control in the Third Reich*, Philadelphia: Temple University Press, 2004.

Arendt, Hannah. *Eichmann in Jerusalem: A Report on the Banality of Evil*, New York: Penguin Books, 1994.

Berger, Peter L. and Thomas Luckmann. *The Social Construction of Reality: A Treatise in the Sociology of Knowledge*, New York: Doubleday, 1967.

Black, Edwin. *IBM and the Holocaust: The Strategic Alliance Between Nazi Germany and America's Most Powerful Corporation*, New York: Crown Publishers, 2001.

Bowker, Geoffrey C. 'How to Be Universal: Some Cybernetic Strategies', *Social Studies of Science* 23 (1993): 107-127.

Bowker, Geoffrey C. and Susan Leigh Star. *Sorting Things Out: Classification and Its Consequences*, Cambridge: MIT Press, 1999.

Butler, Nick. 'The Management of Populations', *Ephemera: Theory and Politics in Organization* 7 (3, 2007): 475-480.

Carey, James W. *Communication As Culture: Essays on Media and Society*, Boston: Unwin Hyman, 1989.

Clynes, Manfred E. and Nathan S. Kline. 'Cyborgs and Space', *Astronautics* (September, 1960): 75-76.

Deleuze, Gilles. 'Postscript on the Societies of Control', in *OCTOBER* 59, Cambridge: MIT Press, (Winter, 1992): 3-7.

Eco, Umberto. *The Open Work*, London: Hutchinson Radius, 1989.

Edwards, Paul N. *The Closed World: Computers and the Politics of Discourse in Cold War America*, Cambridge: MIT Press, 1996.

Elmer, Greg. *Profiling Machines: Mapping the Personal information Economy*, Cambridge, Mass: MIT Press, 2004.

Faubion, J.D. (ed.), *Power, Vol. 3, Essential Works of Foucault 1954-1984*, New York: The New Press, 2000.

Foucault, Michel. *Madness and Civilization; A History of Insanity in the Age of Reason*, New York: Vintage Books, 1973.

– , *The History of Sexuality*, New York: Vintage Books, 1988.

– , *Discipline and Punish: The Birth of the Prison*, New York: Vintage Books, 1995.

– , *The Order of Things: An Archaeology of the Human Sciences*, London and New York: Routledge, 2001:1970.

– , *Archaeology of Knowledge*, New York: Routledge, 2002.

Foucault, Michel, Graham Burchell, Colin Gordon, and Peter Miller. *The Foucault Effect: Studies in Governmentality*, Chicago: University of Chicago Press, 1991.

Foucault, Michel and Colin Gordon. 'The Eye of Power', in *Power/Knowledge: Selected Interviews and Other Writings*, 1972-1977, New York: Pantheon Books, 1980, pp. 146-165.

Gitelman, Lisa. *'Raw Data' Is an Oxymoron*, Cambridge, MA: MIT Press, 2013.

Gonen, Jay Y. *The Roots of Nazi Psychology: Hitler's Utopian Barbarism*, Lexington: University Press of Kentucky, 2000.

Goody, Jack. *The Domestication of the Savage Mind*, Cambridge, New York: Cambridge University Press, 1977.

Grimes, Sara M. and Leslie Shade. 'Neopian Economics of Play: Children's Cyberpets and Online Communities as Immersive Advertising in Neopets.Com', *The International Journal of Media and Cultural Politics* 1 (2005): 181-198.

Gubrium, J.F. and J.A. Holstein. 'Narrative Practice and the Coherence of Personal Stories', *Sociological Quarterly* 39 (1998): 163-187.

Gubrium, Jaber F. and James A. Holstein. 'Analyzing Interpretive Practice', in N.K. Denzin and Y.S. Lincoln (eds), The *Handbook of Qualitative Research*, Thousand Oaks: Sage Publications, 2000.

Hacking, Ian. *The Taming of Chance*, Cambridge, New York: Cambridge University Press, 1990.

– , *The Emergence of Probability: A Philosophical Study of Early Ideas About Probability, Induction and Statistical Inference*, Cambridge, New York: Cambridge University Press, 2006.

Hamilton, Sheryl N. 'Interrogating the Cybernetic Imaginary, Or, Control and Communication in the Human and the Machine', *Communication Studies*, Montreal: Concordia University, 1999.

Haraway, Donna Jeanne. 'Manifesto For Cyborgs: Science, Technology, and Socialist Feminism in the 1980s', *Socialist Review* 80 (1985): 65-108.

– , *Simians, Cyborgs, and Women: The Reinvention of Nature*, New York: Routledge, 1991.

– , *Modest Witness@Second_Millenium, Femaleman©_Meets_oncomouse™: Feminism and Technoscience*, New York: Routledge, 1997.

Hardt, Michael and Antonio Negri. *Empire*, Cambridge: Harvard University Press, 2000.

Heims, Steve J. *John von Neumann and Norbert Wiener: From Mathematics to the Technologies of Life and Death*, Cambridge: MIT Press, 1980.

– , *Constructing a Social Science for Postwar America: The Cybernetics Group, 1946-1953*, Cambridge: MIT Press, 1993.

Hilberg, Raul. *The Destruction of the European Jews*, New York: Holmes & Meier, 1985.

Innis, Harold Adams, *The Bias of Communication*, Toronto: University of Toronto Press, 1991.

Knorr-Cetina, K. *Epistemic Cultures: How the Sciences Make Knowledge*, Cambridge: Harvard University Press, 1999.

Knorr-Cetina, K. and Aaron Victor Cicourel. *Advances in Social Theory and Methodology: Toward an Integration of Micro- and Macro-Sociologies*, Boston: Routledge & Kegan Paul, 1981.

Kogon, Eugen. *The Theory and Practice of Hell: The German Concentration Camps and the System Behind them*, London: Secker & Warburg, 1950.

Koonz, Claudia. *The Nazi Conscience*, Cambridge: Belknap Press, 2003.

Krausnick, Helmut, Hans Bucheim, Martin Broszat, and Hans-Adolf Jacobsen. *Anatomy of the SS State*, London: Collins, 1968.

Krebs, Valdis. 'OSNA – Open Source Network Analysis', talk presented at New Network Theory conference, 28-30 June 2007, Institute of Network Cultures, Amsterdam, http://networkcultures.org/networktheory/1-network-theory/program/.

Kuhn, Thomas S. *The Structure of Scientific Revolutions*, Chicago: University of Chicago Press, 1962.

– , The Structure of Scientific Revolutions, Chicago: University of Chicago Press, 1996.

Lasswell, Harold Dwight, 'The Structure and Function of Communication in Society', in L. Bryson (ed.), *The Communication of Ideas, A Series of Addresses, Religion and Civilization Series*, New York: Jewish Theological Seminary of America and the Institute For Religious and Social Studies, 1948.

– , *Politics: Who Gets what, when, how*, New York: Peter Smith, 1950.

– , *Psychopathology and Politics*, New York: Viking Press, 1960.

– , *Propaganda Technique in the World War*, New York: Garland Pub, 1972.

Lasswell, Harold Dwight, Daniel Lerner, and Hans Speier. *Propaganda and Communication in World History*, Honolulu: Published For the East-West Center By the University Press of Hawaii, 1979.

Lasswell, Harold Dwight and Arnold A. Rogow. *Politics, Personality, and Social Science in the Twentieth Century; Essays in Honor of Harold D. Lasswell*, Chicago: University of Chicago Press, 1969.

Latour, Bruno and Steve Woolgar. *Laboratory Life: The Construction of Scientific Facts*, Princeton: Princeton University Press, 1986.

Lippmann, Walter. *Public Opinion*, New York: Macmillan, 1922.

– , *An Inquiry into the Principles of the Good Society*, Boston: Little Brown and Company, 1937.

– , *The Good Society*, New York: Grosset & Dunlap, 1943.

– , *The Cold War: A Study in U.S. Foreign Policy*, New York: Harper, 1947.

– , *Essays in the Public Philosophy*, Boston: Little Brown, 1955.

– , *Drift and Mastery; An Attempt to Diagnose the Current Unrest*, Englewood Cliffs: Prentice-Hall, 1961.

– , *Public Opinion*, New York: Macmillan, 1965.

– , *Early Writings*, New York: Liveright, 1970.

Lippmann, Walter and Godkin Lectures at Harvard University. *The Method of Freedom*, New York: Macmillan, 1934.

Lovink, Geert and Kenneth C. Werbin. 'Critique of Ranking and Listing: An Email Exchange', in L. Armand and A. Bradley, *TECHNICITY*, Prague: Litteraria Pragensia, 2007.

Lyon, David. *The Electronic Eye*, Minneapolis: Univ. of Minnesota Press, 1994,

– , *Surveillance Society: Monitoring Everyday Life*, Buckingham, Philadelphia: Open University Press, 2002.

Mannheim, Karl, Louis Wirth, and Edward Shils. *Ideology and Utopia; An Introduction to the Sociology of Knowledge*, London, New York: Harcourt Brace and Company, 1936, 1985.

Mayer-Schonberger, Viktor and Kenneth Cukier. *Big Data*, New York, NY: Houghton Mifflin Harcourt Publishing Company, 2013.

Mosco, Vincent. *The Digital Sublime: Myth, Power, and Cyberspace*, Cambridge: MIT Press, 2004.

Ong, Walter J. *Orality and Literacy: The Technologizing of the Word*, London, New York: Routledge, 1991.

Poster, Mark. *The Mode of Information: Poststructuralism and Social Context*, Chicago: University of Chicago Press, 1990.

– , *The Second Media Age*, Cambridge: Polity Press, 1995.

– , *What's the Matter With the Internet?* Minneapolis: University of Minnesota Press, 2001.

– , *Information Please: Culture and Politics in the Age of Digital Machines*, Durham: Duke University Press, 2006.

Pugh, Emerson W. *Building IBM: Shaping an Industry and its Technology*, Cambridge: MIT Press, 1995.

Rabinow P. (ed.). *Essential Works of Foucault 1954-1984, Vol. 3*, New York: The New Press, 2000.

Rapoport, A. *Strategy and Conscience*, New York, NY: Harper and Row, 1964.

– , *Two-Person Game Theory: The Essential Ideas*, Ann Arbor: University of Michigan Press, 1969.

Rose, Ellen. 'The War Machine: IBM and the Holocaust by Edwin Black', *The Antigonish Review* (2001): 91-95.

Schelling, Thomas. *The Strategy of Conflict*, Cambridge: Harvard University Press, 1960.

Senellart M. and A.I. Davidson (eds). *Security, Territory, Population: Lectures at the College de France, 1977-1978*, Houndmills, Basingstoke, Hampshire, New York: Palgrave Macmillan, 2007.

Shade, Leslie. 'Gender and the Commodification of Community: Women.Com and Gurl.Com', in D. Barney and A. Feenberg (eds), *Community in the Digital Age: Philosophy and Practice*, Lanham: Rowan & Littlefield, 2004.

Silverman, David. 'Analyzing Talk and Text', in N.K. Denzin and Y.S. Lincoln (eds), *The Handbook of Qualitative Research*, Thousand Oaks: Sage Publications, 2000.

Simpson, Christopher. S*cience of Coercion: Communication Research and Psychological Warfare, 1945-1960*, New York: Oxford University Press, 1994.

Smith, Bruce Lannes, Harold Dwight Lasswell, and Ralph Droz Casey. *Propaganda, Communication, and Public Opinion: A Comprehensive Reference Guide*, Princeton: Princeton Univ. Press, 1946.

Sobel, Robert. *I.B.M., Colossus in Transition*, New York: Times Books, 1981.

Sofsky, Wolfgang. *The Order of Terror: The Concentration Camp*, Princeton: Princeton University, 1997.

Treichler, Paula A. 'AIDS, Homophobia, and Biomedical Discourse: An Epidemic of Signification', in D. Crimp and L. Bersani (eds), *AIDS: Cultural Analysis, Cultural Activism*, Cambridge: MIT Press, 1988, Pp. 31-86.

– , 'AIDS, HIV, and the Cultural Construction of Reality', in G.H. Herdt, S. Lindenbaum, and Wenner-Gren Foundation for Anthropological Research (eds), *The Time of AIDS: Social Analysis, Theory, and Method*, Newbury Park: Sage Publications, 1992, Pp. 65-98.

Tuchman, Gaye. 'Historical Social Science: Methodologies, Methods, and Meanings', in N. K. Denzin and Y.S. Lincoln (eds), *Strategies of Qualitative Inquiry*, Thousand Oaks: Sage Publications, 1998, Pp. 225-260.

Turkle, Sherry. *The Second Self: Computers and the Human Spirit*, New York: Simon and Schuster, 1984.

– , *Life on the Screen: Identity in the Age of the Internet*, New York: Simon & Schuster, 1995.

Von Neumann, John, *The Computer and the Brain*, New Haven: Yale University Press, 1964.

Von Neumann, John and Arthur W. Burks. *Theory of Self-Reproducing Automata*, Urbana: University of Illinois Press, 1966.

Von Neumann, John and Oskar Morgenstern. *Theory of Games and Economic Behavior*, Princeton: Princeton University Press, 1953.

– , *Theory of Games and Economic Behavior*, New York: Science Editions J. Wiley, 1964.

Waldrop, M. Mitchell. *The Dream Machine: J.C.R. Licklider and the Revolution that Made Computing Personal*, New York: Viking, 2001.

Weizenbaum, Joseph. *Computer Power and Human Reason: From Judgment to Calculation*, San Francisco: W.H. Freeman, 1976.

Werbin, Kenneth C. 'Sometimes a Great Notion: A Reflection on Cybernetics, Isolated Systems, and Open Beings', in Lipika Bansal, Paul Keller, and G. Lovink (eds), *In the Shade of the Commons: Towards a Culture of Open Networks*, Amsterdam, The Netherlands: Waag Society, 2006.

Wiener, Norbert. *Cybernetics, Or, Control and Communication in the Animal and the Machine*, New York: M.I.T. Press, 1948.

– , *The Human Use of Human Beings; Cybernetics and Society*, Boston: Houghton Mifflin, 1950.

– , *The Human Use of Human Beings: Cybernetics and Society*, Garden City, New York: Doubleday, 1954.

– , *I Am a Mathematician, The Later Life of a Prodigy: An Autobiographical Account of the Mature Years and Career of Norbert Wiener and a Continuation of the Account of his Childhood in Ex-Prodigy*, Garden City: Doubleday, 1956.

– , *Invention: The Care and Feeding of Ideas*, Cambridge: MIT Press, 1993.

Williams, Raymond. *Keywords: A Vocabulary of Culture and Society*, London: Fontana/Croom Helm, 1976.

Zureik, Elia and Mark B. Salter (eds). *Global Surveillance and Policing: Borders, Security, Identity*, Cullompton, Portland: Willan, 2005.

www.ingramcontent.com/pod-product-compliance
Lightning Source LLC
Chambersburg PA
CBHW052316220526
45472CB00001B/145